AFTER LIFE IN ROMAN PAGANISM

YALE UNIVERSITY
MRS. HEPSA ELY SILLIMAN
MEMORIAL LECTURES

SILLIMAN MEMORIAL LECTURES

PUBLISHED BY YALE UNIVERSITY PRESS

AFTER LIFE IN ROMAN PAGANISM.

LECTURES DELIVERED AT YALE UNIVERSITY
ON THE SILLIMAN FOUNDATION

BY

FRANZ CUMONT

NEW HAVEN
YALE UNIVERSITY PRESS
LONDON · HUMPHREY MILFORD · OXFORD UNIVERSITY PRESS
MDCCCCXXIII

COPYRIGHT, 1922, BY
YALE UNIVERSITY PRESS

First published, December, 1922.
Second printing, March, 1923.

TO MY FRIEND
GEORGE LINCOLN HENDRICKSON
1888-1922

THE SILLIMAN FOUNDATION

In the year 1883 a legacy of eighty thousand dollars was left to the President and Fellows of Yale College in the city of New Haven, to be held in trust, as a gift from her children, in memory of their beloved and honored mother, Mrs. Hepsa Ely Silliman.

On this foundation Yale College was requested and directed to establish an annual course of lectures designed to illustrate the presence and providence, the wisdom and goodness of God, as manifested in the natural and moral world. These were to be designated as the Mrs. Hepsa Ely Silliman Memorial Lectures. It was the belief of the testator that any orderly presentation of the facts of nature or history contributed to the end of this foundation more effectively than any attempt to emphasize the elements of doctrine or of creed; and he therefore provided that lectures on dogmatic or polemical theology should be excluded from the scope of this foundation, and that the subjects should be selected, rather, from the domains of natural science and history, giving special prominence to astronomy, chemistry, geology, and anatomy.

It was further directed that each annual course should be made the basis of a volume to form part of a series constituting a memorial to Mrs. Silliman. The memorial fund came into the possession of the Corporation of Yale University in the year 1901; and the present volume constitutes the sixteenth of the series of memorial lectures.

PREFACE

AT the invitation of the President of Yale University and of Professor Russell H. Chittenden, chairman of the committee in charge of the Silliman Foundation, the lectures which are here presented to a wider public were delivered in New Haven during the month of March of the year 1921. It was the wish of the committee that I should speak upon some subject from the history of religion. I chose therefore as my theme a matter which had occupied my attention for many years, viz., the ideas current in Roman paganism concerning the lot of the soul after death. The argument has been treated more than once by distinguished scholars and notably—to mention only an English book—by Mrs. Arthur Strong in her recent work "Apotheosis and After Life," a study characterised by penetrating interpretation, especially of archaeological monuments. But we do not yet possess for the Roman imperial epoch a counterpart to Rohde's classical volume, "Psyche," for the earlier Greek period, that is, a work in which the whole evolution of Roman belief and speculation regarding a future life is set forth. These lectures cannot claim to fill this gap. They may however be looked upon as a sketch of the desired investigation, in which, though without the detailed citation of supporting evidence, an attempt at least has been made to trace the broad outlines of the subject in all its magnitude.

The lectures are printed in the form in which they were delivered. The necessity of making each one intelligible to an audience which was not always the same, has made inevitable some repetitions. Cross references have been added, where the same topics are treated in different connections. However, in a book intended primarily for the general reader, the scholarly apparatus has been reduced to a minimum and as a rule indicates only the source of passages quoted in the text.

My acknowledgment is due to Miss Helen Douglas Irvine, who with skill and intelligent understanding of the subject translated into English the French text of these lectures. I wish also to express my gratitude to my friends, Professor George Lincoln Hendrickson, who took upon himself the tedious task of reading the manuscript and the proofs of this book and to whom I am indebted for many valuable suggestions both in matter and in form, and Professor Grant Showerman, who obligingly consented to revise the last chapters before they were printed.

Rome, September, 1922.

CONTENTS

CONTENTS

HISTORICAL INTRODUCTION

THE idea of death has perhaps never been more present to humanity than during the years through which we have just passed. It has been the daily companion of millions of men engaged in a murderous conflict; it has haunted the even larger number who have trembled for the lives of their nearest and dearest; it is still constantly in the thoughts of the many who nurse regret for those they loved. And doubtless also, the faith or the hope has never more imposed itself, even on the unbelieving, that these countless multitudes, filled with moral force and generous passion, who have entered eternity, have not wholly perished, that the ardour which animated them was not extinguished when their limbs grew cold, that the spirit which impelled them to self-sacrifice was not dissipated with the atoms which formed their bodies.

These feelings were known to the ancients also, who gave to this very conviction the form suggested by their religion. Pericles[1] in his funeral eulogy of the warriors who fell at the siege of Samos declared that they who die for their country become like the immortal gods, and that, invisible like them, they still scatter their benefits on us. The ideas on immortality held in antiquity are often thus at once far from and near to our own—*near* because they correspond to aspirations which are not antique or modern, but human, *far* because the Olympians now have fallen into the deep gulf where lie dethroned deities. These ideas become more and more like the conceptions familiar to us as gradually their time grows later, and those generally admitted at the end of paganism are analogous to the doctrines accepted throughout the Middle Ages.

I flatter myself, therefore, that when I speak to you of the beliefs in a future life held in Roman times I have chosen a subject which is not very remote from us nor such as has no relation to our present thought or is capable of interesting only the learned.

[1] Plut., *Pericl.*, 8.

We can here trace only the outlines of this vast subject. I am aware that it is always imprudent to hazard moral generalisations: they are always wrong somewhere. Above all, it is perilous to attempt to determine with a few words the infinite variety of individual creeds, for nothing escapes historical observation more easily than the intimate convictions of men, which they often hide even from those near them. In periods of scepticism pious souls cling to old beliefs; the conservative crowd remains faithful to ancestral traditions. When religion is resuming its empire, rationalistic minds resist the contagion of faith. It is especially difficult to ascertain up to what point ideas adopted by intellectual circles succeeded in penetrating the deep masses of the people. The epitaphs which have been preserved give us too scanty and too sparse evidence in this particular. Besides, in paganism a dogma does not necessarily exclude its opposite dogma: the two sometimes persist side by side in one mind as different possibilities, each of which is authorised by a respectable tradition. You will therefore make the necessary reservations to such of my statements as are too absolute. I shall be able to point out here only the great spiritual currents which successively brought to Rome new ideas as to the Beyond, and to sketch the evolution undergone by the doctrines as to the lot and the abode of souls. You will not expect me to be precise as to the number of the partisans of each of these doctrines in the various periods.

At least we can distinguish the principal phases of the religious movement which caused imperial society to pass from incredulity to certain forms of belief in immortality, forms at first somewhat crude but afterwards loftier, and we can see where this movement led. The change was a capital one and transformed for the ancients the whole conception of life. The axis about which morality revolved had to be shifted when ethics no longer sought, as in earlier Greek philosophy, to realise the sovereign good on this earth but looked for it after death. Thenceforth the activity of man aimed less at tangible realities, ensuring well-being to the family or the city or the state, and more at attaining to the fulfilment of ideal hopes in a supernatural world. Our sojourn here below was conceived as a preparation for another existence, as a transitory trial which was to result in infinite felicity or suffering. Thus the table of ethical values was turned upside down.

"All our actions and all our thoughts," says Pascal, "must

follow so different a course if there are eternal possessions for which we may hope than if there are not, that it is impossible to take any directed and well-judged step except by regulating it in view of this point which ought to be our ultimate goal."[2]

We will attempt first to sketch in a general introduction the historical transformation which belief in the future life underwent between the Republican period and the fall of paganism. Then, in three lectures, we will examine more closely the various conceptions of the abode of the dead held under the Roman Empire, study in three others the conditions or the means which enable men to attain to immortality and in the last two set forth the lot of souls in the Beyond.

    *   *   *   *   *

The cinerary vases of the prehistoric period are often modelled in the shape of huts: throughout, funeral sculpture follows the tradition that the tomb should reproduce the dwelling, and until the end of antiquity it was designated, in the West as in the East, as the "eternal house" of him who rested in it.

Thus a conception of the tomb which goes back to the remotest ages and persists through the centuries regards it as "the last dwelling" of those who have left us; and this expression has not yet gone out of use. It was believed that a dead man continued to live, in the narrow space granted him, a life which was groping, obscure, precarious, yet like that he led on earth. Subject to the same needs, obliged to eat and to drink, he expected those who had been nearest to him to appease his hunger and thirst. The utensils he had used, the things he had cared for, were often deposited beside him so that he might pursue the occupations and enjoy the amusements which he had forsaken in the world. If he were satisfied he would stay quietly in the furnished house provided for him and would not seek to avenge himself on those whose neglect had caused him suffering. Funeral rites were originally inspired rather by fear than by love. They were precautions taken against the spirit of the dead rather than pious care bestowed in their interest.[3]

For the dead were powerful; their action was still felt; they were not immured in the tomb or confined beneath the ground. Men saw them reappear in dreams, wearing their former aspect. They were descried during shadowy vigils; their voices were

[2] *Pensées*, III, 194 (t. II, p. 103, ed. Brunschvigg).
[3] See Lecture I, "Life in the Tomb."

heard and their movements noted. Imagination conceived them such as they had once been; recollection of them filled the memory and to think of such apparitions as idle or unreal seemed impossible. The dead subsisted, then, as nebulous, impalpable beings, perceived by the senses only exceptionally. Here the belief that their remains had not quite lost all feeling mingled with the equally primitive and universal belief that the soul is a breath, exhaled with the last sigh. The vaporous shade, sometimes a dangerous but sometimes a succouring power, wandered by night in the atmosphere and haunted the places which the living man had been used to frequent. Except for some sceptical reasoners, all antiquity admitted the reality of these phantoms. Century-old beliefs, maintained by traditional rites, thus persisted, more or less definitely, in the popular mind, even after new forms of the future life were imagined. Many vestiges of these beliefs have survived until today.

The first transformation undergone by the primitive conception was to entertain the opinion that the dead who are deposited in the ground gather together in a great cavity inside the bowels of the earth.[4] This belief in the nether world is found among most of the peoples of the Mediterranean basin: the *Sheol* of the Hebrews differs little from the Homeric *Hades* and the Italic *Inferi*.

It has been conjectured that the substitution of incineration for inhumation contributed to spreading this new manner of conceiving life beyond the tomb: the shade could not remain attached to a handful of ashes enclosed in a puny urn. It went, then, to join its fellows who had gone down into the dark dwelling where reigned the gods of a subterranean kingdom. But as ghosts could leave their graves in order to trouble or to help men, so the swarms of the infernal spirits rose to the upper world through the natural openings of the earth, or through ditches dug for the purpose of maintaining communication with them and conciliating them with offerings.

The Romans do not seem to have imagined survival in the infernal regions very differently from the survival of the vague monotonous shades in their tombs. Their *Manes* or *Lemures* had no marked personality or clearly characterised individual features. The *Inferi* were not, as in Greece, a stage for the enactment of a tragic drama; their inhabitants had no original life, and in the lot dealt to them no idea of retribution can be discerned.

4 See Lecture II, "The Nether World."

to which we will return in treating of the nether world.[38] These
philosophers do indeed speak of Hades but, faithful to their
habits, while they use traditional terms they give them a new
meaning. "The descent into Hades" is for them simply the de-
parting from life, the transference of the soul to new surroundings. Thus Epictetus, who uses this expression (κάθοδος εἰς Ἅιδου),
clearly states in another passage, "There is no Hades, no
Acheron, no Cocytus, no Pyriphlegethon, but all is filled with
gods and demons."[39] These gods and demons were, however, no
more than personifications of the forces of nature.[40]

The true Stoic doctrine is, then, that souls, when they leave
the corpse, subsist in the atmosphere and especially in its highest
part which touches the circle of the moon.[41] But after a longer
or less interval of time they, like the flesh and the bones, are
decomposed and dissolve into the elements which formed them.

This thought, like Epicurean nihilism, often appears in epitaphs, and shows how Stoic ideas had spread among the people.
Thus on a tombstone found in Moesia we read first the mournful
statement that there is neither love nor friendship among the
dead and that the corpse lies like a stone sunk into the ground.
Then the dead man adds:[42] "I was once composed of earth, water
and airy breath (πνεῦμα), but I perished, and here I rest, having
rendered all to the All. Such is each man's lot. What of it?
There, whence my body came, did it return, when it was dissolved." Sometimes there is more insistence on the notion that
this cosmic breath, in which ours is gathered up, is the godhead
who fills and rules the world. So in this epitaph: "The holy
spirit which thou didst bear has escaped from thy body. That
body remains here and is like the earth; the spirit pursues the
revolving heavens; the spirit moves all; the spirit is nought else
than God."[43] Elsewhere we find the following brief formula,
which sums up the same idea: "The ashes have my body; the
sacred air has borne away my soul."[44] Very characteristic is an
inscription inspired by verses of a Greek poet, on the tomb of a
Roman woman: "Here I lie dead and I am ashes; these ashes are

38 *Cf.* Lecture II, p. 77.
39 Epictetus, III, 13, 15; *cf.* II, 6, 18.
40 Bonhöfer, *Epictet. und die Stoa*, 1890, p. 65.
41 *Cf.* Lecture III, p. 98.
42 *Arch. Epigr. Mitt. aus Oesterreich*, VI, 1882, p. 60; *cf.* Epictetus, *l. c.*
43 CIL, XIII, 8371, at Cologne.
44 CIL, III, 6384: "Corpus habent cineres, animam sacer abstulit aer."

earth. If the earth be a goddess, I too am a goddess and am not dead.''[45]

These verses express the same great thought in various forms: death is disappearance into the depths of divine nature. It is not for the preservation of an ephemeral personality that we must hope. Our soul, a fleeting energy detached from the All, must enter again into the All as must our body: both are absorbed by God,

> ''When that which drew from out the boundless deep
> Turns again home.''[46]

The fiery breath of our intelligence is gathered, as are the matter and the humours of our organism, into the inexhaustible reservoir which produced them, as one day the earth and the heavens will be gathered thither also. All must be engulfed in one whole, must lose itself in one forgetfulness. When man has reached the term of his fate, he faints into the one power which forms and leads the universe, just as the tired stars will be extinguished in it, when their days shall be accomplished. Resistance to the supreme law is vain and painful; rebellion against the irresistible order of things is impious. The great virtue taught by Stoicism is that of submission to the fatality which guides the world, of joyous acceptance of the inevitable. Philosophic literature and the epitaphs present to us, repeatedly and in a thousand forms, the idea that we cannot strive against omnipotent necessity, that the rule of this rigid master must be borne without tears or recriminations. The wise man, who destroys within himself desire of any happenings, enjoys even during this existence divine calm in the midst of tribulations, but those whom the vicissitudes of life drive or attract, who let illusions seduce or grieve them, will at last obtain remission of their troubles when they reach the tranquil haven of death. This thought is expressed by a distich which often recurs on tombs, in Greek and in Latin. ''I have fled, escaped. Farewell, Hope and Fortune. I have nothing more to do with you. Make others your sport.''[47]

---

[45] Dessau, *Inscr. sel.*, 8168; Bücheler, *Carm. epigr.*, 1532; *cf.* 974:
> ''Mortua heic ego sum et sum cinis, is cinis terrast,
> Sein est terra dea, ego sum dea, mortua non sum.''

[46] Tennyson, *Crossing the Bar.*

[47] Bücheler, *Carm. epigr.*, 1498:
> ''Evasi effugi; Spes et Fortuna valete;
> Nil mihi vobiscum. Ludificate alios.''

Cf. Bücheler, 409, 9; 434; *Anthol. Pal.*, IX, 49; 172; Vettius Valens, V, 9 (p. 219, 26, Kroll).

Stoic determinism found support in the astrology which originated in Babylonia and was transplanted to Egypt, and which spread in the Graeco-Latin world from the second century B. C. onwards, propagating its mechanical and fatalistic conception of the universe. According to this pseudo-science, all physical phenomena depended absolutely, like the character and acts of men, on the revolutions of the celestial bodies. Thus all the forces of nature and the very energy of intelligence acted in accordance with an inflexible necessity. Hence worship had no object and prayer no effect. In this way the sidereal divination, which had grown up in the temples of the East, ended in Greece, among certain of its adepts, in a negation of the very basis of religion.[48] It is noteworthy that in the writings left to us there is hardly an allusion to the immortality of the soul. When they speak of what comes after death there is question only of funerals and posthumous glory. We never find in them a promise to the unfortunate, weighed down by misadventure and infirmities, of consolation or compensation in the Beyond. The systematic astrology of the Greeks limits its horizon to this world, although traces of the belief in Hades subsist in its vocabulary and its predictions and although this same astral divination inspired in the mysteries certain eschatological theories, as we shall see later.[49]

* * * * *

The rationalistic and scientific period of Hellenic thought which began, as we have said, with Aristotle, filled the Hellenistic period and continued until the century of Augustus. Towards the end of the Roman Republic faith in the future life was reduced to a minimum and the scepticism or indifference of the Alexandrians was carried into Italy. The mocking verses of an epigram of Callimachus, a man of learning as well as a poet, is well known.[50] "Charidas, what is there down below? Deep darkness. But what of the journeys upwards? All lies. And Pluto? A fable. Then we are lost." Catullus was to say as much, less lightly, with a deeper feeling. "Suns can set and rise again, but we, when our brief light is extinguished, must sleep for an

[48] See my *Oriental religions*, p. 180; 276, n. 51 s.
[49] See Lecture III, pp. 96, 107; VII, p. 176.
[50] Callim., *Epigr.*, 15, 3:

'Ω Χαρίδα τί τὰ νέρθε;—Πολὺ σκότος—Αἱ δ'ἄνοδοι τί;
Ψεῦδος—'Ο δὲ Πλούτων;—Μῦθος—'Απωλόμεθα

eternal night.''[51] The religious belief in retribution in the Beyond was shaken, as all the others were, not only in literary and
philosophic circles but among a large section of the population.
The old tales of the Elysian Fields and Tartarus no longer found
credence, as convincing testimony will show us.[52] Those who
sought to preserve them could do so only by using a daring
symbol which altered their character. But the idea of conscious
survival after death was itself no longer looked upon as sure.
Many who did not go so far as to deny it brutally were firmly
agnostic. When we turn over the pages of the thick volumes of
the *Corpus inscriptionum*, we are struck by the small number
of the epitaphs which express the hope of immortality. The impression received is quite the contrary of that given by going
through our own graveyards or surveying the collections of
Christian epitaphs of antiquity. On by far the larger number
of the tombs the survival of the soul was neither affirmed nor
denied; it was not mentioned otherwise than by the banal formula *Dis Manibus*—so bereft of meaning that even some Christians made use of it. Or else the authors of funereal inscriptions,
like the contemporary writers, used careful phrases which showed
their mental hesitations: ''If the Manes still perceive anything.
. . . If any feeling subsist after death. . . . If there be reward for
the righteous beneath the ground.''[53] Such doubting propositions
are most frequent. The same indecision made people return to an
alternative presented by Plato in the *Apology*,[54] before his ideas
had evolved, and repeat that death is ''an end or a passage,''—
mors aut finis aut transitus,—and no choice is made between the
two possibilities: the question is left open. The future life was
generally regarded as a consoling metaphysical conception, a
mere hypothesis supported by some thinkers, a religious hope
but not an article of faith. The lofty conclusion which ends
Agricola's eulogy will be remembered. ''If,'' says Tacitus,
''there be an abode of the spirits of virtuous men, if, as sages
have taught, great souls be not extinguished with the body, rest
in peace.'' But side by side with the supposition thus hazarded,

51 Cat., V, 4:
        ''Soles occidere et redire possunt;
        Nobis quum semel occidit brevis lux,
        Nox est perpetua una dormienda.''
52 *Cf*. Lecture II, p. 83, and VII, p. 181.
53 Bücheler, *Carm. epigr.*, 180, 1147, 1190, 1339, etc.
54 Plato, *Apol.*, 40c-41c.

the historian expresses the assurance that Agricola will receive another reward for his merits. All that his contemporaries have loved and admired in his character will cause the fame of his deeds to live in men's memory through the eternity of ages.

We here see how the perplexity in which men struggled, when they thought of psychic survival, gave earthly immortality a greater value in the eyes of the ancients. It was for many of them the essential point because it alone was certain. Not to fall into the abyss of forgetfulness seemed a sufficient reward for virtue. ''Death is to be feared by those for whom everything is extinguished with their life, not by those whose renown cannot perish.''[55] That the commemoration of our merits may not cease when the short time of our passage here below has ended, but may be prolonged for as long as the sequence of future generations lasts—this is the deep desire which stimulates virtue and excites to effort. Cicero, when celebrating in the *Pro Archia*[56] the benefits wrought by the love of glory,—from which he was by no means exempt himself,—remarks shrewdly that even philosophers, who claim to show its vanity, are careful to place their names at the beginning of their books, thus showing the worth they attach to that which they exhort others to despise. Even more than today, the hope of a durable renown, the anxiety that their fellows should be busy about them even after their departure, the preoccupation lest their life should not be favourably judged by public opinion, haunted many men, secretly or avowedly dominated their thought and directed their actions. Even those who had played only a modest part in the world and had made themselves known only to a narrow circle, sought to render their memory unforgettable by building strong tombs for themselves along the great roads. Epitaphs often begin with the formula *Memoriae aeternae,* ''To the eternal memory,'' which we have inherited, although the idea it represents no longer has for most of us any but a very relative value.

In antiquity it was first connected with the old belief in a communion of sentiments and an exchange of services between the deceased and their descendants who celebrated the funeral cult. When the firm belief in the power of the shades to feel and act ceased to exist, offerings were made with another intention:

[55] Cic., *Parad. Stoic.*, II, 18: ''Mors est terribilis iis quorum cum vita omnia exstinguntur, non iis quorum laus emori non potest.''

[56] Cic., *Pro Archia*, 11, 26; *cf. Tusc.*, I, 15, 34.

survivors liked to think that he who had gone had not entirely perished as long as his remembrance subsisted in the hearts of those who had cherished him and the minds of those who had learnt his praises. In some way, he rose from the grave in the image made of him by the successors of those who had known him. Epicurus himself stipulated in his will that the day of his birth should be commemorated every month,[57] and under the Roman Empire his disciples were still piously celebrating this recurring feast. Thus this deep instinct of preservation, which impels human beings to desire survival, showed itself even in him who contributed most of all to destroy faith in immortality.

*   *   *   *   *

It is always with difficulty that men resign themselves to dying wholly. Even when reason admits, nay when it desires, annihilation, the subconscious self protests against it; our personality is impelled by its very essence to crave the persistence of its self. Besides, the feelings of survivors rebel against the pain of an unending separation, the definite loss of all affections. In the troubled times which marked the end of the Roman Republic, at a moment when changing fortune periodically turned all the conditions of existence upside down, there grew up a stronger aspiration to a better future, a search, to use the words of the ancients, for a sure haven, in which man, tossed by the storms of life, might find quiet. Thus in the first century B. C. the birth was seen, or rather the rebirth, of a mystic movement which claimed to give by direct communication with God the certainties which reason could not supply. The chief preoccupation of philosophers began to be those capital questions as to the origin and end of man which the schools of the earlier period had neglected as unanswerable. It was above all the Neo-Pythagoreans who gave up pure rationalism, and thus brought Roman thought to admit new forms of immortality.

When the scientific school of the old Pythagorism came to an end in Italy in the fourth century, the sect perpetuated itself obscurely in mysterious conventicles, a sort of freemasonry of which the influence in the Hellenistic period is difficult to measure or circumscribe. It again took on new power in Alexandria under the Ptolemies. In this metropolis, in which all the currents of Europe and Asia were mingled, Pythagorism admitted at this

---

[57] Diog. Laert., X, 16=fragm. 217 Usener; *cf.* Plin., *H. N.*, XXXV, 5.

time many ideas foreign to the teaching of the old master of Samos. This teaching seems not to have set forth a rigid, logically constructed theology, and the points of contact with the beliefs of the East, which its ideas supplied, favoured an accommodating syncretism. Pythagoras was said to have had Plato as a disciple, and Plato was venerated almost as much as the teacher he followed. The powerful structure of Stoic pantheism did not fail to exercise an ascendency over the theorists of the school. This school had been, from its origin, in touch with the Orphic mysteries and those of Dionysos and it remained so, but it was also subject to the more remote influence of Babylonian and Egyptian religions, and particularly of those Chaldean doctrines which the Greeks had learnt to know after Alexander's conquest.

This vast eclecticism, open to all novelties, did not bring about a break with the past. Theology succeeded in effecting a reconciliation with all, even the rudest and most absurd traditions of fable, by an ingenious system of moral allegories. "Divine" Homer thus became a master of piety and wisdom, and mythology a collection of edifying stories. Demonology made it possible to justify all the traditional practices of the cult, as well as magic and divination: everything which seemed incompatible with the new idea of the divinity was ascribed to lower powers. Thus the Pythagoreans could take up the position not of adversaries or reformers but of interpreters of the ancestral religion. They claimed that they remained faithful to the wisdom of the sages who, at the dawn of civilisation, had received a divine revelation, which had been transmitted first to Pythagoras and then to Plato. They felt so sure that they were expressing the thought of these masters, whose authority made law, that they did not hesitate to subscribe the venerated names, by a pious fraud, to their own writings. Nowhere did apocryphal literature have a more luxuriant efflorescence than in these circles.

When the sect was introduced into Rome it sought, according to its wont, to connect itself with old local traditions, and without much difficulty it succeeded. The national pride of the conquerors of Greece could, with some complacency, regard it as Italic. Pythagoras passed for the teacher of King Numa, the religious legislator of the city. Ennius had expressed this philosopher's doctrine in his poems, and altogether, from the time of the ancient republic onwards, the half mythical moralist of Greater Greece enjoyed singular consideration in Rome.[58]

But the first to give new life to the Pythagorean school, which had died in Italy centuries before, was, according to Cicero, his friend, the senator Nigidius Figulus, a curious representative of the scientific religiosity which characterised the sect. This Roman magistrate, a man of singular erudition, was bitten with all the occult sciences. A grammarian, a naturalist and a theologian, he was also an astrologer and magician and, on occasion, a wonder worker. He did not confine himself to theory but gathered about him a club of the initiate, of whom we cannot say whether they were most attracted by scientific curiosity, by austere morals or by mystic practices. Vatinius, the relative and friend of Caesar, and, probably, the spiritualist Appius Claudius Pulcher were the most prominent of this circle of converts.

It is significant that at much the same time the historian Castor of Rhodes claimed to interpret Roman usages by Pythagorism,[59] and the stories establishing a connection between the Roman state and the reformers of Greater Greece were multiplied. In the Augustan age a worldly poet like Ovid[60] thought it permissible to introduce into his *Metamorphoses,* where no digression of the sort was to be looked for, a long speech of Pythagoras explaining vegetarianism and transmigration. A little later Antonius Diogenes, the romancer, found in the same philosophy inspiration for his fantastic pictures of the lot of souls.[61] All this goes to show how powerfully seductive the new sect proved to be as soon as it was revived in Rome.

But it did not lack enemies. Public malignity did not spare these mysterious theosophists who met in subterranean crypts. They were blamed for neglecting the national cult, which had ensured the greatness of the city, in order to indulge in condemned practices or even to commit abominable crimes. It was a more serious matter that their secret gatherings also excited the suspicion of the authorities, and that the partakers were prosecuted as persons who dealt in magic, which was punishable by law. The little Pythagorean church seems not to have been able to maintain itself in the capital for long. In Seneca's time it was dead.[62]

58 Furtwängler, *Die antiken Gemmen,* III, 1900, 257 ss.
59 See Lecture III, p. 97.   60 Ovid, *Metam.,* XV, 60 ss.
61 Rohde, *Der Griech. Roman*[2], p. 270 s.
62 Sen., *Quaest. nat.,* VII, 32, 2.

But Pythagorism continued to find adepts in the empire and soon returned to Rome. Under Domitian, Apollonius of Tyana made the East resound with his preaching and miracles, and although thrown into prison by this emperor he was in favour with his successors. Under the Antonines, the false prophet Alexander of Abonotichos, unmasked by Lucian, claimed to be a new incarnation of the sage of Samos, whose wisdom he pretended to reveal in his mysteries. The literary tradition of the sect maintained itself until the third century, when it was absorbed by Neo-Platonism. In a period of syncretism, the originality of this philosophy resided less in its doctrine than in its observances, and when its conventicles were dissolved, it easily merged itself in the school which professed to continue it. During its long life Pythagorism had indeed had a powerful influence, not only on the system of Plato and Plotinus, but also on the Oriental cults which spread under the empire. It had supplied the first type of the learned mysteries in which knowledge ($\gamma\nu\tilde{\omega}\sigma\iota\varsigma$) is at once the condition and the end of sanctification.[63] Possibly it even penetrated into Gaul at an early date, by way of Marseilles, and was thus known to the Druids.

It would certainly be a mistake to look upon Pythagorism as a pure philosophy, like Epicureanism and Stoicism. Its sectaries formed a church rather than a school, a religious order, not an academy of sciences. From a recent discovery in Rome, if my interpretation of the monument is right,[64] we have learnt that the Pythagoreans met in underground basilicas, constructed on the model of Plato's cavern, in which, according to the great idealist, the chained men see only the shades of the higher realities.[65] A foundation sacrifice, that of a dog and a young pig, was made before this basilica was constructed. Its stucco decoration is borrowed almost entirely from Greek mythology or the ceremonies of the mysteries. Secret rites and varied purifications had to be accomplished in it; hymns accompanied by sacred music were sung; and from a chair within the apse the doctors gave esoteric teaching to the faithful. They taught them the symbols in which the truths of faith and the precepts of conduct, formerly revealed by Pythagoras and the other sages, were handed down in enigmatic form. These remote disciples interpreted all the myths of the past, and especially the Homeric

[63] See Lecture IV, p. 121.
[64] *Revue archéologique*, 1918, VIII, p. 52 ss.
[65] Plato, *Republ.*, VII, p. 514.

poems, by psychological or eschatological allegories. They laid down, as definite commandments, a rule of strict observance which included all the acts of daily life. At dawn, after he had offered a sacrifice to the rising Sun. the pious man must decide on the way in which his day was to be employed. Every evening he must make a threefold examination of conscience, and, if he had been guilty of any sin of omission or commission, must make an act of contrition. He was obliged to follow a purely vegetarian diet and to practise many abstinences, to make repeated prayers, to meditate lengthily. This austere and circumstantial system of morals would ensure happiness and wisdom on earth and salvation in the Beyónd.

All the Neo-Pythagoreans agree in stating that the human soul is related to God and therefore immortal. Many, like the Stoics, look upon it as a parcel of the ether, an effluvium of burning and luminous fluid which fills the celestial spaces and shines in the divine stars. Others, who are nearer to Plato, believe it to be immaterial and define it as a number in movement. Always, generation is regarded as a fall and a danger for the soul. Enclosed in the body as in a tomb, it runs the risk of corruption, even of perishing. Earthly existence is a hard voyage on the stormy waters of matter, which are perpetually rolling and surging. Thus a fundamental pessimism looked upon life here below as a trial and a chastisement; a radical dualism placed the body in opposition to the divine essence residing in it. The constant care of the sage was to keep his soul from pollution by its contact with the flesh. He abstained from meat and other foods which might corrupt it; a series of tabus protected it against all contagion. Ritual purifications restored to it its purity (ἀγνεία) which was continually threatened. The unwearying exercise of virtue, the scrupulous practice of piety preserved its original nature. Music, which caused it to vibrate in harmony with the universe, and science, which lifted it towards divine things, prepared its ascension to heaven. Meditation was a silent prayer, which placed reason in communication with the powers on high. Seized by love for the eternal beauties, it rose in its transports even in this life to God, identified itself with Him and so rendered itself worthy of a blessed immortality.[66]

When the death determined by destiny occurred, the soul escaped from the body in which it was captive but kept its bodily form and appearance, and this simulacrum (εἴδωλον) appeared to

[66] See below, Lecture VIII, p. 209 ss.

men in dreams and after evocations. According to some Pythagoreans, this subtle form was distinct from the soul ($\psi\nu\chi\acute{\eta}$), which ascended immediately to the higher spheres. Others believed that, like a light garment, it wrapped the soul, which was for some time constrained to dwell here below.[67] After this shade had remained beside the body or somewhere near the tomb for a certain number of days, it rose in the atmosphere in which contended winds, water and fire, and was purified by the elements. This zone, the lowest circle of the world, was what fable had called hell (*Inferi*), and it was of this passage from one circle to that next it that poets spoke when they told of the Styx and Charon's boat.[68] When the soul had been purified it was borne, uplifted by the winds, to the sphere of the moon. Here lay the boundary of life and death, the limit which divided the residence of the immortals, where all was harmony and purity, from the corrupt and troubled empire of generation. Thus the luminary of the night was the first dwelling of the Blessed, and there lay the Elysian Fields of the poets, Proserpina's kingdom where rest the shades. And the Fortunate Islands, of which the ancients sung, were no other than the sun and the moon, celestial lands bathed by the waters of the ether.[69]

The shade remained in the moon or was dissolved there, and pure reason rose to the sun whence it came forth, or even reached the summit of the heavens where reigned the Most High. A helpful escort, called by mythology Hermes the Soul-Guide, or *psychopompos,* led the elect to these Olympian peaks. There they regained their true country, and as birth had been to them a death, so their death was their rebirth. They enjoyed the contemplation of the luminous gods. They were rapt by the ravishing tune of the harmony of the spheres, that divine melody of which earthly music is but a feeble echo.[70]

Some souls were kept on the banks of the Styx and could not cross it : in other words, they were constrained to remain on the earth. The dead who had not had religious burial must linger beside their neglected bodies for a hundred years, the normal span of a human life, before they were admitted to the place of purgation, where they would sojourn for ten times that period.[71]

[67] See Lecture VI, p. 167; *cf.* III, p. 103.
[68] See Lecture II, p. 81.
[69] See, for all this, Lecture III, p. 96 s.; *cf.* VIII, p. 195.
[70] See Lecture VIII, p. 212.
[71] See Lecture I, p. 66.

In the same way those who had died young or whose days had been cut short by violence would not enter the purgatory before the due term of their life.[72] But especially the souls of the criminal and the impious were thus condemned to wander, restless and in pain, through the lower air, which they filled with their multitude. It was these demoniac spirits who returned as dismal phantoms to frighten the living, who were evoked by wizards and who revealed the future in oracles. Demonology accounted for all the aberrations of magic and divination. These spirits rose to the aerial purgatory after they had for long years tormented and been tormented, but they could not reach the moon, which repelled them; they were condemned to reincarnation in new bodies, either of men or of beasts, and were once again delivered to the fury of the passions. These passions are the Erinyes, of whom poets sung, that in Tartarus they burnt criminals with their torches and scourged them with their whips. For there was no subterranean hell: Hades was in the air or on our earth, and the infernal sufferings described by mythology were the various tortures inflicted on the souls condemned to transmigration.[73]

This religious philosophy, which, by a symbolism transforming the meaning of the traditional beliefs, reconciled these with men's intelligence, did more than any other to revive faith in immortality. Many enlightened men, like Cicero and Cato, had sought consolation for the misfortunes of this world and a hope for the Beyond in reading Plato, but Plato's proof of immortality could convince only those already convinced.[74] Pythagorism, on the other hand, offered to restless souls a certainty founded on a revelation made to ancient sages, and it satisfied at once the Roman love for order and rule, and the human love for the marvellous and the mysterious. The evidence of the effect of this philosophy is still recognisable, although it often has not been recognised, in the compositions decorating many sepulchral monuments and in the wording of several epitaphs. A tombstone found at Philadelphia in Lydia is particularly curious.[75] It bears a representation of the Y symbol, that is, of the diverging roads between which man must choose when he leaves childhood behind him. On the one side earthly travail leads the virtuous man to eternal rest; on the other softness and debauchery bring the

72 See Lecture V, p. 133.
73 See Lecture III, pp. 73, 81; VII, p. 181 s.
74 *Cf.* Cic., *Tusc.*, I, 11, 24.
75 See Lecture VI, p. 151.

vicious man to a gulf into which he falls. A metrical epitaph, found at Pisaurum (Pesaro), hints covertly at the ideas of the school. This commemorates a child who, in spite of his youth, had learnt the dogmas of Pythagoras and read "the pious verses of Homer" as well as the philosophers, and had studied in Euclid the sacred science of numbers. His soul, runs the inscription,[76] "goes forward through the gloomy stars of deep Tartarus towards the waters of Acheron," a sentence which can be understood only on the supposition that Tartarus and Acheron had for the author a figurative meaning and lay in the depths not of the earth but of the sky.

*　　　*　　　*　　　*　　　*

The belief in a celestial immortality which was thus propagated by the half philosophical, half religious sect of the Pythagoreans was to find a powerful interpreter in a thinker who had a predominant influence over his contemporaries and the succeeding generation—in Posidonius. We know little of his life. Born at Apamea in Syria, about the year 135, he early left his native country, of which he seems to have kept a poor opinion, and as a young student in Athens he attended the lectures of the older Stoic Panaetius. The universal curiosity which was to make him a scholar of encyclopaedic knowledge soon impelled him to take long journeys, in which he even reached the shores of the Atlantic and studied the tides of the ocean. Upon his return he opened a school in the free city of Rhodes and there numbered Cicero among his hearers. When he died at the age of eighty-four the prestige he enjoyed both in the Roman world and among the Greeks was immense. He owed his intellectual ascendancy as much to the marvellous variety of the knowledge which he displayed, as philosopher, astronomer, historian, geographer and naturalist, as to his copious, harmonious and highly coloured style.

A theologian rather than a logician, a scholar rather than a critic, he did not construct an original metaphysical system comparable to those of the great founders of schools. But Posidonius was the most prominent representative of that syncretism which, as we have seen, showed itself in the Pythagoreans before his day and which reigned in the world about him, because men were weary of the sterile discussions of opposing thinkers. He gave the support of his authority and his eloquence to the eclecticism

[76] Bücheler, *Carm. epigr.*, 434.

which reconciled the principles of the ancient Greek schools. Moreover, his Syrian origin led him to combine these doctrines with the religious ideas of the East, which had with astrology given the Hellenes a new conception of man and of the gods.[77]

It is exactly here that Posidonius is important from the point of view of our subject: his tendencies represent a direct reaction against the scepticism of his master Panaetius, who denied both the survival of the soul[78] and the possibility of divination. Posidonius introduced into Stoicism momentous ideas derived at once from Pythagorism and from Eastern cults, and sought to establish them firmly by connecting them with a system of the world, which his vast intelligence had sought to understand in all its aspects. His faith in immortality is strictly related to his cosmography and receives support from his physics.

It was this system of the world which was, thanks to Ptolemy's authority, to perpetuate itself on the whole until the time of Copernicus. We will here give a broad outline of its essential features, because the eschatological doctrines were to remain for centuries connected with it. The terrestrial globe was held to be suspended, motionless, in the centre of the universe, surrounded by an atmosphere formed of the three other elements and reaching to the moon. That part of the atmosphere which was near the earth was thickened and darkened by heavy vapours rising from the soil and the waters. Above, there moved a purer and lighter air which, as it neared the sky, was warmed by contact with the higher fires. Still higher were ranged the concentric spheres of the seven planets, wrapped in ether, a subtle and ardent fluid—first the moon, which still received and gave back the exhalations of the earth,[79] then Mercury and Venus, the two companions of the sun in his daily course. The fourth place, that is, the middle point of the superimposed heavens, was occupied by the luminary of the day,—here Posidonius forsakes Plato and follows the Chaldeans,—the burning heart of the world, the intelligent light which is the source of our minds.[80] Above the sun moved the three higher planets— Mars, Jupiter and Saturn. And these seven wandering stars were surrounded by the sphere of the fixed stars, which were animated by constant and uniform movement. That sphere

[77] Cf. my *Astrology and Religion*, 1912, p. 83 ss.
[78] See above, p. 13.
[79] See Lecture III, p. 98.
[80] See below, Lecture III, p. 100 ss.

marked the world's boundary: beyond it there was only void or the ether.

The universe, as this philosophy imagined it, had therefore well-defined limits: when men raised their eyes to the constellations of the firmament, they thought they perceived its end. The depths of the sky were not then unfathomable; he who sank his gaze in them was not seized with giddiness at the abysses nor bewildered by inconceivable magnitudes, and was not tempted to cry with Pascal:[81] "The eternal silence of these boundless spaces affrights me." Nor was the universe then a multiplicity of heavenly bodies moving to an unknown goal and perpetually transformed, transitory manifestations of an energy developed for undiscoverable ends. The conception formed of the world was static, not dynamic. It was a machine of which the wheels turned according to immutable laws, an organism of which all the parts were united by reciprocal sympathy as they acted and reacted on each other.

This organism was alive, penetrated throughout by the same essence as the soul which maintains our life and thought. This soul was an igneous breath of which the moral corruption was conceived quite materially. When it gave itself up to the desires of the senses, to corporeal passions, its substance thickened and was troubled, and the mud of this pollution adhered to it like a crust. When the soul left the body at the time of death, it became a spirit like the multitude of demons who peopled the atmosphere. But its lot varied in accordance with its condition. If it were laden with matter, its weight condemned it to float in the densest air, the damp-charged gas which immediately surrounded the earth, and its very composition then caused it to reincarnate itself in new bodies.[82] But if it had remained free from all alloy its lightness caused it to pass immediately through this heavier layer of air and bore it to the higher spaces. It stopped in this ascension when, within the ether which was about the moon, it found itself in surroundings like its own substance. Some elect beings, the divine spirits of the sages, kept such purity that they rose through the ether as far as the highest astral spheres. In this system the doctrine of immortality is seen to be closely knit up with cosmography.

[81] Pascal, *Pensées*, III, 206 (t. II, p. 127, Brunschvigg): "Le silence éternel de ces espaces infinis m'effraie."

[82] See Lecture III, p. 98; VI, p. 161 s.; VII, p. 184.

If Posidonius has largely borrowed these ideas from the pla-tonising Pythagorism of his period, he forsook this philosophy on an essential point. As a Stoic he did not admit the transcend-ency of God. For him, God was immanent in the universe; the seat of the directing reason of the world ($\dot{\eta}\gamma\epsilon\mu o\nu\iota\kappa\acute{o}\nu$) was the sphere of the fixed stars, which embraced all other spheres and determined their revolutions. There too, at the summit of the world but not outside it, the spirits of the blessed gathered; from these high peaks they delighted to observe earthly happenings; and when a pious soul tried to rise to them, these succouring heroes, like our saints, could lend their aid and protection.

This philosophy did not draw its power of persuasion only from its logical consistency, which satisfied reason, but it also made a strong appeal to feeling. Posidonius caused a broad stream of mystical ideas, undoubtedly derived from the beliefs developed by the astral religions of the East, to flow into the arid bed of a Stoicism which had become scholastic. For him, reason was not enclosed in the body, even when it sojourned here below; it escaped from it to pass with marvellous swiftness from the depths of the sea to the ends of the earth and the top of the heavens; it flew through all nature, learning to know physical laws and to admire the divine order ever more and more. Above all it could never weary of the sight of the glowing constellations and their harmonious movements. It felt with emotion, as it gave itself up to contemplating them, its kinship with the celestial fires; it entered into communion with the higher gods. In enthusiastic terms, echoed by his imitators, Posidonius described the ecstasy which seized him who left the earth, who felt himself transported to the midst of the sacred chorus of the stars and who followed their rhythmic evolutions. In these transports, the soul did not only win to infinite power, but also received from heaven the revelation of the nature and cause of the celestial revolutions. Thus even in this life it had a foretaste of the beatitude which would belong to it after death when reason, rid of the weak organs of the senses, would directly perceive all the splendours of the divine world and would know its mysteries completely.[83]

This theology attributed to man a power such as to satisfy his proudest feelings. It did not regard him as a tiny animalcule who had appeared on a small planet lost in immensity, nor did

[83] See Lecture IV, p. 127; VIII, p. 210.

it, when he scrutinised the heavens, crush him with a sense of his own pettiness as compared with bodies whose greatness surpassed the limits of his imagination. It made man king of creation, placed him in the centre of a still limited world of which the proportions were not so vast that he could not travel all over his domain. If he could tear himself from the domination of his body, he became capable of communicating with the visible gods who were almost within his reach and whom he might hope to equal after his passage here below. He knew himself to be united to them by an identity of nature which alone explained how he understood them.

"Quis caelum possit, nisi caeli munere, nosse
Et reperire deum, nisi qui pars ipse Dei est?"[84]

"Who could know heaven save by heavenly grace, or find God if he were not himself a part of God?"—words of the Roman poet who echoes Posidonius' teaching.

* * * * *

It is easy to understand that such ideas were readily adopted at a time when human minds, tired of inconclusive disputes, despaired of ever reaching truth by their own strength. The astral mysticism eloquently preached by Posidonius was to influence all the later Stoicism. Seneca in particular, in the numerous passages in which he speaks of the misery and baseness of life in the body and celebrates the felicity of the pure souls who live among the stars, shows the imprint of the philosopher of Apamea. And this philosopher also exerted a far-reaching action beyond the narrow circle of the school. The erudition of the antiquarian Varro, the poems of Virgil and Manilius and the biblical exegesis of Philo the Jew, all drew on him for inspiration. But the author in whom we can best discern his influence is his pupil Cicero, the abundance of whose writings allows us to follow the evolution of his thought, which is characteristic of the whole society of his time.

It is beyond doubt that Cicero was an agnostic for the greater part of his life. His mind found satisfaction in the scepticism of the New Academy, or rather he adopted towards the future life the received attitude of the world in which he lived, where the problem of the soul's origin and destiny was regarded as not only insoluble but also idle, as unworthy to absorb the minds of men

(So Isk Fowler)

[84] Manilius, II, 115.

who should devote their energies to the service of the state. The question of the cult to be rendered to the Manes had been settled once for all by the ancient pontifical law. Old Rome distrusted speculations as to the Beyond because they dangerously diverted thought from actual realities. But Cicero, by his study of the writings of his master Posidonius and by his intercourse with the senator Nigidius Figulus, a fervent adept of Pythagorism,[85] had been brought into contact with the stream of mystical ideas which was beginning to flow through the West. Gradually, as he grew older and life brought him disappointments, his thought was more attracted to religious ideas.[86] In 54, when he had given up political life, he composed the *Republic*, an imitation of Plato's work on the same subject. As Plato had introduced the myth of Er the Armenian at the end of his work, so his Roman imitator concludes with the puzzling picture of "Scipio's Dream," where the destroyer of Carthage receives the revelations of the conqueror of Zama. The hero, from the height of the celestial spheres, expounds that doctrine of astral immortality which was common to the Pythagoreans and to Posidonius. It is given as yet only as a dream, a vision the truth of which is in no way guaranteed. But in 45 B. C. Cicero suffered a cruel loss in the death of his only daughter Tullia. His grief persuaded him that this beloved being still lived among the gods. Even while he accused himself of unreasonable weakness, he ordered that not a tomb but a chapel (*fanum*), consecrating her apotheosis, should be raised to this young woman. The letters he wrote at this time to Atticus, from the shores of the Pomptine Marshes, in the solitude of Astura, apprise us of his most intimate feelings. He gave vent to his sorrow in writing a *Consolatio*, and in its preserved fragments we see him strangely impressed by the Pythagorean doctrines: he speaks of the soul, exempt from all matter, as celestial and divine and therefore eternal, of the soul's life here below as a penalty inflicted on it because it is born to expiate anterior crimes (*scelerum luendorum causa*).

Cicero's sensitive spirit, troubled by the perplexing problem of our destiny, did not turn to the old discredited beliefs but to the new conceptions which a mystical philosophy had brought from the East. *Hortensius* and the *Tusculans*, written in this

---

[85] See above, p. 22.

[86] Lehrs, *Populäre Aufsätze aus dem Altertum*, 1875, p. 349 ss.; Fowler, *Religious Experience of the Roman People*, p. 382 ss.

period of his life, show us the empire which the Neo-Stoicism of his master and the Neo-Pythagorism of his fellow-senator then exercised over his mind, saddened and disillusioned as he was, and show us too how he sought consolation for the private and public ills which were overwhelming him in the luminous doctrine of a blissful survival.

This spiritual evolution is an image of the great change which was about to take place in the Roman world.

*   *   *   *   *

Stoic philosophy, although its maxims had been popularised by education and literature, was almost as incapable of exercising a wide influence on the deep masses of the people as the esoteric theosophy revealed in the aristocratic conventicles of the Pythagoreans. The urban "plebs," to which slavery and trade had given a strong admixture of Eastern blood, and the peasants of the rural districts, where the gaps caused by depopulation were filled up by a foreign labour supply, were beginning at the end of the Republican period to hear new dogmas preached, dogmas which were winning an ever increasing number of believers. The ancient national cults of Greece and Rome aimed above all at ensuring civic order and earthly welfare, and paid small regard to the spiritual perfection of individuals and their eternal future. But now exotic cults claimed to reveal the secret of immortality to their adepts.[87] The Oriental mysteries, propagated in the West, united in the promise of securing holiness in this life and felicity in the next, while they imparted to their initiates the knowledge of certain rites and required submission to certain precepts. Instead of the fluctuating and disputable beliefs of philosophers as to destiny in the Beyond, these religions gave certainty founded on divine revelation and on the faith of countless generations attached to them. The truth, which the mysticism of the thinkers looked to find in direct communication with heaven, was here warranted by a venerable tradition and by the daily manifestations of the gods adored. The belief in life beyond the grave, which had in ancient paganism been so vague and melancholy, was transformed into confident hope in a definite beatitude. Participation in the occult ceremonies of the sect was an infallible means of finding salvation. A society that was weary of doubt received these promises eagerly, and the old

[87] *Cf.* my *Oriental religions in Roman paganism*, Chicago, 1911, p. 39 ss.

beliefs of the East combined with an eclectic philosophy to give a new eschatology to the Roman Empire.

The salvation ensured by the mysteries was conceived as identification with the god venerated in them. By virtue of this union the initiate was reborn, like this god, to new life after he had perished, or, like him, escaped from the fatal law of death which weighs on humanity. He was "deified" or "immortalised," after he had taken part, as actor, in a liturgical drama reproducing the myth of the god whose lot was thus assimilated to his own. Purifications, lustrations and unctions, participation in a sacred banquet, revelations, apparitions and ecstasies—a complicated series of ceremonies and instructions helped to bring about this metamorphosis of the faithful whom a higher power absorbed or penetrated with its energy. We shall return to this sacramental operation which made pious souls equal to the divinity.[88]

There is another point on which, in the course of this historical introduction, we must dwell a little longer, namely, the evolution undergone by the conception of the Beyond taught in the different mysteries and the share of philosophy in the transformation. For if in the various sects the liturgy was usually preserved with scrupulous fidelity, its theological interpretation varied considerably as time passed. In paganism much doctrinal liberty was always combined with respect for rites.

Some of the mysteries often gave in their beginnings a rather coarse idea of the future life, and the pleasures which might be enjoyed therein were very material. The ancient Greek conception, going back to Orphism, was, as we have seen, that of a subterranean kingdom divided into two contrasted parts—Tartarus where the wicked, plunged in a dark slough or subjected to other pains, suffering the chastisement of their faults, on the one side; on the other, the Elysian Fields, those flowered, luminous meadows, gay with song and dance, in which the blessed pursued their favourite occupations, whether they were allowed to dwell there for ever, or whether they awaited there the hour fixed for their rebirth on earth.[89] This eschatology, which had become the common possession of the Hellenes, was certainly that of the mysteries of Greece and in particular of the mysteries of Eleusis. But these mysteries were never more than local religions: how-

[88] See Lecture IV, p. 118 ss.
[89] See Lecture II, p. 76; VII, p. 171.

ever numerous were the initiates attracted by their renown, they were bound to the soil where they were born. Thus their influence was very limited in the Roman period and cannot be compared with that of the universal cults which were propagated throughout the Mediterranean world. As for Orphism, which was never connected with any one temple, it is doubtful whether it still constituted an actual sect, and if it did, it certainly spread over a very narrow field. Its influence was perpetuated chiefly because it was absorbed by Pythagorism.

Among the mysteries propagated in the West, the most ancient were those of the Thraco-Phrygian gods, Dionysos and Sabazios, who were indeed looked upon as identical. We know that in 186 B. C. a *senatus consultum* forbade the celebration of the Bacchanalia in Italy, and in 139 some sectaries of Jupiter Sabazius, who identified this god with the Jahve-Sabaoth of the Jews, were expelled from Rome by the praetor at the same time as the "Chaldeans." The cult practised by the votaries of Bacchus or Liber Pater, whose confraternities were maintained until the end of paganism, differed profoundly from the Dionysos worship of ancient Greece: a number of Oriental elements had been introduced into it; in particular, the relations between Dionysos and Osiris, which go back to a very remote period, had become singularly close in Egypt. However, many reliefs on tombstones and the celebrated paintings found in the catacombs of Praetextatus prove that the cults of the Thraco-Phrygian gods remained faithful to the old idea of a future life. The shade went down into the bowels of the earth, never again to leave them. If judged worthy, it took part in an eternal banquet, of which the initiate received a foretaste on earth, in the feasts of the mysteries. Sacred drunkenness, a divine exaltation, was the pledge of the joyous intoxication which the god of wine would grant in Hades to the faithful who had united themselves to him.[90]

In 205, towards the end of the second Punic war, the cult of Cybele, the Great Mother of the Gods, and of Attis, her associate, was transported from Pessinus in Phrygia and officially adopted by the Roman people. The great feasts of this religion were celebrated in March about the equinox and commemorated the death and resurrection of Attis, the emblem of vegetation, which, after it has withered, flowers again in the spring. The faithful associated their own destiny with the lot of their god: like him

[90] See Lecture IV, p. 120; VIII, p. 204.

they would be reborn to a new life after they had died. Their doctrines on this point were certainly transformed as time passed, for no Oriental cult which spread in the West underwent more evolution, since none was more fundamentally barbarous when it came from Asia. Originally, Cybele was the goddess of the dead, because Mother Earth receives them into her bosom. Every Phrygian tomb is a sanctuary and its epitaph a dedication: often the graves are consecrated to the goddess and bear her image or that of the lion, her substitute. Often too the tombstone has the shape of a door, the door of the subterranean world whither the dead descend. The belief seems to have been held that the deceased were absorbed in the Great Mother who had given them birth, and that they thus participated in her divinity. She brought forth corn and grapes for men and thus sustained them day by day, and the bread and wine, taken in the meal which was the essential act of the initiation, would ensure immortality to those who were of the mystery. "Thou givest us the food of life with unfailing constancy," says a prayer, "and when our soul departs we will take refuge in thee. Thus all that thou givest, always falls to thee again."[91]

Towards the end of the Republic the mysteries of Isis and Serapis, which had come from Alexandria and had already spread through the south of Italy, established themselves in Rome and maintained themselves there in spite of opposition from the senate. Under the Empire, the Egyptian religion displayed all the pomp of its liturgy in magnificent temples and had a number of votaries in every province. The cult of Osiris, of which that of Serapis was a form, was originally a cult of the fields, like that of Attis, and the great feast which its adherents celebrated in autumn recalls the Phrygian spring feasts. The death of Osiris, whose body had been torn to pieces by Seth, was mourned; and when Isis had found the scattered fragments of the corpse, joined them together and reanimated it, noisy rejoicing followed the lamentation. Like the initiates of Cybele and Attis, those of Isis and Serapis were associated with the passion and resurrection of their god. And, in the same way, the oldest conception of immortality in these mysteries was that the de-

---

[91]   "Alimenta vitae tribuis perpetua fide,
        Et cum recesserit anima in te refugiemus,
        Ita, quicquid tribuis, in te cuncta recidunt."

(*Anthol. Lat.*, ed. Riese, I, p. 27.)

parted went down into the infernal regions, where a man became
another Serapis, a woman another Isis, which is to say that they
were assimilated to the gods who had granted them salvation.[92]
This is why on numerous funeral reliefs the dead man, who
has become a hero and is shown lying on a couch, bears on his
head the bushel (*modius*) which is the attribute of Serapis.
In consequence, however, of the identification of this god with
Dionysos, the joys beyond the grave are also represented as a
feast in the Elysian Fields at which the great master of banquets
presides.[93]

All these mysteries conceive immortality as a descent of the
dead into Hades. For them, the kingdom of the dead lies in the
bosom of the earth. Those who have been initiated will there
enjoy a felicity made up of purely material pleasures, or they
will be identified with the powers who reign over the nether world
and will have part in their divine life. It will be noticed how
closely this last conception approached to that of ancient
Stoicism, according to which the various parts of the human
organism, dissociated by death, were to regain their integrity
in the divine elements of the universe.

Quite another doctrine was propagated by the Syrian cults
and the Persian mysteries of Mithras, which spread in the West
in the first century of our era. These religions taught that the
soul of the just man does not go below the ground but rises to
the sky, there to enjoy divine bliss in the midst of the stars in
the eternal light. Only the wicked were condemned to roam the
earth's surface, or were dragged by the demons into the dusky
depths in which the spirit of evil reigned. Opinions differed as
to the region of heaven in which the souls of the elect dwelt. The
"Chaldeans," who looked upon the sun as the master and the
intelligence of the universe, made him the author of human
reason, which returned to him after it had left the body, while
for the priests of Mithras the spirit rose, by way of the planetary
spheres, to the summit of the heavens. We will have to examine
later the different forms of astral immortality.[94] But you will
already have noticed how nearly this immortality, as formulated
by the Iranian and Semitic sects, approximated to the doctrine
taught by Pythagorism and adopted by Neo-Stoicism.

[92] See Lecture IV, p. 122.
[93] See Lecture VIII, p. 202.
[94] See Lecture III, p. 96 ss.

This meeting of the two doctrines was not an effect of chance. The idea that souls are related to the celestial fires, whence they descend at birth and whither they reascend at death, had probably been borrowed by the ancient Pythagoreans from the astral religions of the East. Recent research seems to have established the fact of its Chaldeo-Persian origin. But the Greek philosophers, according to their wont, defined and developed this idea in an original way. In the Hellenistic period, when they adopted astrology, they were subject for the second time to the ascendancy of the scientific religion of the "Chaldeans"; and, in their turn, they reacted on the Oriental cults when these spread in the Graeco-Roman world. We have sure evidence that the mysteries of Mithras were, in particular, strongly affected by the influence of the Pythagorean sect, which was itself organised like a kind of mystery. In a more general way, philosophy introduced into the mysteries ethical ideas and, instead of the purely ritualistic or rather magical means of salvation, some moral requirements became necessary to earn immortality.

There is here a mass of actions and reactions of which the details escape us; but we can form some idea of such a syncretism from the remains of the theological writings attributed to Hermes Trismegistus, from the writings, that is, which are supposed to contain the revelations of the Egyptian god Thot. This professedly Egyptian wisdom includes a number of ideas and definitions which are characteristic of Posidonius and Neo-Pythagorism. The Greek and the Egyptian elements are so closely associated in it that it is very difficult to separate the one from the other. We find another example of the same mixture in the "Chaldaic Oracles," which were probably composed about the year 200 of our era and which became one of the sacred books of Neo-Platonism. Unlike the Hermetic writings, this collection of verses does indeed seem to have belonged to a sect practising an actual cult: its greater part is taken up with mythology, and the fantastic mysticism of the East is more prominent here than in the Hermetic lore, but the mind of the compiler of these revelations was also penetrated by the ideas which the Greek masters had widely circulated.

The tenet of astral immortality, which philosophy shared with the cults emanating from Syria and Persia, imposed itself on the ancient world. It is curious to notice how it was introduced into the theology of the very mysteries to which it was at first foreign: Attis ended by becoming a solar god, and thenceforward it was in the heights of heaven that Cybele was united to the souls she had prevented from wandering in darkness and had saved from hell. The priests of the Alexandrian divinities were similarly to explain that the dead had not their dwelling in the interior of our globe, but that the "subterranean" (ὑπόγειος) kingdom of Serapis was situated beneath the earth, that is, in the lower hemisphere of heaven, bounded by the line of the horizon.[95]

According as the Oriental religions were more largely propagated, faith in a new eschatology spread gradually among the people; and although memories and survivals of the old belief in the life of the dead in the grave and the shade's descent into the infernal depths may have lingered, the doctrine which predominated henceforward was that of celestial immortality.

The distance separating the age of Augustus from that of the Flavians on this point can be measured by reading Plutarch's moral works (about 120 A. D.). A constant preoccupation with religious matters, and in particular a learned curiosity as to the cults of the East, shows itself in this Greek of Chaeronea, living in a country which, in its pride in its own past, had more than any other resisted the invasion of exoticism. Further, the eclectic philosopher likes to insert in his dissertations myths in which, after the fashion of Plato, he expounds the lot of souls in the Beyond and their struggle to rise heavenwards. An attempt has been made to prove—wrongly, I think—that he is here inspired by Posidonius. These apocalytic visions, which claim to reveal truths previously ignored, are not taken from that well-known writer; they have a religious imprint which betrays sacerdotal influence, and the philosophic ideas they contain are those which were part of the common wisdom of the Pythagoreans and the mysteries.

There doubtless still were in the second century Stoics, like the Emperor Marcus Aurelius, for whom the future life was a mere hypothesis, or at most a hope (p. 14), as well as sceptics, like Lucian of Samosata, whose irony mocked all beliefs. But gradually their number diminished and the echo of their voices grew feebler. Faith in survival deepened as present life came to seem a burden harder and harder to bear. The pessimistic idea that birth is a chastisement and that the true life is not that passed on earth, imposed itself in proportion to the growth of

[95] See Lecture II, p. 79.

public and private ills and to the aggravation of the empire's social and moral decline. In the period of violence and devastation which occurred in the third century, there was so much undeserved suffering, there were so many unjust failures and unpunished crimes, that men took refuge in the expectation of a better life in which all the iniquity of this world would be retrieved. No earthly hope then brightened life. The tyranny of a corrupt bureaucracy stifled every attempt at political progress. Science seemed exhausted and no longer discovered unknown truths; art was struck with sterility of invention and reproduced heavily the creations of the past. An increasing impoverishment and a general insecurity constantly discouraged the spirit of enterprise. The idea spread that humanity was smitten by incurable decay, that society was on the road to dissolution and the end of the world was impending. All these causes of discouragement and pessimism must be remembered in order to understand the dominance of the old idea, then so often repeated, that a bitter necessity constrains the spirit of man to enclose itself in matter, and that death is a liberation which delivers it from its carnal prison. In the heavy atmosphere of a period of oppression and powerlessness, the despondent souls of men aspired with ineffable ardour to the radiant spaces of heaven.

*   *   *   *   *

The mental evolution of Roman society was complete when Neo-Platonism took upon itself the office of directing minds. The powerful mysticism of Plotinus (205-262 A. D.) opened up the path which Greek philosophy was to follow until the world of antiquity reached its end. We shall not undertake to notice in this place the discrepancies of the latest teachers who theorised about the destiny of souls. In the course of these lectures we shall have occasion to quote some of the opinions of Porphyry, the chief disciple of Plotinus, and of his successor Jamblichus, who was, like himself, a Syrian. We will here do no more than indicate broadly what distinguished the theories of this school from those which had hitherto been dominant.

The system generally accepted, by the mysteries as by philosophy, was a pantheism according to which divine energy was immanent in the universe and had its home in the celestial spheres. The souls, conceived as material, could in consequence rise to the stars but did not leave the world. The Neo-Pythagoreans themselves had not had a very firmly established doctrine on this point: while some of them stated that reason was incorporeal, others, as we have seen (p. 24), admitted with the Stoics that it was an igneous substance. It is true that even in paganism the appearance can be discerned of the belief in a Most High (Ὕψιστος) or an unknown god (Ἄγνωστος), whom some people supposed to dwell above the starry heavens, beyond the limits of the world, and towards whom pious spirits could rise. The revivers of Platonic idealism asserted the transcendence of God and the spirituality of the soul more strongly and clearly. A whole chapter of the *Enneades* of Plotinus is taken up with refuting those who held the soul to be material.[96] As a principle of life and movement, it is stated to be immortal by its very essence, so that if it kept its purity perfect, it would find after its passage here below eternal felicity in the intelligible world.

The Neo-Platonists preserved the idea, which had previously been admitted, that this intellectual essence comes down to earth through the planetary spheres and the atmosphere, and that as it sinks in the luminous ether and the damp air, it becomes laden with particles of the elements through which it passes. It surrounds itself with a garment or, as it is sometimes called, with a vehicle (ὄχημα) which thickens as it gradually draws near us.[97] This subtle body, the seat of the passions and of feeling, is intermediary between the spiritual principle which has issued from God and the flesh in which it is to enclose itself, and for certain philosophers it survives death and accompanies the soul to the Beyond, at least if the soul, not being free from earthly admixture, cannot wholly leave the world of sense, and therefore rises only to the planetary circle or to that of the fixed stars.

When the soul has suffered even more from the taint to which its contact with matter, the source of evil, exposes it, it is doomed to reincarnate itself in a new body and again to undergo the trial of this life. When it has become incurably corrupt and burdened with evil, it goes down into the depths of Hades.

Following Plato, Plotinus and his successors have adopted the Pythagorean doctrine of metempsychosis. They have even developed it, as we shall see,[98] together with the whole pessimistic and ascetic conception of life, the conception which looks at

[96] *Enn.*, IV, 7.
[97] See Lecture III, p. 106; VI, p. 169.
[98] See Lecture VII, p. 184 ss.

birth as a pain and a fall, a temporary subjection to a body from which emancipation must be sought. It is only after this liberation that the soul can reach perfect wisdom; it must no longer be troubled by the senses if it is to attain to the end of existence, to union with God.

This union can be realised even during this life in moments of ecstasy, in which the soul rises above thought and gives itself up entirely to love for the ineffable Unity in which it is absorbed. Like many other mystics, Plotinus disdains the ceremonies of positive cults: they were superfluous to the sage who could of himself enter into communion with the supreme Being. But even his disciple Porphyry conceded a greater value to rites and initiations. If they were powerless to lead the partakers of mysteries to the highest degree of perfection, their effect yet was to render men worthy to live among the visible gods who people heaven.[99] But only philosophical wisdom could rise to the intelligible world and the Unknowable.

The principle of a mystical relation between man and the divinity was to lead Neo-Platonism to more and more reverence for religious traditions. For it was held that in the past the revelation of truth had been granted by Heaven not only to divine Plato and the sages of Greece, but to all the founders of barbarous cults and authors of sacred writings. They all communicated profound teaching, which they sometimes hid beneath the veil of allegory. Inspired by the symbolism of the Pythagoreans, the last representatives of Greek philosophy claimed to rediscover the whole of Platonic metaphysics and the Platonic doctrine of immortality in the myths and rites of paganism. The speeches of Julian the Apostate on the Sun-King and the Mother of the Gods are characteristic examples of this bold exegesis, destitute of all critical and even all common sense, which was adopted by the last champions of the old beliefs.

*　　　*　　　*　　　*　　　*

These aberrations of Neo-Platonic thought must not hide the school's historical importance from us, any more than the excesses of the superstitious theurgy which invaded it. When it revived Plato's idealism, it produced a lasting change in the eschatological ideas which prevailed in paganism, and it deeply influenced even the Christian doctrines of immortality held since

[99] See Lecture IV, p. 108; VIII, p. 212.

the fourth century. This will be better seen, we hope, in the course of these lectures.[100] It may be said that the conception of the lot of souls which reigned at the end of antiquity persisted on the whole through the Middle Ages—the immaterial spirits of the just rising through the planetary spheres to the Supreme Being enthroned above the zone of the fixed stars; the posthumous purification of those whom life has sullied in a purgatory intermediary between heaven and hell; the descent of the wicked into the depths of the earth where they suffered eternal chastisement. This threefold division of the universe and of souls was largely accepted at the time of the Empire's decline by pagans and by Christians, and after long centuries it was again to find magnificent expression in Dante's "Divine Comedy." Before it could be destroyed astronomy had to destroy the whole cosmography of Posidonius and Ptolemy on which it was based. When the earth ceased to be the centre of the universe, the one fixed point in the midst of the moving circles of the skies, and became a tiny planet turning round another heavenly body, which itself moved in the immensity of space, among an infinity of similar stars, the naïve conception formed by the ancients of the journey of souls in a well-enclosed world could no longer be maintained. The progress of science discredited the convenient solution bequeathed to scholasticism by antiquity, and left us in the presence of a mystery of which the pagan mysteries never had even a suspicion.

100 See Lecture II, p. 90; IV, p. 109; VIII, p. 196 ss., 206.

I

AFTER LIFE IN THE TOMB

WHEN Cicero in his *Tusculans*[1] first touches on the question of the immortality of the soul, he begins by citing in its support the fact that belief in it has existed since earliest antiquity. He states that unless the first Romans were convinced that man was not reduced to nought, when he left this life, and that all feeling was not extinguished in death, there could be no explanation of the rules of the old pontifical law as to funerals and burials, rules the violation of which was regarded as an inexpiable crime. This remark is that of a very judicious observer. There subsist in the funeral rites of all peoples, in the ceremony of mourning established by the religious law or by tradition, customs which derive from archaic conceptions of life beyond the tomb and which are still followed although their original meaning is no longer understood. Modern learning has sometimes successfully sought to elucidate them, borrowing light from the practices of savage peoples and from European folk-lore. We will not enter the domain of these researches, for since our special purpose here is to expound the ideas as to immortality held in later times, we have to consider only the beliefs which were still alive in that period. A false interpretation supplied by a philosopher may have more historical value for us than the true explanation of an institution which had lost its meaning.

But even among the ideas which were neither obliterated nor discredited, conceptions which originated at very different dates have to be distinguished.

[1] Cic., *Tusc.*, I, 12, §27.

The doctrines of paganism, like the soil of our planet, are formed of superimposed strata. When we dig into them we discover successive layers under the upper deposits of recent alluvia. Nothing was suddenly destroyed in ancient religions; their transformations were never revolutionary. Faith in the past was not entirely abolished when new ways of believing were formed. Contradictory opinions could exist side by side for a long time without any shock being caused by their disagreement; and it was only little by little and slowly that argument excluded one way of thinking to give place to the other, while there were always hardy survivals left, both in thought and in customs. Thus the beliefs as to the future life which were current under the Roman Empire present a singular mixture, coarse ideas going back to the prehistoric period mingling with theories imported into Italy at a late date.

We will today examine the oldest of all the ways of considering survival in the Beyond: life in the tomb.

*　　　*　　　*　　　*　　　*

Ethnology has proved that among all peoples the belief that the dead continue to live in the tomb has reigned, and sometimes still reigns. The primitive man, disconcerted by death, cannot persuade himself that the being who moved, felt, willed, as he does, can be suddenly deprived of all his faculties. The most ancient and the crudest idea is that the corpse itself keeps some obscure sensitiveness which it cannot manifest. It is imagined to be in a state like sleep. The vital energy which animated the body is still attached to it and cannot exist without it. This belief was so powerful in Egypt that it inspired a whole section of the funeral ritual and called forth the infinite care that was taken to preserve mummies. Even in the West it survived vaguely, and traces of it might still be discovered today. Lucretius combats this invincible illusion of men who, even while they affirm that death extinguishes all feeling, keep a secret uneasiness as to the suffering which their mortal remains may undergo and are

frightened by the idea that their bodies may be eaten by
worms or carnivorous animals. They cannot separate
themselves from this prone body, which they believe is
still their self. Why, continues the poet, would it be more
painful to be the prey of wild beasts than to be burnt by
the flame of the pyre, to freeze lying on the icy slab of the
grave or to be crushed by the weight of heaped-up earth?[2]
This very fear that the earth may weigh heavily on those
who are deposited in the grave shows itself among many
peoples who inter their dead, and was expressed in Rome
by a formula so very usual that it was recalled in epitaphs
by initials only: "*S(it) t(ibi) t(erra) l(evis)*," "May
earth be light for thee." Until the Empire Stoic philosophers could be found who upheld that the soul endures
only for the time for which the body is preserved.[3]

But experience proved that the corpse decomposed
rapidly in the soil, all that remained of it being a skeleton
bereft of the organs of sensation. When the custom of incineration, followed in Italy from the prehistoric period,
became practically general in Rome, the destruction of the
body took place regularly before the eyes of those present. Thus men reached the belief that those near and dear
to them, whom they sometimes saw again in their dreams
or seemed to feel beside them, who were kept alive at
least in memory, differed from the beings of flesh and
bones whom they had known. From those material individuals subtle elements detached themselves, filled with
a mysterious force which subsisted when the human
organism had crumbled to dust or been reduced to ashes.
It was this same principle which temporarily departed
from persons who lost consciousness in a faint or a
lethargy. If this light essence did not leave a dying man
at the moment of his death—whether or not it could
escape from his body immediately was indeed uncertain
—it was set free by the funeral fire,[4] but it still inhabited

---

2 Lucretius, III, 890 ss.
3 Servius, *Aen.*, III, 68.
4 Servius, *ibid*.

the tomb in which his remains rested. The idea that it was somehow attached to his remains had taken root in men's minds, and even literature bears witness to the persistence of this deeply implanted popular belief. Propertius,[5] when cursing a woman, desires that "her Manes may not be able to settle near her ashes." And at Liternum in Campania, where Scipio Africanus caused himself to be buried because, as he said, he did not wish to leave even his bones to his ungrateful country, the grotto was shown where he rested and where, so men believed,[6] "a serpent kept guard over his Manes."

This primitive conception of the persistence of a latent life in the cold and rigid corpse or of its passage to a vaporous being like the body, is connected with the belief that the dead retain all the needs and feelings which were previously theirs. The funeral cult, celebrated at the tomb, is born of this belief. It proceeds from fear as much as from piety, for the dead are prone to resentment and quick in vengeance. The unknown force which inhabits them, the mysterious power which causes them to act, inspired great awe. If the natural course of their existence had been interrupted, especially if they had died before their time, they were suspected of being victims of some mischievous enchantment; their sickness was looked upon as an invasion of maleficent spirits provoked by spells. The wrath of those who had thus been torn from their homes and their wonted way of life was to be dreaded. Loud outbursts of grief followed by prolonged manifestations of mourning must prove to them, in the first place, that they were truly lamented and that no attempt had been made to get rid of them. Then, in their new abode to which they were conveyed, they must be ensured a bearable existence, in order that they might remain therein quietly and not trouble their families nor punish, by some intrusion, those who neglected them. Solicitude for the beloved, the desire to prevent their suffer-

---

[5] Propertius, IV, 5, 3: "Nec sedeant cineri Manes." *Cf.* Lucan, IX, 2.
[6] Pliny, *H. N.*, XVI, 44, §234; *cf.* Livy, XXXVIII, 53.

ing, the hope of obtaining their protection, partly account
for the origin and maintenance of these practices, but they
were above all inspired by the terror which spirits called
forth, as is proved by the fact that they were the same for
all the departed without distinction, for those who had
been loved and those who had been hated.

The tomb is the house of the dead. This is an idea
common to the whole ancient world, going back in Italy
beyond the foundation of Rome. The prehistoric cemeteries of the first iron age have yielded a number of
cinerary urns exactly reproducing the various types of
huts which sheltered the tribes who then peopled the
peninsula. The burial places of the Etruscans are often
on the plan of their dwellings, and Roman epitaphs leave
no doubt as to the persistence of the conviction that the
dead inhabit the tomb. The diffusion of Oriental cults
revived archaic beliefs on this point as on many others.
The name "eternal house" (*domus aeterna*), borrowed
from the Egyptians and the Semites, often occurs in funeral inscriptions of the imperial period.[7] One text even
specifies that this is "the eternal house in which future
life must be passed."[8] The tomb is thus no mere passage
through which the soul goes on its way to another region
of the world; it is a lasting residence. "This," says an
inscription, "is our certain dwelling, the one which we
must inhabit."[9] In the *Aeneid,* a cenotaph is raised to
Polydorus, whose body had been lost, and his "soul" is
installed there by a funeral ceremony,[10] for the shade
which has no sepulchre wanders, as we shall see, about the
earth. But when a fine monument is given to a dead man,
he is happy to be able to offer hospitality there to passers-
by and invites them to stay on their way. Sometimes he is

[7] *Cf.* my *Oriental religions,* p. 240.

[8] CIL, I, 1108: "Domum aeternam ubi aevum degerent."

[9] Bücheler, *Carm. epigr.,* 1555: "Haec certa est domus, haec est colenda
nobis."

[10] Virg., *Aen.,* III, 67: "Animam sepulcro condimus." *Cf.* Pliny, *Epist.,*
III, 27, 12: "Rite conditis Manibus."

imagined as in a bedchamber, where he sleeps an endless sleep,[11] but this is not the primitive nor the dominant idea. This idea, on the contrary, was that his rest was at least not unbroken, since he had many requirements. It was necessary not only to ensure him a roof but also to provide for his support, for he had the same needs and tastes beneath the ground as he had upon it. Therefore the clothes which covered him, the jewels which adorned him, the earthen or bronze vessels which decked his table, the lamps which afforded him light, would be placed beside him. If he were a warrior he would be given the arms he bore, if a craftsman the tools he used; a woman would have the articles necessary to her toilet, a child the toys which amused him; and the amulets, by the help of which all that was maleficent would be kept away, were not forgotten. "It is against common sense," says Trimalchio in Petronius' romance,[12] "to deck the house of the living and not to give the same care to the house which we must inhabit for a longer time." In fact, the larger number of the articles of furniture and household use preserved in our museums come from tombs, which, in the climate of Egypt, have sometimes been able to yield up to us, intact, some precious volume intended for a mummy's bedside book.

But the tombs have kept for us only a small part of the offerings made to those who were leaving this world, for often their wardrobe and implements were delivered with them to the flame of the pyre in the belief that somehow they would find them again in the Beyond. Lucian relates that a husband loved his wife so dearly that at her death he caused all the ornaments and the clothes which she liked to wear to be buried with her. But seven days after her death, as, stretched on a couch, he was silently reading Plato's *Phaedo*, seeking therein solace for his grief, his wife appeared, seated herself beside him, and re-

[11] See above, Introd., p. 10; Lecture VIII, p. 192.

[12] Petronius, 71: "Valde enim falsum vivo quidem domos cultas esse, non curari eam ubi diutius nobis habitandum est."

proached him for not having added to his offering one of
her gilt slippers which had been left behind a chest.
The husband found it there, and hastened to burn it in
order that the poor woman might no longer remain half
barefooted.[13]

Above all, the dead must be offered food, for the shade,
like the human body which it replaces, needs nourishment
for its subsistence. Its feeble and precarious life is quick-
ened and prolonged only if it be constantly sustained. The
dead are hungry; above all they are thirsty. Those whose
humours have dried, whose mouths have withered, are
tortured by the need to refresh their parched lips. It
therefore is not enough to place in the tombs the drinks
and dishes, the remains of which have often been found
beside skeletons; by periodic sacrifices the Manes must be
supplied with fresh food also. If they are left without
nourishment they languish, weak as a fasting man, almost
unconscious, and in the end they would actually die of
starvation. This is why the flesh of victims was, in funeral
sacrifices, wholly destroyed by fire, none of it being
reserved for those present. People always retained the
conviction that the offerings burnt on the altar or the
libations poured into the grave were consumed by him
for whom they were intended. Often there is in the tombstone a circular cavity, the bottom of which is pierced
with holes; the liquid poured into it went through the perforated slab and was led by a tube to the urn which held
the calcinated bones. It is comprehensible that an unbe-
liever protested against this practice in his epitaph. "By
wetting my ashes with wine thou wilt make mud," he
says, "and I shall not drink, when I am dead."[14] But how
many other texts there are which show the persistence of
the ancient ideas! "Passer-by," says a Roman inscription, "the bones of a man pray thee not to soil the monu-

---

[13] Lucian, *Philopseudes*, 27; *cf.* Dessau, *Inscr. sel.*, 8379, 1. 50 ss.

[14] Kaibel, *Epigr. Graeca*, 646=Dessau, *Inscr. sel.*, 8156; *cf.* Lucian,
De luctu, 19.

ment which covers them; but if thou be benevolent pour wine into the cup, drink and give me thereof.'"[15]

If the dead ask for fresh water, with which to quench their insatiable thirst, they are above all eager for the warm blood of victims. This sacrifice to the dead was at first often a human sacrifice of slaves or prisoners, and barbarous immolations of this kind had not entirely disappeared even in the historic period. When, after the taking of Perugia, Octavius, on the Ides of March (that is, on the anniversary of the slaying of Julius Caesar), caused three hundred notables of the town to be slaughtered on Caesar's altar,[16] this collective murder, inspired by political hatred, perpetuated an old religious tradition. Fights of gladiators, whose blood drenched the soil, originally formed part of the funeral ceremonies by which the last duty was paid to the remains of an illustrious personage. It is said that these sacrifices were intended to provide him who had gone to the other world with servants and companions, as the offering of a horse gave him a steed, or else that, in case of violent death, they were meant to appease the shade of a victim who claimed vengeance. And doubtless these ideas, which correspond to conceptions already evolved, contributed to keeping this cruel custom in force. But originally the object of this sacrifice, as of the sacrifice of animals, was essentially to ensure the duration of the undefinable something which still inhabited the tomb.

Among all the peoples of antiquity the blood was looked upon as the seat of life;[17] the vapour which rose from the warm red liquid, flowing from a wound, was the soul escaping therewith from the body; and therefore when blood was sprinkled on the soil which covered the remains of a relative or a friend, a new vitality was given to his shade. With the same motive women were wont to scratch their faces with their nails in sign of mourning.[18]

---

[15] Bücheler, *Carm. epigr.*, 838=Dessau, *op. cit.*, 8204.

[16] Sueton., *Aug.*, 15.   [17] *Cf.* p. 52, n. 20, and Lecture IV, p. 118.

[18] Servius, *Aen.*, III, 67.

This ancient conviction that fresh blood was indispensable to the dead, was maintained in some countries with surprising tenacity. In Syria, as late as the seventh century of our era, Christians insisted, in spite of episcopal objurgations, on immolating bulls and sheep on tombs, and in Armenia, where these practices were sanctioned by the national clergy, the faithful remained persuaded that the dead found no happiness in the other life unless the blood of victims had been made to flow for them on the days fixed by tradition.[19]

Other libations performed in the funeral rites of the Greeks, as of the Romans, were intended to produce the same effect, the libations, namely, of wine, milk and honey. The use of wine has been explained as that of a substitute for blood, as wine is red. Servius even interprets the purple flowers which Aeneas threw on the tomb of his father Anchises by the same association of ideas, as an "imitation of blood in which is the seat of life."[20] Many proofs could be cited of the fact that wine has often taken the place of the liquid which flows in our veins, but its use in connection with the dead can be explained also by its own virtue. It is the marvellous liquid which gives divine drunkenness and which in the mysteries ensures immortality to such as are, thanks to this sacred draught, possessed by Bacchus.[21] In the same way it vivifies the Manes to whom it is poured out. Similarly *melikraton,* a mixture of milk and honey, is the food of the gods, and when the dead absorb it, they too become immortal.

Such is the first meaning of these offerings, one which was never quite forgotten. Their object is the infusion of new vigour into the enfeebled shades who slumber in the tomb. This intention can also be discerned in the fact that the same offerings are used in magic, which often preserved ideas abolished or superseded in religion. In order

[19] *Cf. Comptes-rendus Acad. des Inscr.,* 1918, p. 284 s.

[20] Servius, *Aen.,* V, 79: "Ad sanguinis imitationem, in quo est sedes animae." *Cf.* II, 532.

[21] See above, Introd., p. 35, and Lecture VIII, p. 204.

to evoke the phantoms, the necromancers dug a ditch and
poured blood, wine, milk and honey into it. These liquids
had an exciting effect on the spirits of the dead, arousing
them from their torpor, and the wizard took advantage of
it to question them.

Precautions lest the dead should ever suffer from lack
of nourishment were multiplied. In order that they might
be fed on other days than those of sacrifices, all over the
ancient world it was customary to place food on their
tombs—eggs, bread, beans, lentils, salt, flour, with wine.
Hungry vagrants did not always respect their offerings
but would help themselves to the proffered viands.

*   *   *   *   *

The institution which is most characterised by the persistence of the ancient ideas of life in the tomb is however that of the funeral banquets. These family repasts,
which had previously been celebrated among the Etruscans, took place in Rome on the grave immediately after
the funeral (*silicernium*) and were repeated on the ninth
day following (*cena novemdialis*). In Greece and in the
East the ceremony took place thrice, on the third, ninth
and thirtieth or on the third, seventh and fortieth day.
Everywhere it was subsequently renewed every year on
the anniversary of the death and on several other fixed
dates, as on that of the *Rosalia* in May, on which it was
customary to decorate the tombs with roses. Memorial
monuments of some importance are often found to include, beside the burial chamber, a dining-room (*triclin-
ium*) and even a kitchen (*culina*). The importance
attached to these meals is proved by several wills which
have been preserved, and which make considerable endow-
ments to ensure their perpetuity. For instance, at Ra-
venna a son bequeaths a sum of money to a college on
condition that its members annually scatter roses on his
father's grave and feast there on the Ides of July.[22]
When Aurelius Vitalio had built at Praeneste a family

[22] CIL, XI, 132=Dessau, 7235.

tomb, surmounted by a room with a terrace, he wrote a
letter in incorrect Latin to the brothers of the society to
which he belonged: "I ask you, my companions, to refresh
yourselves here without quarrelling."[23] An African settled in Rome similarly writes to his relatives and friends,
"Come here in good health for the feast, and rejoice
together."[24] And in Gaul a will commands that the burial
vault be furnished and receive a bed with coverings and
cushions for the guests who have to meet on the memorial
days.[25]

These funeral repasts go back to a prehistoric antiquity. They are found in India and in Persia as well as
among the European peoples. They are doubtless as
ancient as wedding and festal banquets. Among the Egyptians and the Etruscans it was even customary to place the
representation of a perpetual feast on the walls of a tomb
in order to secure to the dead person the relief it gave.
The shade of a guest might well be pleased with the like-
ness of dishes.

It was believed that at funeral feasts the Manes of
ancestors came to sit among the guests and enjoyed with
them the abundance of the food and wines. Lucian tells of
repasts of this kind, which he witnessed in Egypt, at which
the dried mummy was invited to eat and drink at the table
of his kin.[26] In Greece, even in the Roman period, those
present at the feast used to summon the dead to it by
name. An epitaph of Narbonne jokingly expresses the
vulgar idea as to the participation of the deceased in the
banquet: "I drink and drink again, in this monument,"
says the dead man, "the more eagerly because I am
obliged to sleep and to dwell here."[27]

23 CIL, XIV, 3323=Dessau, 8090: "Hoc peto aego a bobis unibersis
sodalibus ut sene bile refrigeretis."
24 CIL, VI, 26554=Dessau, 8139.
25 Dessau, 8379.
26 Lucian, De luctu, 37.
27 Dessau, 8154=CIL, XII, 5102=Bücheler, Carm. epigr., 788:
    "[Eo] cupidius perpoto in monumento meo,
    Quod dormiendum et permanendum heic est mihi."

Nothing is further from our spiritual ideas as to the holiness of graveyards than the conviviality occasioned by the cult of the departed; among the guests crowned with flowers, the drinks went round (*circumpotatio*) and soon produced a noisy intoxication. Do not think this was an abuse due to a relaxation of morals and which came into being in later times. The character of these funeral banquets was such from the beginning, and such it has remained down to modern times in many countries. You all know the practice of the Irish "wake" which has been preserved even in the United States.

For it was long believed that the dead had their part in the merriness and inebriation of the companions at table and were thus consoled for the sadness of their lot. "Thou callest," says Tertullian,[28] "the dead careless (*securos*) when thou goest to the tombs with food and delicacies, but thy real purpose is to make offerings to thyself, and thou returnest home tipsy." And indeed, as we shall see,[29] these feasts were no longer of profit to the dead only but to the living also, because there came to be a confusion between them and the Bacchic communions in which wine was a drink of immortality.

No religious ceremony was more universally performed in the most diverse regions of the Empire than this cult of the grave. At every hour of every day families met in some tomb to celebrate there an anniversary by eating the funeral meal. Peoples remained strongly attached to practices the omission of which would have seemed to them dangerous as well as impious, for the spirits of the dead were powerful and vindictive.

It is therefore not surprising that these practices persisted in the Christian era in spite of the efforts of the clergy to suppress them. St. Augustine reprimands those who, like pagans, "drink intemperately above the dead" —these are his words—"and who, while serving meals to

28 *De testim. animae,* 4.
29 See below, Lecture VIII, p. 203 s.

corpses, bury themselves with these buried bodies, making a religion of their greed and their drunkenness."[30]

In the East, however, ecclesiastical authority tolerated a custom which it could not uproot, contenting itself with forbidding the abuse of wine and recommending a moderation the absence of which might often be deplored. Ecclesiastical authority also insisted that a part of the feast should be given to the poor, thus giving a charitable character to the old pagan practice.[31] Therefore in many countries, and especially in Greece and in the Balkans, the habit has survived to this day, not only of placing food on tombs, but also of eating there on certain anniversaries, with the idea that the dead in some mysterious way share and enjoy the meal.

*   *   *   *   *

In Rome, in historical times, the funeral repast might be taken not at the tomb but in the house. Among the feasts celebrated by the confraternities in honour of some dead benefactor, on the dates fixed by his last will, many were held in the meeting-place of the guild. But the belief continued in the real presence of him whose "spirit was honoured,"[32] and whose statue or picture often adorned the banqueting hall.

From the earliest period, the spirit of the dead was indeed not regarded as inseparable from his remains or as a recluse cloistered in the tomb. He dwelt there but could issue thence, although for long it was believed that he could not go far away but remained in the neighbourhood of the burial place. He was brought back to it by the necessity of taking food, which was no less indispensable to him than to men. He returned, therefore, to it, as a dweller returns to his home, to repair his energies and to rest. This idea that the soul wandered around its "eter-

[30] Augustine, *De mor. eccles.*, 34: "Qui luxuriosissime super mortuos bibant et epulas cadaveribus exhibentes super sepultos se ipsos sepeliant et voracitates ebrietatesque suas deputent religioni."

[31] *Constitutiones Apostol.*, VIII, 42.

[32] Dessau, 8375: "Colant spiritum meum."

nal house" often caused pains to be taken to surround
this house with a garden. Sometimes such a garden was
planted with a practical object: it was a vineyard, an
orchard or a rose-garden which supplied the wine, fruit
or flowers necessary for the offerings to the dead.[33] But
elsewhere a mere pleasure-garden, with shady groves,
bowers, pavilions and sparkling fountains, surrounded
the burial place. The care which the living took to fix,
by their will, its extent and its planting is a measure of
the intensity of their conviction that their shade would
take pleasure in refreshing itself in this quiet haunt.
There, about the tomb, it would enjoy the delights which
would afterwards be transported to the Elysian Fields,
as we shall see later.

The cult of the grave has not ceased in these days; the
ancient rites have not been discontinued. Tombstones are
still surrounded with flowers; they are decked with
wreaths; in Italy lamps are kept burning over them. But
the reasons which established these customs have disappeared; for us they are no more than a way of betokening
our care for the beloved, of piously showing our intimate
feelings by outward signs and marking the duration of
our regrets and our memories. They are survivals which
have lost all the concrete and real meaning which they
had in the far-off days when men believed that a being
like themselves sojourned in the place in which bones or
ashes were deposited.

The dead were not then cut off from the society of the
living; the connection between them and their surroundings was not broken; the continuity between the hour
which preceded and that which followed their decease
was not interrupted. It has often been remarked that in
this respect ancient ideas were profoundly different from
ours. Those lost to sight did not then cease to partake
of the life of their families; they remained in communication with their friends and their kin, who met

[33] *Cf.* Petronius, 71: "Omne genus poma volo sint circa cineres meos et
vinearum largiter"; Dessau, 8342 ss.; below, Lecture VIII, p. 200.

together in their new dwelling, and an effort was made to
render their isolation less hard to bear by bringing them
into touch with many people. Our dead rest in peaceful
and remote graveyards where no noise or din may trouble
the tranquil mood of afflicted visitors. The Romans placed
their dead along the great roads, near the gates of towns,
where there was press of passers-by and the rolling of
chariot-wheels. Their wish was not, when they buried
them beside the most frequented highways, to recall their
destiny to mortals, although philosophers have thus explained the custom.[34] On the contrary, they wanted to
cause those who were no more to forget their own destiny.
"I see," says an epitaph,[35] "and I gaze upon all who go
and come from and to the city." "Lollius has been
placed," we read elsewhere,[36] "by the side of the road in
order that all passers-by may say to him, 'Good day,
Lollius.' "

The inscriptions in which the dead speak, addressing
those who stop before their monuments, are innumerable.
They console such as continue to love them, thank those
who are still busy on their behalf and express wishes for
their happiness, or else they impart to their successors
the wisdom acquired by experience of life. Often they take
part with them in a dialogue, answering their greetings
and wishes: "May the earth be light on thee!"—"Fare
thou well in the upper world";[37] or else: "Hail Fabianus."—"May the gods grant you their benefits, my
friends, and may the gods be propitious to you, travellers,
and to you who stop by Fabianus! Go and come safe and
sound! May you who crown me with garlands or throw me
flowers, live for many years!"[38]

*   *   *   *   *

Thus throughout antiquity, in spite of the evolution of

[34] Varro, *Lingu. Lat.*, VI, 49 (45).
[35] *Arch. epigr. Mitt. aus Oesterreich*, X, 1886, p. 64.
[36] Dessau, 6746.
[37] *Ibid.*, 8130.
[38] *Ibid.*, 1967; *cf.* 8139.

ideas as to the future life, the persuasion always remained invincible that the spirits of the dead moved about among men. These disincarnate intelligences, which were, however, provided with light and swift bodies, did not let themselves be imprisoned in the tomb. They fluttered unceasingly around living beings, causing them to feel the effects of their presence. There is here, mingled with the primitive idea that a mysterious being, like it in appearance, has its place in the ground beside the buried corpse, the other and equally ancient idea that the soul is a breath exhaled by the dead at the moment when they expire. To breathe is the first act which marks the life of a newly born infant and to cease to breathe is the first sign which betokens the extinction of life. Primitive people therefore naturally thought that the principle which animated the body was a breath, which entered it at birth and left it at death. The very name which denotes the vivifying essence is in most languages witness to the general predominance of this conception. Ψυχή in Greek is connected with ψύχω, "to blow"; the Latin *animus* or *anima* corresponds to ἄνεμος, "wind," and in the Semitic languages *nefeš* and *ruah* have a similar meaning. At the moment in which man expired, his soul escaped through his mouth and floated in the ambient air. The Pythagoreans, when they taught that "the air is full of souls,"[39] were conforming to an old belief which is not Greek only but universal. When Virgil[40] shows us Dido's sister, at the time of the queen's suicide, receiving the last breath which floats on her dying lips, he is lending a Roman custom to the Carthaginians, the custom of the last kiss which, according to a widely held belief, could catch on its way the soul which was escaping into the atmosphere.

This soul was often imagined as a bird in flight and we will see elsewhere the conclusions drawn from this naïve conception.[41] Here we wish merely to indicate how the

[39] Diog. Laert., VIII, 32; *cf.* Servius, *Aen.*, III, 63; Lecture VI, p. 160.
[40] Virg., *Aen.*, IV, 685.
[41] See Lecture VI, p. 157.

idea of the aerial soul was combined with that of the
spirit inhabiting the tomb. This shade or simulacrum of
those who were no longer of this world, but who still
existed, since they showed themselves to the living in
their previous guise, was a body like the wind—intangi-
ble, invisible, save when it thickened like clouds or smoke.
A multitude of these vaporous beings, innumerable as
past generations, moved unceasingly on the earth's surface, and, above all, roamed around the tombs, where they
were retained by their attachment to their bodies.
Whether, like the Greeks, men identified them with the
"demons," or, like the Romans, called them "Manes
gods," "*genii*" or "*lemures*," or by other names, the
unanimous opinion was that their power was superior to
that of mankind and that they caused it to be felt by a
constant intervention in the affairs of human society.

It was generally held that if the required cult were not
rendered them, they would punish this neglect with wrath,
but that they showed their benevolence to those who deserved it by zeal in serving them.[42] The dead were capable, like the living, of gratitude as well as of resentment. The greater had been their power in this world, the
more considerable it remained in the other, and the more
advantage there was in securing their protection or even
their co-operation.

Servius reports the existence of the singular belief that
souls had to swear to Pluto never to help those they had
left behind them on earth to escape from their destiny.[43]
Such was, then, the extent of their supposed power. But
all the dead were not, like some of the heroes who had become the equals of the gods, capable of performing prodigious deeds. Many, gifted with less force, were concerned
with lesser interests; they did no more than protect their
family, the domestic hearth and the neighbouring field,
and render small daily services. "Farewell, Donata, thou

[42] *Cf.* Porph., *De abstin.*, II, 37.
[43] Servius, *Georg.*, I, 277; *cf.* Dessau, 8006.

who wast pious and just," says an epitaph, "guard all thy kin."[44]

The idea that the ancestors become the tutelary spirits of their descendants who were faithful to their duty to them, goes back to the remotest antiquity and probably lies at the foundation of the cult of the Lares.[45] But the field of action of these genii was multiple, since they were a multitude, and their functions underwent a further development when they were considered to be the equivalents of the demons of the Greeks. "The souls of the dead," Maximus of Tyre[46] tells us, "mingle with all kinds of men, with every destiny, thought and pursuit of man; they support the good, succour the oppressed and punish the criminal." Plotinus, recalling the universal custom of paying cult to those who have gone, adds: "Many souls which belonged to men do not cease to do good to men when they have left the body. They come to their aid especially in granting them revelations."[47]

The wish is therefore entertained to see in dreams those who have left an empty place in the family dwelling or the marriage couch. A woman whom a murder has separated from her young husband prays the most holy Manes to be indulgent to him and to allow her to see him again during the hours of the night.[48] But it was not only in dreams that men hoped to descry again those who were lost to sight. "If tears are of any avail," says another epitaph, "show thyself by apparitions (*visis*)."[49] Is it a question here also of nocturnal apparitions? Perhaps; but the belief that the spirits of the dead returned to the earth and made themselves visible to people who were wide awake met with very little incredulity among the

[44] CIL, VIII, 2803*a*: "Donata, pia, iusta, vale, serva tuos omnes."

[45] Margaret Waites, *American journ. of archaeol.*, 1920, 242 ss.

[46] Maxim. Tyr., *Diss.*, IX (XV), 6.

[47] Plotinus, *Enn.*, IV, 7, 20.

[48] Dessau, *Inscr. sel.*, 8006. "Manus mala" means probably a murder produced by witchcraft; *cf. ibid.*, 8522; Lecture V, p. 135.

[49] CIL, II, 4427: "Lacrimae si prosunt, visis te ostende videri."

ancients. It was not only the common man who accepted it; most thinkers upheld this opinion. Lucian[50] shows us a meeting of philosophers in which no one doubts "that there are demons and phantoms and that the souls of the dead do wander on earth and show themselves to whom they please." A single fact will suffice to prove how general was this conviction. The sober historian Dio Cassius[51] relates that in his time, more precisely in the year 220 A. D., a demon (who was evidently a flesh and blood impostor) appeared in the Danubian countries in the form of Alexander the Great. He was followed by four hundred Bacchantes carrying the thyrsus and the nebris. This troop went through all Thracia without doing any harm to the inhabitants, who hastened to give them shelter and food, and not a single official dared oppose their passage. Arrived near Chalcedon, the pseudo-Alexander made a strange sacrifice one night, burying a wooden horse, and thereupon immediately disappeared.

Like modern spiritualists, the ancients saw in these apparitions an irrefutable proof of the after life. "Thou who doubtest the existence of the Manes," we read on the tomb of two young girls, "invoke us after making a vow and thou wilt understand."[52] Revelations were indeed to be expected of the wisdom of the disincarnate souls. In spite, therefore, of the laws forbidding magic, necromancy never ceased to be practised. By a nocturnal sacrifice, analogous to that offered on tombs (p. 52) and by the virtue of their incantations, the wizards obliged the dead to appear before them and answer their questions. The poets and romancers liked to introduce in their works descriptions of the atrocious ceremonies which were intended to give momentary life even to a corpse and cause it to pronounce oracles.

The dead in these scenes often appear as restive and

[50] Lucian, *Philopseudes*, 29.
[51] Dio Cassius, LXXIX, 18.
[52] Dessau, *Inscr. sel.*, 8201*a*: "Tu qui legis et dubitas Manes esse, sponsione facta invoca nos et intelleges."

even hostile beings who were forced to such actions by the power of witchcraft. The dominant feeling among all peoples is indeed that the dead are unhappy and therefore malevolent. They were believed to be excessively sensitive: great care must be taken to do nothing to offend them. If their rights were overlooked, if they were forgotten, they showed their wrath by sending illnesses and scourges to the guilty. This unpleasant and sometimes cruel, even ferocious character of the Manes is very marked in Rome, perhaps in consequence of the influence of the Etruscans or the beliefs concerning after life. A legend had it that the ceremonies of the *Parentalia* having on one occasion been omitted, the plaintive ghosts scattered about the town and the fields and caused many deaths.[53] What we know of the rites performed at the *Lemuria* and at funerals shows that they tended to protect the house against the spirits haunting it and to rid it of them. "The dead are welcome neither to the gods nor to men," says an old Latin inscription.[54] To the family *Lares* who protected a household, the *larvae* were opposed, the wandering phantoms who spread terror and evil. "Spare thy mother, thy father and thy sister," we read on a tomb, "in order that after me they may celebrate the traditional rites for thee."[55] This hostile character attributed to inhabitants of the tombs explains the custom of placing in them leaden tablets on which curses were written calling down the most frightful ills on enemies. A large number of these *tabellae defixionum* in Greek and Latin have been found and they prove the frequency of this practice, which has perhaps an Oriental origin.[56] But the *devotio* to the Manes gods is an old Roman ceremony, which proceeds from the idea that they

[53] Ovid, *Fast.*, II, 546.

[54] CIL, I, 818=VI, 10407e=Dessau, 8749: "Mortuus nec ad deos nec ad homines acceptus est." *Cf.* CIL, X, 8249.

[55] CIL, VI, 12072: "Parce matrem tuam et patrem et sororem tuam Marinam, ut possint tibi facere post me sollemnia."

[56] Audollent, *Defixionum tabellae*, 1904.

endeavour to tear the living from the earth and draw them to themselves.

*   *   *   *   *

There is one class of the dead which is peculiarly noxious, those namely who have not been buried. The ideas connected with them are so characteristic of the oldest conception of immortality that these ἄταφοι or *insepulti* deserve to detain us for a few moments.

From the most ancient times the beliefs reigned among all the peoples of antiquity that the souls of those who are deprived of burial find no rest in the other life. If they have no "eternal house" they are like homeless vagabonds. But the fact that the dead had been buried did not suffice; their burial must also have been performed according to the traditional rites. Perhaps the liturgical formulas were supposed to have power to keep the shade in the tomb, as other incantations could summon it thence. Above all, however, it was believed, as we have already stated, that when the dead had not obtained the offerings to which they had the right, they suffered and that their unquiet spirits fluttered near the corpse and wandered upon the surface of the earth and the waters, taking vengeance on men for the ills men had inflicted on them.

The denial of interment was thought to be the source of infinite torment for the dead as for the living, and to throw earth on abandoned corpses was a pious duty. The pontiffs, who believed the sight of a corpse made them unclean, might not for all that leave it unburied if they happened to find one on their way. To bury the dead has remained a work of mercy in the Church, and in Rome a confraternity still exists which brings in from far away the dead found lying in the desert Campagna. The pain represented by lack of burial was the worst chastisement called down by imprecations on enemies on whom vengeance was desired. Among believers it gave rise to an anxiety comparable with that which the refusal of the last sacrament now causes to Roman Catholics. In the Greek cities, as in Rome, the law often condemned to it those who had committed suicide or had been executed, hoping thus to divert desperate and outrageous men from their fatal design by the apprehension of a wretched lot in the Beyond.[57] Sometimes the law merely laid down that the guilty must not be interred in the soil of their country, an almost equally terrible penalty, since it cut them off from the family cult, by which their descendants could give satisfaction to their Manes. When, therefore, through some accident, a traveller or soldier died abroad or was shipwrecked at sea, his body was, when possible, brought back to his country, or, if this could not be done, a cenotaph was raised to him, and his soul was summoned aloud to come and inhabit the dwelling prepared for it. When cremation became general in Rome, the old pontifical law invented another subterfuge which allowed the ancient rites to be accomplished: a finger was cut from the body before it was carried to the pyre, and earth was thrown three times on this "resected bone" (os resectum).

Against these ancient beliefs, which were the source of so much anguish and so many superstitions, the philosophers fought energetically. First the Cynics and then the Epicureans and the Stoics endeavoured to show their absurdity. They are fond of quoting the answer of Theodore the Atheist to Lysimachus who was threatening him with death without burial—"What matters it whether I rot on the earth or under it?" Since the corpse was unconscious and without any sensibility, it was indeed of no consequence whether it were burnt or buried, eaten by worms or by crows. Why should it be a misfortune to die abroad? Only the living had a country; the whole earth was the dwelling of the dead. If such cares troubled men they were the victims of the invincible illusion that the body retained capacity to feel even beyond the grave.

The very frequency with which these commonplaces of

[57] See below, Lecture V, pp. 143, 145.

the school are repeated shows how tenacious were the prejudices which they attempted to eradicate. Here, as in other connections, the renewal of Pythagorism supervened at the end of the Republic to favour the persistence of the old beliefs. A doctrine, to which Plato alludes,[58] taught that souls which had not been appeased by funeral rites, had to wander for a hundred years, the normal term of a human life. Confined in the air near the earth, they remained subject to the power of magicians. Especially if the wizards had been able to obtain possession of some portion of the corpse, whence the soul could not entirely detach itself, they gained influence over it and could constrain its obedience. When this century of suffering had elapsed, these souls were admitted to a place of purification, where they sojourned ten times longer, and when these thousand years had passed they returned to reincarnate themselves in new bodies. We will see in another lecture[59] that the Pythagoreans enunciated analogous theories as to the lot of children swept off before their time and of men who died a violent death.

Virgil describing the descent of Aeneas into the infernal regions recalls these Pythagorean speculations when he shows us the miserable crowd of the unburied shades fluttering for a hundred years on the bank of the Styx before they obtained from Charon their passage to its other shore.[60]

Favoured by these new tendencies of philosophy, the unreasoning apprehension inspired by omission of burial subsisted under the Empire, not only among the ignorant many, but also in the most enlightened classes. This fear explains why everyone took extreme care to have a tomb built for himself and to ensure, if he could, that funeral ceremonies were celebrated in it, why many epitaphs threaten with judicial penalties and divine punishments

---

58 Plato, *Republ.*, X, 615 A B; *cf.* Norden, *Aeneis Buch VI*, p. 10.

59 See Lecture V, p. 134.

60 Virg., *Aen.*, VI, 325 ss: ''Inops inhumataque turba. . . . Centum errant annos volitantque haec litora circum.''

the sacrilegious offenders who should violate the grave, and why such a number of popular colleges were founded, of which the principal object was to secure decent obsequies to their members. The rules of the *cultores* of Diana and Antinoüs at Lanuvium stipulate that when a slave dies and his master maliciously refuses to deliver his body for burial, a *"funus imaginarium"* be made for him, that is, that the ceremony be celebrated over a figure representing the dead man and wearing his mask.[61] From this "imaginary" burial effects were expected as beneficent as those results are maleficent which a wizard anticipated when he fettered and pierced a waxen doll to work a charm.

From the stories of the gravest writers we perceive what lot was believed to threaten the unfortunate who were burnt or interred without the rites being observed. After Caligula's murder his corpse was hastily shovelled into the ground in a garden on the Esquiline (*horti Lamiani*), but then the keepers of this park were terrified by apparitions until the imperial victim's sisters caused his body to be exhumed, and buried it in accordance with the sacred rules.[62] Pliny the Younger in one of his letters seriously relates a story which seems to have been often repeated, for we find it, little changed, in Lucian.[63] There was in Athens a haunted house which remained empty, no one daring to live in it because several of its tenants had died of fright. In the silence of the night a noise was heard as of clanking iron; then a horrible spectre moved forward in the shape of an emaciated old man, bearded and hairy, rattling the chains which were about his feet and legs. A philosopher dared to take this house, and he settled himself there one evening, resolved to keep himself awake by working. The ghost appeared to him, came towards him with its usual clatter, signed to him to follow and disappeared in the courtyard. When daylight came,

[61] Dessau, *Inscr. sel.*, 7213=CIL, XIV, 2112, II, 4.
[62] Sueton., *Calig.*, 59; *cf.* Plautus, *Mostell.*, III, 2.
[63] Pliny, *Epist.*, VII, 27; Lucian, *Philopseudes*, 31.

a hole was dug in the place where the phantom had van-
ished, and a skeleton in fetters was found. The bones were
taken up and burned according to the rites, and thereafter nothing troubled the quiet of the house. Lucian, in
his version of this ghost story, specifies the philosopher
as a Pythagorean and shows him repelling the apparition
by the virtue of his spells. The Pythagoreans were indeed
often necromancers, convinced defenders of spiritualism,
in which, as we have said (p. 62), they sought an immediate proof of the immortality of the soul, and by their
doctrines they contributed to keeping alive the superstitious fear attached to omission of burial.

But they were no more than theorists as to a belief
which was widespread and which the invasion of Oriental
magic was to revive. The curse-tablets often evoke,
together with other demons, "those who are deprived of
a sacred tomb" (ἄποροι τῆς ἱερᾶς ταφῆς).[64] They associate
them with those who have died before their time or by a
violent death.[65] Heliodorus[66] the romancer, a priest of
Emesa in Syria, who probably lived in the third century,
pictures for us a very characteristic scene: a child has
been killed; a wizard takes its body, places it between two
fires, and performs a complicated operation over it, in
order to restore it to life by his incantations and to obtain
a prediction of the future. "Thou forcest me to rise again
and to speak," the child complains, "taking no thought
for my funeral and thus preventing me from mingling
with the other dead." For the shades of the nether world
rejected one who had been left unburied.[67]

These ancient beliefs, which the East shared with the
West, were, more or less modified, to survive the downfall of paganism. If the Christians of the first centuries
no longer feared that they would go to join the shades
who wandered on the bank of the Styx, they were still

[64] Audollent, *Defixionum tabellae*, 27, l. 18; *cf.* 22 ss.
[65] See Lecture V, p. 135.
[66] Heliodorus, *Aeth.*, VI, 15.
[67] See Lecture VIII, p. 193.

pursued by the superstitious dread that they would have no part in the resurrection of the flesh if their bodies did not rest in the grave.[68] Nay, the terrors of former ages still haunt the Greeks of today. The people remain persuaded that those who have not had a religious funeral return to wander on the earth, and that, changed to bloody vampires, they punish men, and in particular their kin, for their neglect.[69] A nomocanon of the Byzantine Church orders that if the body of a ghost be found intact, when disinterred, its maleficent power thus being proved, it be burnt and a funeral service with an offering of meats be afterwards celebrated for its soul. This is exactly what was done in antiquity in order to appease the dead who had not been buried according to the rite, *rite conditi.*

[68] Leblant, *Epigraphie chrétienne de la Gaule*, 1890, 52 ss.
[69] Lawson, *Modern Greek folklore*, 1910, p. 403.

II

THE NETHER WORLD

AMONG most peoples the primitive idea of an after life in the grave was enlarged into the conception of a common existence of the dead in the depths of the earth. The dead man does not stay confined in the narrow dwelling in which he rests; he goes down into vast caverns which extend beneath the crust of the soil we tread. These immense hollows are peopled by a multitude of shades who have left the tomb. Thus the tomb becomes the antechamber of the true dwelling of the spirits who have departed; its door is the gate of Hades itself. Through the tomb, the great company of the beings who have been plunged in the darkness of the infernal regions remains in communication with those who still sojourn in our upper world. The libations and offerings made by the survivors on the grave descend to this gloomy *hypogeum* and there feed and rejoice those for whom they are intended. Until the time of the Roman Empire, nay, to the end of antiquity, the common man believed in this wonder.[1] To attempt to define the means by which it was brought about would be vain. These were beliefs which went back so far and were so deeply rooted in the mind of the people that men accepted them without seeking to explain them.

In Rome, the idea that the spirits of the dead inhabit a common dwelling in the nether world existed from the time when the city had its beginnings. It kept in religion a coarsely naïve form which proves how archaic it was.

[1] Lucian, *De luctu*, 9.

According to a rite borrowed by the Romans from the Etruscans, a pit was dug in the centre of the city, when the latter's foundations were laid, in order to make the *Inferi* communicate with the upper world. First fruits and other gifts were thrown into the pit, as well as a clod of the earth of the settlers' native country. Thus they restored their broken contact with the Manes of their ancestors. In all probability this hole was formed of a vertical pit ending in a chamber with an arched roof curved like the heaven—hence the name *mundus* given to it. The key of the vault of this lower cellar was formed of a stone, the *lapis Manalis,* which could be raised in order to let the spirits pass. Three times a year, on the twenty-fourth of August, the fifth of October and the eighth of November, this ceremony took place: the door of hell was opened and the dead had free access to the atmosphere. These days were therefore sacred, *religiosi,* and all business was suspended on them.

Recently the *mundus* of the ancient *Roma Quadrata* was believed to have been discovered during excavations of the Palatine, but the underground space in question is probably only a silo or a cistern. Other pits used for the cult of the dead existed elsewhere in the city. It has recently been suggested that the altar of the god Consus, which was hidden in a ditch in the middle of the Circus Maximus and uncovered during the races, was one of these mouths of hell and like that shown in representations of the funeral games of the Etruscans.[2]

But on certain days the souls of the dead rose to the earth's surface of themselves, although nothing had been done to make their coming thither easier, and they then had to be appeased by sacrifices. This was what happened from the thirteenth to the twenty-first of February, during the *Parentalia,* when the souls of ancestors were honoured, and on the ninth, the eleventh and the thirteenth of May, the dates of the *Lemuria,* on which, at mid-

[2] Piganiol, *Revue d'histoire et de litt. religieuses,* VI, 1920, p. 335 ss.

night, according to a prescribed ceremonial, the father of the family nine times threw black beans to the *Lemures* to keep them away from the house.

Lemures and *Manes* are used only in the plural: these words stand for the vague conceptions formed of the shades of the dead who dwelt beneath the ground. These were a nameless crowd, hardly individualised, not distinguishable from the fleeting phantoms who fluttered about the tombs. The Romans were a people of little imagination, and their infernal mythology remained rudimentary until the time when they borrowed from the Greeks the picturesque stories about the adventures of travellers to Hades and the blessings and misfortunes which there awaited them.

Originally no idea of retribution was attached to this descent of the dead into the infernal regions; it was neither their merits nor their demerits which determined their condition. On the contrary, the inequalities of human society were perpetuated: a nobleman kept a higher rank than that of his servants; each man in some sort continued his occupations, even preserved his tastes and his passions. Existence in the Beyond was conceived as a mere prolongation of earthly life. It is to this idea, which was generally entertained, that the old custom corresponds of placing in the grave the implements and other objects which a dead man was in the habit of using. We have already touched on this point in speaking of life in the tomb (p. 49), but the things deposited beside the corpse were not only those which could be used by the dweller of the "eternal house." If he were a powerful lord his chariot, his horses and his arms would be buried with him;[3] a hunter would be supplied in the other world with his spears and his nets;[4] a craftsman with the tools of his trade; a woman with the objects which enabled her to spin and to weave. These funeral customs were more than a tradition, followed without reference to the reasons

[3] *Cf.* Lucian, *De luctu*, 14.
[4] *Cf.* Dessau, 8379.

inspiring it. Among the Greeks, as among the Romans, the idea survives persistently, in poetic descriptions of the Elysian Fields, that each man will there keep the character and retain the habits which distinguished him before his death. Virgil, taking his inspiration from Pindar, shows us the blessed occupied by the contests of the palestra, by song and poetry and by chariot races; for, he tells us, the passion which the dead had in life for arms and for horses still pursues them when they have been buried in the earth.[5] Ovid[6] sketches with rapid touches an analogous picture. "The shades," he says, "wander bloodless, bodiless, boneless; some gather in the forum, others follow their trades, imitating their former way of life." And this is no fancy due to the poet's imagination. An awkward epitaph of a young, probably Syrian, slave[7] tells us that he is glad still to be able to discharge his service zealously in the retired place where dwells the god of the infernal abode. In these instances we find, in spite of the transformation undergone by eschatological ideas as a whole, a survival of the old conception of the destiny of the dead.

We have not to seek far to discover how this transformation took place. It was provoked by the desire to subject souls to different treatment according to their deserts, and to distribute them in distinct compartments in which they would be rewarded or punished in accordance with their past works. It was much prior to the Roman period, going back to the distant age at which Orphic theology, with its sanctions beyond the grave, modified Homeric tradition and popular religion in Greece. In the West the doctrine which imposed itself with the Hellenic civilisation on peoples of foreign race was ready-made. It spread through the south of Italy by

[5] *Aen.*, VI, 653 ss.

[6] Ovid, *Metam.*, IV, 443 ss.

[7] Bücheler, *Carm. epigr.*, 1186:
"Sed in secessum numinis infernae domus
Oficiosus tandem ministerio laetatur suo."

way of the colonies of Greater Greece in which Pythagorism came to its full power. It is in this country that some of the Orphic tablets intended as guides to the dead in their journey through the infernal realm have been discovered in the tombs;[8] and the great amphorae of a later date, bearing representations of scenes of Hades, which were also found in southern Italy, show the importance which continued to be attached there to the idea of the future life. In Campania, Lake Avernus was even regarded as one of the entrances to the nether world, through which Ulysses and Aeneas had descended.

The Greek doctrines were also introduced among the Etruscans and combined with the beliefs of this people as to an underworld in which the Manes of the dead were threatened by horrible demons and protected by beneficent genii. This Greek influence and its alliance with the native traditions appear in Etruria in a great number of funeral monuments on which we find represented many figures which, according to mythology, peopled the kingdom of Pluto. One of the most significant is the fine sarcophagus, discovered a few years ago at Torre San Severo near Bolsena, which seems to date from the third century B. C.[9] The two long sides hold corresponding reliefs, the one showing Achilles' sacrifice of the Trojan prisoners on the grave of Patroclus, the other the sacrifice of Polyxena, last of Priam's daughters, on the tomb of Achilles. These scenes, borrowed from the Greek epic poetry, are placed between two Etruscan demons, winged figures which bear serpents and are male on one side and female on the other. The small sides are decorated by two scenes from the Odyssey, the myth of Circe changing the companions of Ulysses into animals—perhaps an allusion to metempsychosis—and Tiresias' evocation of the shades of the dead, the Elysian Fields being curiously indicated. This instance—and many others might be cited—shows

8 See below, Lecture VI, p. 148.
9 *Monumenti Antichi*, XXIV, 1917, pp. 5-116.

how closely the Hellenic legends of Hades had been intermingled with Etruscan demonology.

This Greek conception of the infernal regions, which
literature and art were to popularise and perpetuate even
after credence had ceased to be given to it, remains
familiar to us. Taken altogether and in the large, it is that
of a kingdom imagined as an imitation of the cities of our
world, in which, however, there reigns such a rigorous
justice as is on our poor earth no more than a dream of
minds morally disposed. This underground state, of
which the frontier is defended by an unbridged river, the
Styx, is governed by powerful rulers, Pluto and Proserpina. It has its judges, Minos, Aeacus and Rhada-
manthus; its executioners, the Erinyes or Furies; and its
prison, Tartarus, surrounded by high walls. This jail, in
which the guilty, laden with chains, suffer the torments
enacted in Greece by the penal laws or others more
atrocious,[10] is distinctly contrasted with the abode of the
good citizens who freely enjoy in delightful gardens all
the pleasures which make the joy of human beings.

Books treating of the "Descent into Hades," of which
a considerable number were in circulation, and the poets'
descriptions embroidered various patterns around this
central design. There was a whole mythological and theological efflorescence which peopled with more and more
numerous figures the fantastic kingdom occupying the
great cavern of the earth. Infinite variations were imagined on a traditional theme, of which, however, even
certain details were preserved from age to age with a
surprising fidelity. Lucian in his satirical description of
Charon and his boat reproduces types fixed in the sixth
century before our era, for, as has been observed, his
picture is in exact agreement with the recently discovered
fragment of a black-figured vase.[11]

Although in our sources infernal topography is occa-
sionally somewhat confused, certain essential features,

10 See below, Lecture VII, p. 172 s.
11 Furtwängler, *Archiv für Religionswissenschaft*, VIII, 1905, p. 191 ss.

which we will here merely indicate, can be recognised in
it. We will return to them one after the other, and speak
of them in greater detail, in later lectures. When the
souls, or rather the shades, descend to the depths of the
earth, they reach first a provisional abode where they
await a decision as to their lot, an intermediate region
through which all of them pass but in which some are kept
for a considerable time.[12] They then cross the Styx, and a
road which is also common to all of them leads them to
the court which determines their lot.[13] This judging of
the dead is foreign to Homeric poetry: the idea of it was
perhaps borrowed by Greece from Egypt, but from
ancient Orphism onwards it was an essential element of
infernal eschatology. Infallible judges, from whom no
fault is hid, divide into two companies the multitude of
the souls appearing before them. The guilty are constrained to take the road to the left which leads to dark
Tartarus, crossing its surrounding river of fire, the
Pyriphlegethon. There those who have committed inexpiable crimes are condemned to eternal chastisement.[14]
But the road to the right leads the pious souls to the
Elysian Fields where, among flowered meadows and
wrapped in soft light, they obtain the reward of their
virtues, whether, having attained to perfection, they are
able to dwell for ever with the heroes, or whether, being
less pure, they are obliged to return later to the earth in
order to reincarnate themselves in new bodies after they
have drunk the water of Lethe and lost the memory of
their previous existence.

*   *   *   *   *

The philosophical criticism of the Greeks had early
attacked these traditional beliefs, but such negative attitude became more definite among the thinkers of the surpassingly rationalistic period which came after Aris-

[12] See Lecture I, p. 66.
[13] See Lecture VI, p. 151.
[14] See below, Lecture VII, p. 172 ss.

totle.[15] The Peripatetics, who admitted at most the survival of reason, rejected in consequence all the myths dealing with the descent of the shades into the kingdom of Pluto. The Epicureans were even more radical, for, as we have seen (p. 7), they condemned the soul to dissolution at the moment of death, thus destroying the very foundation of the belief in Hades. Their campaign against stories in which they saw only the lugubrious inventions of priests and poets, was one of the capital points of their polemics against popular religion, and they flattered themselves that by destroying faith in the pains of Tartarus they freed mankind from vain terrors which obsessed its minds and poisoned its joys. The Stoics, we know (p. 13), taught that the soul is a burning breath of the same nature as the ether and as the stars which shine in the sky. As to whether this ardent fluid was lost after death in the universal fire, or kept its individuality until the final conflagration of the world, the doctrine of the Porch varied. But one thing was certain: the fiery nature of the soul must prevent it from going down into the underground and impel it to rise to higher spheres. If it were weighed down by its contact with the body and laden with matter, it might float for some time in the dense air surrounding the earth but could never descend into its depths.[16] The impossibility of admitting literally the truth of the stories as to the infernal realm was thus proved.

The same psychological doctrine as to the soul's kinship with the fire of the heavenly bodies was admitted in the Alexandrian age by the sect which paid one and the same veneration to Pythagoras and to Plato and was thus more attached than any other to belief in immortality. It gave in, to some extent, to contemporary rationalism and was brought to modify its ideas as to life beyond the grave. Ancient Pythagorism, the heir of Orphism, made much of the sufferings reserved for sinners in the infer-

15 See Introd., p. 6.
16 See Introd., p. 29.

nal abysses. A book attributed to Periktione still shows the daughter who has despised her parents as condemned to suffer, beneath the earth and in the company of the impious, the eternal evil inflicted by "Dike and the gods of down below."[17] But in the first century before our era the pseudo-Timaeus of Locri declares that such tales are fictions—salutary, it is true—imagined by Homer in order to divert from evil those to whom truth alone was not a sufficient guide.[18] The only penalty which can overtake the sinning soul is, according to these Neo-Pythagoreans, metempsychosis, which forces it to reincarnate itself in a fleshly prison.[19]

This doctrine of transmigration claims to transport hell to earth and to explain, as moral allegories, all the fables which the poets had invented.[20] The *Inferi* are nothing else than the dwellings of our globe, which is the lowest of the nine circles of the world. The true Hades is the wicked man's life in which he is tortured by his vices. The rivers of hell—Cocytus, Acheron, Pyriphlegethon and Styx—are anger, remorse, sadness and hate, which cause man to suffer. The Furies are the passions, scourging him with whips and burning him with torches; and similarly an ingenious interpretation is given to each of the pains suffered by Tantalus, Sisyphus, the Danaïdes and the others.[21]

This exegesis led finally to an absolute denial of the existence of hell, but such radical scepticism was in too flagrant contradiction to the old beliefs to be willingly accepted by the minds which remained attached to them. Hence arose attempts to bring these beliefs into harmony with the psychology generally admitted.

A first theory, to which we will have to return when

[17] Mullach, *Fragm. phil. Graec.*, II, p. 33.
[18] Tim. Locr., *De anim. mundi*, 17, p. 104 D; *cf.* Schmekel, *Mittlere Stoa*, 1892, p. 435.
[19] *Cf.* Lecture VII, p. 178 ss.
[20] *Cf.* on this doctrine *Revue de philologie*, XLIV, 1920, p. 230 ss.
[21] *Cf.* Lecture VII, p. 181.

speaking of the nature of the surviving souls,[22] seems to
have been invented in Alexandria and to have been inspired by Egyptian religion.[23] The authors who first
allude to it, one Greek and one Roman, are contemporaries who wrote about the year 200 B. C., the critic
Aristarchus and the poet Ennius, but the transmission of
the doctrine can be traced through literary traditions
down to the end of antiquity. It divides the human composite not into two but into three parts—the body, the
soul and the shade. The body is destroyed beneath the
earth; the soul, which is a particle of the divine ether,
rises after death towards its place of origin; but a form
($\epsilon\check{\iota}\delta\omega\lambda o\nu$) of subtle matter detaches itself from the corpse,
and it is this semblance (*simulacrum*) or shade (*umbra*)
which goes down to the infernal regions. The existence
of these regions could thus be maintained, but they were
no longer held to receive the celestial principle which
gave intelligence.

Others allowed that it was impossible that the earth
should contain subterranean caverns large enough to
hold Tartarus, the Elysian Fields and the infinite multitude of the dead. But they explained that the word sub-
terranean ($\dot{\upsilon}\pi\acute{o}\gamma\epsilon\iota o\varsigma$) had been misunderstood, that it denoted not the bowels of the earth but the lower half of the
terrestrial globe, the southern hemisphere, which was
unknown to the ancients, or even the whole celestial
hemisphere, curved below this globe which hung motionless in the centre of the universe.[24] This hemisphere is
always invisible,—so the ancients might say,—which is
exactly the sense of the word Hades ($=\dot{a}\epsilon\iota\delta\acute{\eta}\varsigma$). The
Axiochos, an apocryphal work attributed to Plato, was
first to reveal this doctrine, claiming that it had been communicated to Socrates by the Mage Gobryes. It was in
reality borrowed by the Greeks of the Alexandrian age
from the astral theology of the Semitic peoples. Accord-

---

[22] See Lecture VI, p. 167.

[23] *Cf. Rev. philol., l. c.,* p. 237 ss.

[24] On this doctrine see *Comptes rendus Acad. Inscriptions,* 1920, p. 272 ss.

ing to this theology the world is divided into two halves
by the line of the horizon; the upper hemisphere is the
domain of the living and the higher gods, the lower that
of the dead and the infernal gods. Descent to it and ascent
from it are by way of two gates, situated west and east,
where the sun appears and disappears. The marshes of
the Acheron, the river Styx, and Charon and his boat are
constellations which the souls cross when they have
passed through the "gate of Hades."

The ancient Greeks had placed the Islands of the
Blessed, whither the heroes were borne by the favour of
the gods, somewhere far away in the ocean. These islands
were now supposed to lie in the Antipodes, in the unknown half of the earth. All the poets' stories of the fragrant and melodious gardens of this abode of delights
were applied to these marvellous countries which no
sailor had ever reached.[25] On the other hand, Tartarus
was placed at the bottom of the celestial abysses, near the
lowest point of the lower hemisphere, that is, diametri-
cally opposite to Olympus, the dwelling of the gods, who
were throned on the summit of the starry vault. It was
into this sombre gulf that the wicked were flung; there
yawned the bottomless pit in which the demons of the
dusky world inflicted eternal torture on the guilty.

This theory claimed to bring the ancient Hellenic
beliefs into agreement with the cosmography of astrono-
mers, but this cosmography itself undermined the foundations of the system, in so far as it refuted the hypothesis of a physical opposition between the two halves of
the universe. It was observed that a single sky revolved
about our earth; that the same atmosphere, composed of
the same elements, enveloped it entirely; that every part
of it was, in turn, equally in the light and in the shade.
Therefore physical phenomena must be identical over the
whole surface of our globe; the climate of the Antipodes
must be like that of our lands; if the Antipodes were

25 *Cf.* Lecture VI, p. 155.

peopled, it was by races like those of men and the beasts. Their inhabitants therefore were not the dead but living beings. The marvels of the Fortunate Isles did not exist and there was no reason for regarding the lower rather than the upper part of the heavens as the vast reservoir of souls.

The doctrine which placed the subterranean kingdom of Pluto and Proserpina on the other side of the earth and in the other celestial hemisphere, made a poor resistance to this criticism of the Alexandrian geographers. If it did not entirely disappear, if its transmission can be followed down to the end of antiquity and even to the Middle Ages, it never was so widespread nor so active as another doctrine claiming to reconcile the beliefs of the past with accepted science.

*   *   *   *   *

This bold doctrine transported the whole subterranean world above the earth's surface. We shall see, in the next lecture, on celestial immortality (p. 96), that the Pythagoreans conceived the idea of placing the Elysian Fields in the moon, and that the Fortunate Isles were similarly explained by them as being the sun and the moon bathed by the fluid of the ether. The *Inferi* were thus the lower space, that is, the space extending between the sphere of the moon, which was the limit of the world of the gods, and our globe, which was the centre of the cosmic system. In the *Inferi* the souls which had to suffer the chastisement of their faults were kept prisoners; they could not win to the stars but wandered plaintively on the earth's surface and especially about their own tombs, and then rose through the atmosphere in which, little by little, they were purified by the elements. Allegorical interpretations found a place for the infernal rivers in this new topography of the Beyond: Acheron was explained as being the air, the Pyriphlegethon as the zone of hail and fire, and the meanderings of the Styx became the circles of the universe. We shall have occasion to return to the passage of the soul through this aerial purgatory and its ascension to the Elysian Fields of the sky.[26]

This cosmological interpretation of the tales referring to Hades had a more powerful influence than the moral allegory which did too much violence to tradition in claiming to make our earthly life the mythological hell. The doctrine that the *Inferi* were in the atmosphere was adopted by Stoicism at least from the time of Posidonius and was therefore widely believed from the end of the Roman Republic onwards. Even the mysteries, which first kept alive the belief in a subterranean kingdom of the infernal gods, did not escape the influence of these new ideas and were brought to adapt their esoteric teaching to them.[27]

The transformation of ancestral beliefs by this theology cannot today be better apprehended than from the sixth book of the Aeneid. Virgil, when he relates the descent of Aeneas into the abode of the shades, is inspired by the *Nekyia* of the Odyssey and other poetic tales. He remains apparently faithful to mythological and literary tradition, retaining the conventional decoration, the unvarying geography of the infernal kingdom; but he does not admit the literal truth of these beliefs of an earlier time; he is aware of the figurative sense given by the philosophers to the old fables of Hades. At the risk of seeming to contradict himself, he recalls this learned eschatology—the purification, the ascension and the transmigration of souls—in connection with what might have been no more than the story of a marvellous journey to the country of the dead. The unity of the conception and the composition is the less seriously compromised because it was believed that the ancient poets themselves had wished to indicate these truths in their verses under the veil of allegory. The descent to the nether world has therefore a much loftier bearing in Virgil than a mere

[26] See Lecture VII, p. 185; *cf.* VI, p. 161 s.
[27] See Introd., p. 38 s.

embellishment. It is the expression of a conviction or at least a hope, not only a brilliant fiction based on an old poetic theme.

*   *   *   *   *

However, the symbolical interpretations of the pagan theologians who respected tradition and the purely negative criticism of the sceptics led finally to a common result, to the destruction, namely, of the ancient beliefs, even when it was claimed that they were being saved. Whether the souls were held captive in the other hemisphere or in the atmosphere, or whether they were condemned to reincarnation in a body, Hades was transformed either to the lower sky, the air or the earth, and the early conception of a subterranean world, whither the dead who had been laid in the grave descended, was abolished. There are abundant texts to prove that from the end of the Roman Republic this belief had lost its grip on many minds. Cicero[28] claims that there was not an old woman left foolish enough to fear the deep dwellings of Orcus and the gloomy regions peopled by the livid dead. "No one is childish enough," Seneca repeats,[29] "to fear Cerberus and the phantoms which appear in the form of skeletons." "That there are Manes," says Juvenal,[30] "a subterranean kingdom, a ferryman armed with a pole, and black frogs in the gulfs of the Styx, that so many thousands of men can cross the dark water in a single boat," these are things in which everyone had ceased to believe except very young children. Pliny[31] brings forward a paradoxical argument, that, had there been infernal regions, the zeal of the miners who had dug deep galleries in the ground would have pierced their boundaries; and even the devout Plutarch, when he comes to speak of the punishments reserved by mythology for

28 Cic., *Tusc.*, I, 21, 48; *cf.* I, 6, 10; *Nat. deor.*, II, 2, 5.
29 Sen., *Epist.*, 24, 18.
30 Juvenal, *Sat.*, II, 149 ss.
31 Pliny, *H. N.*, II, 63, §158.

the wicked, sees in them only nurses' tales to frighten babies.[32]

The multiplicity of this testimony and its precision allow no doubt that not only the educated classes but a large portion of the population rejected the fables as to the nether world. These fables were in any case a foreign importation in the Latin world. Moralists, while they ceased to believe in them for themselves, sometimes pretended to retain them in order to inspire the people with salutary fear, but Tartarus had lost much of its terror for those it should have kept from ill-doing.

Is this to say that these ideas no longer found credence anywhere? A faith which has long dominated minds disappears hardly and leaves persistent traces behind it in customs and feeling. Thus we find that, more or less everywhere, the practice was perpetuated of placing in the mouth of the corpse a piece of money which served, it was said, to pay Charon for the crossing of the Styx.[33] Excavators have found these coins in many Roman tombs. But they are doubtless evidence of no more than a traditional rite which men performed without attaching a definite meaning to it.

Moreover, the metrical epitaphs continue to speak of the Elysian Fields and of Tartarus, of Styx and of Acheron; they complain of the cruelty of Pluto who bears away mortals before their time, or of the Parcae or Fates who cut the thread of their days; they mention the avenging Furies, the sufferings of Tantalus, Sisyphus and Ixion. But these are no more than ready-made formulas of poetical language, literary reminiscenses or traditional metaphors. Yet sometimes this infernal mythology is curiously developed. Thus a long inscription on a Roman tomb describes a young man descending from the ether in order to announce to those near and dear to him that he has become a celestial hero and has not to go to Pluto's kingdom. "I shall not wend mournfully to the floods of

---

[32] Plutarch, *Non posse suaviter vivi sec. Epic.*, 27, p. 1105.
[33] *Cf.* Lucian, *De luctu*, 10.

Tartarus; I shall not cross the waters of Acheron as a shade, nor shall I propel the dusky boat with my oar; I shall not fear Charon with his face of terror, nor shall old Minos pass sentence on me; I shall not wander in the abode of gloom nor be held prisoner on the bank of the fatal waters.''[34] This epitaph dates from the century of Augustus, but did its author, any more than the writers of that time, believe in the reality of the beings with which he peoples Hades? He decorates his language with a literary ornament which Christian poetry was later to inherit. This poetry did not hesitate to employ these pagan commonplaces, which had passed from hand to hand until they were so worn out that their first meaning had been effaced. The Renaissance and the age of modern classicism were again to use and to abuse them.

The sculpture of tombs continued in the same way often to reproduce the ancient models. Sarcophagi sometimes show us the dead man led by Hermes, guide of souls, and coming into the presence of Pluto and Proserpina.[35] We also see on funeral monuments Charon in his boat, the typical sufferings of Tantalus, whose eager lips cannot reach the flowing water, Ixion turning on his wheel, Sisyphus labouring under the weight of his rock and, above all, the Danaïdes eternally pouring water into a perforated vase.[36] But it is probable that these traditional figures were repeated without any very strong faith being held as to the real existence of the personages which they

[34] Bücheler, 1109, v. 19-24:
"Non ego Tartareas penetrabo tristis ad undas,
Non Acheronteis transvehar umbra vadis,
Non ego caeruleam remo pulsabo carinam,
Nec te terribilem fronte timebo Charon,
Nec Minos mihi iura dabit grandaevus et atris
Non errabo locis nec cohibebor aquis.''
[35] See, for instance, *Jahresh. Instit. Wien,* XVII, 1914, p. 133 ss.; or *Hermes,* XXXVII, 1902, p. 121 ss.
[36] *Cf.* Jahn, *Darstellungen der Unterwelt auf Sarkophagen,* in *Ber. Gesellschaft Wiss. Leipsig,* 1856, p. 267 ss.; Reinach, *Répertoire des reliefs,* III, 391; Berger, *Revue archéol.,* 3ᵉ serie, XXVI, 1895, p. 71 ss.

represented; indeed it was proposed only to show them as symbols which had to be interpreted allegorically.

If we had no other evidence than funeral poetry and art of the persistence of the beliefs of the past, the testimony would have to be accepted very cautiously. But other more convincing proofs assure us that popular faith clung, with characteristic tenacity, to the ancient conception of the *Inferi*. Without believing precisely in the strange tortures inflicted on the wicked heroes of mythology, the man in the street was still vaguely persuaded that the souls went down from the tomb to some deep places where they received rewards and punishments. Suetonius[37] relates that when the death of Tiberius became known in Rome the people "prayed Mother Earth and the Manes gods to give the dead man no other dwelling than that of the impious." The Oriental slaves brought the same convictions from their countries like many other old beliefs which had faded away in the West. The romancer Heliodorus, a Syrian priest, shows us in his novel his heroine invoking "the demons who on the earth and under the earth watch over and punish unrighteous men,"[38] her prayer being that, after the iniquitous death which threatened her, they might receive her. The same conviction appears in the funeral inscriptions of the East. Thus an epitaph of Elaiousa in Cilicia[39] adjures "the heavenly god, the Sun, the Moon and the subterranean gods who receive us." The common idea was that a dead man can be excluded from the dwelling of the shades and condemned to wander miserably on the earth. In the same way the thought is often expressed in the magic papyri of Egypt that the deceased were plunged into the dark gulfs underground and there became demons whom the wizard called up, when he summoned them by his incantations. Even in Greece, where

[37] Sueton., *Tiberius*, 75, 1: "Terram matrem deosque Manes orarent, ne mortuo sedem ullam nisi inter impios darent."

[38] Heliodorus, *Aeth.*, VIII, 9, p. 231, 10, Bekker.

[39] *Jahresh. Instit. Wien*, XVIII, 1915, Beiblatt., p. 45.

rationalistic criticism had penetrated far deeper among the people, Plutarch, while he reports that few people were still really afraid of Cerberus, the lot of the Danaïdes and other bugbears of Hades, adds, however, that for fear of such pains recourse was had to purifications and initiations.[40]

This belief in the existence of Hades, maintained in the lower strata of the population in spite of the inroads made on it and of its partial supersession by other doctrines, was to acquire new strength from the rebirth of Platonism, which looked upon the writings of the "divine" master as inspired. In several passages Plato spoke with so much precision of the dwelling of the souls in the bowels of the earth that even the subtlety of his later interpreters found difficulty in giving another meaning to his text, although the attempt was made by some of them. Therefore effort was directed to defending the doctrine of the infallible sage by refuting the objections raised against it by his adversaries. The Stoics had held, as we have seen (p. 77), that the soul, being a "fiery breath," had a natural tendency to rise in the air and could not sink into the ground. But Porphyry[41] objected that in lowering itself from heaven towards our world it had become impregnate with the atmospheric damp and thus had grown heavier, and that if during its passage in the body it became laden with the clay of a sensual life, if it wrapped itself in a material cloak, its density came to be such that it was dragged down into the dusky abysses of the earth. "It is true," says Proclus,[42] "that the soul by force of its nature aspires to rise to the place which is its natural abode, but when passions have invaded it they weigh it down and the savage instincts which develop in it attract it to the place to which they properly belong, that is, the earth." According to Proclus,[43] who claims to

---

40 Plutarch, *Non posse suaviter vivi sec. Epic.*, 27, p. 1105.
41 Porph., *Sent.*, 29 (p. 13, Mommert).
42 Proclus, *In Remp. Plat.*, II, p. 126, 10 ss., Kroll.
43 Proclus, *ibid.*, II, p. 131, 20 ss.

interpret Plato faithfully, the soul after death is judged
somewhere between the sky and our globe; if it be declared worthy it enjoys a life of blessedness in the celestial spheres; if, on the other hand, it deserve penalties,
it is sent to a place beneath the ground. Elsewhere, de-
fining his thought,[44] he affirms that the various parts of
Hades and the subterranean courts and the rivers of
whose existence Homer and Plato appraise us, should not
be regarded as vain imaginations or fabulous marvels. As
the souls which go to heaven are distributed among
several and different resting-places, so we must believe
that for souls still in need of chastisement and purification underground dwellings, whither penetrate numerous
effluvia of the super-terrestrial elements, are thrown
open. It is these effluvia that are called "rivers" or "currents." Here too various classes of demons hold empire,
some of them avengers, some chastisers, some purifiers
and some executioners. Into this abode, the farthest from
that of the gods, the sun's rays do not penetrate. It is
filled with all the disorder of matter. Therein is the
prison, guarded by demons who ensure justice, of the
guilty souls hidden beneath the earth.

It is not by their faithfulness to Plato's doctrine, which
in truth they alter, but by the mere logic of their system
that the last Greek philosophers are led to admit what
their predecessors rejected. Sometimes, more or less un-
consciously, they were under a religious influence. The
Platonist Celsus believed in the eternal pains of hell but
invoked only the authority of "mystagogues and theologians" in support of this article of faith.[45] The opposition between the obscure retreats of the Manes and the
bright dwellings of Olympus is old, and naturally became
prominent as the belief spread, first that heroes, and
afterwards that all virtuous spirits, rose to the eternal
spaces.[46] But the religion which formulated the strictly

[44] Proclus, *In Remp. Plat.*, I, 121, 23 ss., Kroll.
[45] Orig., *Contra Celsum*, VIII, 48 s.
[46] See Lecture IV, p. 113 ss.

consequent doctrine of an absolute antithesis between the luminous kingdom where the divinities and the beneficent genii were seated, and the dark domain of the Spirit of Evil and his perverse demons, was Persian Mazdeism. The resplendent heights where the gods had their thrones were to be after death the abode of those who had served piously. On the other hand, those who had contributed to increase evil on the earth, were to be flung into the murky abysses in which Ahriman reigned. Iranian dualism imposed this eschatological conception on a section of Alexandrian Judaism; it was admitted by many Pythagoreans, then by the gnostic sects and later by Manicheism. But above all it was widely propagated under the Roman Empire by the mysteries of Mithras. We find then put forth the doctrine that the demons are divided into two armies, incessantly at war with each other, one good and one evil. The good army is subject to celestial powers and comes down to earth to give succour and support to the faithful. The evil army obeys an anti-god ($\dot{\alpha}\nu\tau\dot{\iota}\theta\epsilon$os) and issues from the bowels of the earth in order to scatter misery, sin and death among men.[47] The souls of the dead become like one or the other of these two opposing classes of demons. When they are virtuous and pure they rise to the luminous ether where dwell the divine spirits. If, on the contrary, they are vicious and defiled they go down into the underground depths where the Prince of Darkness commands; like the maleficent demons who people this hell they suffer and cause to suffer.

It was at this compromise that paganism stopped when it reached the term of its evolution. Oriental dualism imposed on it its final formula. It no longer admitted, like the ancients, that all the dead must go down from the grave into immense hollows dug in the bowels of the earth, and it no longer made the Elysian Fields and Tar-

---

[47] Porph., *De abstin.*, 38 ss.; *cf.* Bousset, *Archiv für Religionswiss.*, XVIII, 1915, p. 134 ss., and Andres in *Realencycl.*, Supplementband, III, 315.

tarus two contiguous domains of the kingdom of Pluto. Nor did it transport them both, side by side, as the pagan theologians of the beginning of our era would have done, to the atmosphere and the starry spheres. It separated them radically, cutting the abode of the souls into two halves, of which it placed one in the luminous sky and the other in subterranean darkness. This was also the conception which, after some hesitation, became generally accepted by the Church, and which for long centuries was to remain the common faith of all Christendom.

III

CELESTIAL IMMORTALITY

THE astral religion which became predominant in the Roman Empire may be considered as an intermediary, a connecting link, between the old anthropomorphic paganism and the Christian faith. Instead of moral—or, if you prefer, immoral—beings, stronger than man but subject to all the passions of man, it taught the adoration of the heavenly powers who act on nature, and so led mankind to the worship of the Power who is beyond the heavens. This influence of the astral cults of the East can be clearly perceived in the evolution of the ideas as to future life, and this above all constitutes the historical importance of the subject which I venture to treat in this lecture.

Beliefs which are spread among many peoples of the world relate the immortality of the soul to the heavenly bodies. It was for long naïvely imagined that a new sun was created every evening, or at least every winter, and a new moon born each month, and traces of this primitive idea survived in the religion of antiquity and persist even in our modern speech. But when it was realised that the same celestial luminaries reappeared and resumed their ardour after their fires had died and they had ceased to shine, that the stars which were lit at sunset were those which had been extinguished at dawn, their lot was related to that of man, destined like them to be reborn, after death, to a new life. Various savage tribes thus associate the heavenly bodies, and especially the moon, with the resurrection of the dead. The wan circle which sheds its vague light in the darkness of night causes phantoms to appear to haunt vigils and dreams, and is therefore the power which presides over life beyond the tomb. Among the Greeks of the most ancient period Hecate was at one and the same time the goddess of the moon, the summoner of ghosts and the queen of the infernal realm. In the East astrological ideas mingled with this mythology. It was taught that the moon's cold and damp rays corrupted the flesh of the dead and thus detached from it the soul which finally abandoned the corpse. The Syrians, at the critical times in which the moonbeams exercised a more active influence on this separation, offered sacrifices on tombs, and the threefold commemoration of the dead on the third, the seventh and the fortieth day in a part of the Eastern Church had its earliest origin in these offerings of the sidereal cults.[1]

There was also a very widely held belief, which has survived in European folk-lore, that each man has his star in the sky. This star is dazzling if his lot be brilliant, pale if his state of life be humble. It is lit at his birth and falls when he dies. The fall of a shooting star therefore denotes a person's death. This popular idea existed in antiquity. Pliny the Naturalist reports it, although he denies its truth,[2] and it was again combated in the fifth century by Eusebius of Alexandria. "Were there then only two stars in the time of Adam and Eve," asks the bishop, "and only eight after the Flood when Noah and seven other persons alone were saved in the Ark?"[3] The formulas of epitaphs and the very usages of language show how current was the belief that each man was, as we still say, born under a good or an evil star. *Astrosus* was the Latin equivalent of our *unlucky*. This doctrine of a rudimentary astrology was incorporated in the general system of learned genethlialogy. Although this latter attributed a predominant influence to the planets and the signs of the zodiac, it also taught, in accordance with popular opinion, that each of the most brilliant stars

[1] *Cf. Comptes rendus Acad. Inscriptions*, 1918, p. 278 ss.
[2] Pliny, *H. N.*, II, 8, § 28.
[3] Eusebius Alex., in *Patr. Graeca*, LXXXVI, 1, p. 453.

(λαμπροὶ ἀστέρες) ensures riches, power and glory to the newly born child, if it be in a favourable position at his birth.[4]

But side by side with this general conception of a relation between the life of the stars and that of men, a much more precise idea is met with from the first. The soul was, as we shall see,[5] often conceived by the ancients as a bird preparing for flight. Where would it alight when it had passed through the air except on the heavenly bodies which were still imagined as quite near the earth? The paintings on an Egyptian tomb of a late period, found at Athribis, show us the soul of the dead man fluttering with those others like him in the midst of the constellations.[6]

The belief was widely spread that the spirits of the dead went to inhabit the moon. In the East this faith retained a very crude form which certainly went back to a most primitive paganism. We find it in India as well as in Manicheism, which arose in Mesopotamia in the third century, but which admitted many ancient traditions into its doctrine. "All who leave the earth," says an Upanishad, "go to the moon, which is swollen by their breath during the first half of the month." The Manicheans similarly affirmed that when the moon was in the crescent its circumference was swelled by souls, conceived as luminous, which it drew up from the earth, and that when it was waning it transferred these souls to the sun. Using an idea much earlier than his time,[7] Mani also stated that the boat of the moon, which plied in the sky, received a load of souls which every month it transferred to the sun's larger vessel. The association established in Syro-Punic religions between the moon and the idea of immortality is marked by the abundance in Africa of funeral monuments bearing the symbol of the crescent, either alone or

---

[4] *Cat. codd. astrol. Graec,* V, pars. 1, p. 196 ss.
[5] See below, Lecture VI, p. 157.
[6] Flinders Petrie, *Athribis,* London, 1908 (52 A. D.).
[7] *Cf.* below, Lecture VI, p. 154.

associated with the circle of the sun and the star of Venus.[8] These astral symbols are identical with those already used by the Babylonians. But it is not only among the Semitic peoples that we find the crescent on tombs, either alone or accompanied by other figures: it is of frequent occurrence, notably in Celtic countries. Possibly the Druids placed in the moon the other world where men pursued an existence uninterrupted by death.

As for the sun, the idea most commonly accepted was that the dead accompanied him on his course and went down with him in the west to an underground world. There, during the night, this enfeebled heavenly body recovered his strength, and there the dead too were revived. The power of this faith in ancient Egypt is known: the souls embarked on the boat of Ra, and with him, after they had accomplished the circle of the heavens, went down through a crevice of the earth or beyond the ocean. This was the first origin of the rôle of "psychopomp" which we shall find attributed to the solar god.

Finally many peoples believed that souls, after plying through air and space, inhabited the sky in the form of brilliant stars. The multitude of the stars scintillating in the firmament was that of the innumerable spirits who had left the world. They pressed in a dense crowd, especially in the long luminous track of the Milky Way, which was, *par excellence,* the dwelling of the dead. Other traditions saw in this band across the sky the highroad which the dead travelled to gain the summit of the world.[9] A vestige of this ingenuous conception is retained in the very name, "Milky Way."

*   *   *   *   *

These ideas as to the lot of the soul after death, which were spread among a number of different peoples, may

[8] Toutain, *Revue des études anciennes,* XIII, 1911, p. 166 ss.; *cf. ibid.,* p. 379 s.

[9] See below, p. 104, and Lecture VI, p. 153.

also have existed in primitive Greece but we have no proof that they were current there. As the Hellenes granted to the stars only a restricted and secondary place in their anthropomorphic religion, so in early times they had no belief, or scarcely any, in the ascent of souls to the starry sky. This doctrine was entirely strange even to the earliest Ionian thinkers. Recent research has made it more and more probable that these conceptions were introduced into Greece from the East, where astrolatry was predominant.[10] Pausanias[11] claimed to know that the Chaldeans and the Magi of India were the first to assert that the human soul is immortal, and that they convinced the Hellenes, and in particular Plato, of this doctrine. Such an affirmation, in this form, is certainly false, but it contains an element of truth. The tenet of astral immortality is ancient in the East: it probably took form in Babylon about the sixth century, when Persian Mazdeism, which believed that the righteous were lifted up to the luminous dwelling of the gods, came into contact with the sidereal religion of the Chaldeans. It was propagated in Greece especially by the Pythagoreans, for whom the soul had a celestial origin, being, as we have seen (p. 24), a fiery principle, a particle of the ether which lights the divine fires of heaven. This spark, which descended at birth in the body, which it heated and animated, reascended after death to the upper regions, whence it had come forth. Aristophanes in his *Peace*[12] greets the apparition of a new star, that of the Pythagorean poet, Ion of Chios, who had recently died, asking ironically if it be not true that "when someone dies he becomes like the stars in the air." This is the most ancient precisely dated mention of stellar immortality (421 B. C.), and it cannot be doubted that the doctrine was that of Ion himself. Plato received it from the Pythagoreans and makes very clear allusions to it.

[10] E. Pfeiffer, *Studien zum antiken Sternglauben*, 1916, p. 113 ss.

[11] Pausanias, IV, 32, 4.

[12] Aristophanes, *Peace*, 832 ss.

The fundamental idea on which it rests, the idea that the psychic essence is the same as the fire of the heavenly bodies, is at the root of all oriental astrology, which claims to explain by astral influence the formation of character. This idea of a relationship (συγγένεια) between the soul and the stars does not in Greece belong to the old basic popular beliefs. It was introduced thither by the philosophers, who, as we shall see, drew from it very important theological conclusions. According to them, it was owing to this identity of nature that the soul was capable of knowing the gods and of aspiring to join them.[13] This doctrine took on new power when astrology succeeded in imposing itself on the Alexandrian world, and it is significant that we find it clearly formulated by an adept of this pseudo science, the famous Hipparchus, in the second century before our era. "Hipparchus," says Pliny,[14] "will never receive all the praise he deserves, since no one has better established the relation between man and the stars, or shown more clearly that our souls are particles of the heavenly fire." Pythagorism and Stoicism, and after them the Syrian and Persian mysteries, were to popularise this conception throughout the ancient world. In certain regions, as in Gaul, it undoubtedly found pre-existing native beliefs with which it combined, and in religion and among theologians it assumed multiple forms. We shall try to distinguish its chief aspects, dealing successively with lunar, solar and stellar immortality.

*   *   *   *   *

The Pythagoreans, perhaps transforming a belief of the Greek people as to Selene's rôle, but more probably inspired by Oriental speculations, held that souls, when they had been purified by air, went to dwell in the moon. To the question, "What are the Isles of the Blessed?" the orthodox doctrine of the sect answered, "The sun

[13] See below, Lecture IV, p. 111; cf. Introd., p. 24.
[14] Pliny, H. N., II, 26, § 95.

and the moon.'"[15] For them the heavenly bodies were moving islands washed by a luminous fluid, which their swift motion caused to sound about them. These thinkers, who debated all the scientific hypotheses, accepted the plurality of worlds. The heavenly bodies were other earths surrounded by air and rolling in the boundless ether. The moon in particular was designated as the "ethereal" or "Olympic earth," and in the moon lay the Elysian Fields, the meadows of Hades, in which the shades of the heroes rested. Pythagoras himself, promoted to the rank of an immortal spirit, rejoiced there among the sages. Persephone, assimilated to Artemis, reigned over this kingdom. Did not the moon, like her, transfer itself alternately above and below the earth? The planets were this huntress's hounds which, ever in chase, were scouring the fields of space around her in every direction.

The authors of Pythagorean apocalypses peopled the mountains and valleys of the moon with fantastic animals, stronger than ours, and with strange plants, more vigorous than those of our globe. The inhabitants of the moon, fed on the vapours of the atmosphere, were not liable to human needs. In his "True Histories," Lucian[16] parodied these mad imaginings with comic exaggeration and ludicrous obscenity.

A curious fragment of Castor of Rhodes gives an instance of an unexpected application of these beliefs.[17] This historian, who lived at the end of the Republic, had the idea of interpreting Roman customs by the Pythagorean doctrines which Nigidius Figulus and his circle of theosophists had brought back into fashion (p. 22). In particular he explained by this method the ivory *lunulae* (crescents) which decorated the senators' shoes. They recalled, he says, that noble souls inhabited the moon after death and trod on its soil.

---

[15] Jamblich., *Vit. Pyth.*, XVIII, 82=Diels, *Vorsokratiker*, I³, p. 358, 18; *cf.* Plut., *De genio Socr.*, 22, p. 590 C; Hierocles, *In Aur. carm.*, end.

[16] Lucian, *Verae hist.*, I, 10 ss.

[17] Castor, fragm. 24 and 25, Müller.

The eclectic Stoics of the same period, and especially Posidonius of Apamea, gave this lunar eschatology a place in their system, and undertook to justify it by the physical doctrines of the Porch. According to them, souls, which are a burning breath, rose through the air towards the fires of the sky, in virtue of their lightness.[18] When they reached the upper zone, they found in the ether about the moon surroundings like their own essence and remained there in equilibrium. Conceived as material and as circular in form, they were, like the heavenly bodies, nourished by the exhalations which arose from the soil and the waters. These innumerable globes of a fire endowed with intelligence formed an animated chorus about the divine luminary of night. The Elysian Fields did not, in this theory, lie in the moon itself, which was no longer an earth inhabited by fantastic beings, but in the pure air *about* the moon whither penetrated only souls no less pure. This idea was to last until the end of paganism, although other eschatological doctrines then met with more favour. The emperor Julian in the beginning of his satire on the Caesars describes them as invited to a banquet held, as was proper, on a lower level than the feast of the gods, who met at the summit of heaven. "It seemed fitting," he says,[19] "that the emperors should dine in the upper air just below the moon. The lightness of the bodies with which they had been invested and also the revolutions of the moon sustained them."

The zone of the moon, the lowest of the seven planetary spheres, in which the serene ether touches our own foggy atmosphere, is the frontier between the world of the gods and that of men, the border between immortality and the generated, the line of demarcation between the life of blessedness and the death which our earthly existence really is. Aristotle had already noted the distinction between the two halves of the universe, the one active and the other passive, the heavens formed of unalterable

[18] See Introd., p. 29, and Lecture VI, p. 162.
[19] Julian, *Caes.*, p. 307 c.

ether and subject neither to progress nor to corruption, and our sublunary world composed of four elements, our world in which all is born, is transformed and dies. Neo-Pythagoreans and Neo-Stoics liked, in insisting on this opposition, to show the contrast between the splendour and the darkness, the serenity and the trouble, the constancy and the mutability, the truth and the error, the happiness and the misery, the peace and the war, which reigned respectively in the dwelling of the gods and in the abode of men, whither souls descending to earth penetrated so soon as they had crossed the circle of the moon. In imitation of Plato[20] this sublunary world is shown as a dark cave in which the captive souls, plunged in obscurity, aspire to see again the light from on high.

The funeral monuments of the imperial period have retained numerous traces of these beliefs. As we have already said (p. 94), the crescent often appears on them, either alone or together with other symbols. Other tombstones are still more expressive. A Roman relief, preserved in Copenhagen, is particularly characteristic: the bust of a little girl appears on it placed on a large crescent and surrounded by seven stars.[21] On this an inscription recently found at Didyma might serve as a commentary: "Standing before this tomb, look at young Chorô, virgin daughter of Diognetos. Hades has placed her in the seventh circle,"[22] that is, in the circle of the moon, which is the lowest of the seven planets.

We see that philosophy and physics had united to transform the old belief in the ascent of souls to the moon. The intervention of theories claiming to explain the systems of the world is still more marked in the other doctrines of astral immortality. It was this blending

---

[20] Plato, *Rep.*, VII, p. 514.

[21] Reproduced in my *Études syriennes*, 1917, p. 87; *cf.* below, p. 139.

[22] Wiegand, in *Abhandl. Akad. Berlin*, 1908, *Bericht*, VI, p. 46:

Στὰς πρόσθε τύμβον δέρκε τὴν ἄνυμφον
κόρην Διογνήτοιο νηπίην Χοροῦν,
ἣν θῆκεν ''Αιδης ἐν κύκλοισῑν ἑβδόμοις. . . .

which made them strong enough to impose themselves on the minds of men. By their agreement with contemporary science, they satisfied reason and faith at the same time. But as all this theology really rested on a wrong cosmography, its lot was bound up with that of a false conception of the universe, and the two fell together.

*　　*　　*　　*　　*

The first of these doctrines appears to us the most reasonable because it is founded on the primordial rôle of the sun in our world. It was born in the East when the Chaldean priests deprived the moon of the pre-eminence originally ascribed to it, and recognised the unequalled importance of the sun in the cosmic system.[23] These astronomical theologians deduced from this recognition a theory which includes something like an anticipation of universal gravitation, and which was to prove seductive both by its greatness and by its logic. It spread through the ancient world in the second and first centuries B. C. There are some signs that the Pythagoreans, who were much addicted to the study of the heavenly bodies, were the first to adopt it, and with the propagation of Oriental astrology it obtained a wide diffusion in the West.

The sun, placed in the fourth rank or the middle of the planetary spheres,[24] like a king surrounded by his guards, was believed alternately to attract and repel the other celestial bodies by the force of his heat, and to regulate their harmonious movements as the coryphaeus directed the evolutions of a chorus. But since the stars were looked upon as the authors of all the physical and moral phenomena of the earth, he who determined the complicated play of their revolutions was the arbiter of destinies, the master of all nature. Placed at the centre of the great cosmic organism, he animated it to its utmost limits, and was often called the "heart of the world" whither its heat radiated.

[23] See *La théologie solaire du paganisme romain* in *Mém. sav. étrangers Acad. Inscr.*, XII, 1909, p. 449 ss.

[24] *Cf.* Introd., p. 28.

But this well-ordered universe could not be directed by a blind force, and therefore the sun was an "intelligent light" (φῶς νοερόν). The pagan theologians looked upon him as the directive reason of the world (*mens mundi et temperatio*). The Pythagoreans saw in him Apollo Musagetes, the leader of the chorus of the Muses, who were placed in the nine circles of the world and whose accord produced the harmony of the spheres. Thus he became the creator of individual reason and director of the human microcosm. The author of generation, he presided over the birth of souls, while bodies developed under the influence of the moon. The radiant sun constantly sent down sparkles from his flaming circle to the beings he animated. The vital principle which nourished men's material envelope and caused its growth was lunar, but the sun produced reason.

Inversely, when death had dissolved the elements which formed the human composite, when the soul had left the carnal prison which enclosed it, the sun once more drew it to himself. As his ardent heat caused vapours and clouds to rise from the earth and the seas, so he brought back to himself the invisible essence which animated the body. He exercised on the earth both a physical and a psychical attraction. Human reason reascended to its original source and returned to its divine home. The rays of the god were the vehicles of souls when they rose aloft to the higher regions.[25] He was the anagogue (ἀναγωγεύς) who withdrew spirits from matter which soiled them.

Just as he sent the planets away from him and brought them back by a series of emissions and absorptions, so he caused his burning effluvia to descend to the beings whom he called to life, and so he gathered them after their death that they might rise to him once more. Thus a cycle of migrations caused souls to circulate between the sky and the earth, as the stars alternately drew away from and returned to the radiant focus, heart and spirit of the

25 See below, Lecture VI, p. 160.

Great All, which called forth and directed their eternal revolutions. It is easy to understand how this coherent and, it may be said, magnificent theology, founded on the discoveries of ancient astronomy at its zenith, imposed on Roman paganism the cult of the invincible Sun, the master of all nature, the creator and saviour of man.

A mass of literary evidence and a number of figured monuments prove how powerful became, under the Roman Empire, the belief that the sun was the god of the dead. Old mythological traditions combined with Chaldean theology and were propagated with the Eastern religions. It was imagined that the deceased, and in particular the emperors, were borne to heaven on the chariot of Helios, or that the eagle, the king of the birds and the servant of the sovereign sun, carried off their souls to bear them to his master. Elsewhere it was the griffin of Apollo or the solar phoenix who was the bearer of the dead or the symbol of immortality. A funeral altar of Rome even bears the characteristic inscription, *"Sol me rapuit,"* "the Sun has seized me up."[26]

You will probably ask how men succeeded in reconciling this solar immortality with the doctrine which made the moon the abode of the dead. The Greeks, following the Orientals, had been able to make a lunar-solar calendar, and they also constructed an eschatology in which the two great heavenly bodies both played part. They were the two divinities whose help the priests promised to "those who were about to die."[27] This eschatology is founded on the astrological idea that the moon presides over physical life, over the formation and decomposition of bodies, but that the sun is the author of intellectual life and the master of reason. The doctrine also includes the belief we have already explained elsewhere,[28] that when souls leave the earth, they are still surrounded by a subtle

[26] CIL, VI, 29954; see below, Lecture VI, p. 157 ss.

[27] Commodian, VIII, 10: "Sacerdotes . . . numina qui dicunt aliquid morituro prodesse."

[28] See Introd., p. 24 s.; *cf.* below, Lecture VI, p. 167.

fluid which retains the appearance of the persons whom they formerly animated. The pagan theologians thus admitted that the souls which came down to earth assumed in the sphere of the moon and in the atmosphere these aerial bodies which were regarded as the seat of the vital principle. Inversely, when they rose again to heaven, the function of the moon was to dissolve and to receive these light envelopes, as on earth its damp rays provoked the corruption of the corpse. The soul, thus becoming pure reason ($\nu o\hat{\nu}s$), ascended to the sun, the source of all intelligence. According to others the formation of the soul's integument was begun and its reabsorption was completed in the planetary spheres, and this is why the Neo-Platonist Jamblichus[29] placed the Hades of mythology between the sun and the moon. These theories are not the product of pure philosophical speculations, but have their roots in the old astral religion of the Semites. The mysteries of Mithras, the Chaldaic oracles, and above all Manicheism shared the belief in a lunar-solar immortality of which the source certainly goes back to the tenets of the "Chaldean" priests.

* * * * *

Solar immortality is a learned doctrine, the fruit of the astronomical theories which made the king-star the centre and the master of the universe. It was such as to find acceptance with theologians and philosophers and to be spread by the Oriental mysteries. But it never succeeded in eliminating or overshadowing the old popular idea that the souls of the dead dwell in the midst of the glittering constellations. A trace of the double conception is found in the Stoic school. For certain of the masters of this school the directing reason of the world, the ἡγεμονικόν, has its principal seat in the sun, for others in the sphere of the fixed stars. In the same way the poets, Lucan addressing Nero, and Statius addressing Domitian, hesitatingly ask if these emperors will ride in the

[29] Lydus, *De mensib.*, IV, 149 (p. 167, 25, Wünsch.).

flaming chariot of Phoebus or if they will assume Jupiter's sceptre in the highest heaven.[30] The Neo-Pythagoreans admitted that souls could rise to the Most High (εἰς τὸν Ὕψιστον), that is to say, to the supreme God who was enthroned at the summit of the world.[31] It was, moreover, very anciently held among the Greeks that Olympus was in the outer circle enveloping the world, and until the end of antiquity we find the Elysian Fields were transported to the zone of the constellations and in particular to the Milky Way. This is, for instance, the doctrine of Cicero as shown in the dream of Scipio.

So the old popular idea that the soul became a star, which in Greece was accepted by the ancient Pythagoreans, still subsisted. According to mythology this was the happy lot reserved for heroes. We have whole books which tell us how these heroes at the end of their career were transformed to brilliant stars in reward for their exploits. "Catasterism" draws a moral conclusion from ancient tales. Hercules, Castor and Pollux, Perseus and Andromeda and many others had deserved such metamorphosis. It did not therefore seem bold to assign to the eminent men of the present the same destiny as to the great figures of the past, and no one was shocked by the supposition that their divine spirits might be added to the number of the "visible gods." This was, in particular, a lot worthy of the princes who had deserved apotheosis. At the death of Caesar a comet appeared. It was thought to be the dictator's soul which had been received among the Immortals, and Ovid[32] does not hesitate to show us Venus descending, invisible, into the senate, snatching this soul from the pierced body and bearing it aloft to the sky. There Venus feels the soul become inflamed and sees it escape from her breast to fly beyond the moon and turn into a trailing comet. Hadrian, in his grief for the death

[30] Lucan, *Phars.*, I, 45; Statius, *Theb.*, I, 27; *cf.* my *Études syriennes*, 1917, p. 97 s.

[31] Diog. Laert., VIII, 31.

[32] Ovid, *Metam.*, XV, 840 ss.; *cf.* 749.

of Antinous, let himself be persuaded that a star had just appeared which was the deified soul of his favourite.[33] But as in Greece "heroification" was finally awarded by the will of families to every one of their members whose loss they mourned, so "catasterism" was in the end accorded to deceased persons of very moderate deserts. "Nearly the whole heaven," says Cicero, "is filled with mankind."[34] In an inscription of Amorgos[35] a young man, carried off by the Fates at the age of twenty, thus addresses his mother: "Weep not; for of what use is weeping? Rather venerate me, for I am now a divine star which shows itself at sunset." And at Miletus[36] a child of eight years old, whom Hermes has led to Olympus, contemplates the ether and shines in the midst of the stars, "rising every evening to the horn of the Goat. By the favour of the gods he protects the young boys who were his playfellows in the rude palaestrae."

Epitaphs so precise in expression are exceptional. On the other hand, numerous epigraphic and literary texts declare that the soul of some dead person has risen to the stars to live there with the Immortals, but leave the position of this soul undetermined. It is stated to have flown towards the vast sky, to have been received by the ether, to be living at the summit of the world and following the revolutions of the celestial armies. But the place where the blessed thus come together, that one of the upper spheres in which their meeting takes place, is left uncertain. Their dwelling was known to be somewhere very high above us, but men did not willingly venture to fix its exact situation.

The heathen theologians wished however to bring order and precision into this astral eschatology. As they had combined the doctrines of lunar and solar immortality,

[33] Cassius, Dio, LXIX, 11, 4.

[34] Cic., *Tusc.*, I, 12, 28: "Totum prope caelum nonne humano generi completum est?"

[35] *Revue de philologie*, XXXIII, 1909, p. 6 = IG, XII, 7, 123.

[36] *Revue de phil.*, *ibid.*; cf. Lecture V, p. 139.

so they attempted to bring both into agreement with stellar immortality. When Lucian in the beginning of his "Icaromenippus" shows us his hero passing over three thousand stadia from the earth to the moon, where he makes a first halt, rising thence five hundred parasangs to the sun, and then ascending from the sun to heaven, Jupiter's citadel, through the space travelled in a full day by an eagle in rapid flight, he is giving us a humorous parody of the journey which some men ascribed to souls. This idea that the soul thus rises to Paradise by three stages was widely entertained in the East, and it was notably held by Mazdeism. A trace of this belief seems to linger in the passage of the Second Epistle to the Corinthians in which Saint Paul tells that he has been lifted "to the third heaven."[37]

The Platonists sometimes adopted the same conception and combined it with psychological ideas, a development of those we recalled in connection with solar immortality (p. 103). It was held that when the soul came down to earth it first received an ethereal garment of almost immaterial purity; then, imagination being added to reason, a solar fluid surrounded it; then a lunar integument made it subject to the passions; and finally a carnal body was the cause of its ignorance of divine truths and of its blind foolishness. It successively lost with these wrappings the inclinations or faculties which were bound with them, when after death it went back again to the place of its origin.[38]

The conception of the triple ascension of souls rested fundamentally on a rudimentary astronomy, for it confused the five planets with the fixed stars, discriminating from both only the sun and the moon. But for long the system which divided the heavens into seven superimposed spheres, enveloped by an eighth sphere which was the limit of the universe, had imposed itself not only on

[37] II *Cor.* 12, 2.

[38] Porph., *Sent.*, 292 (p. 14, Mommert); Proclus, *In Remp.*, I, p. 152, 17, Kroll; *In Tim.*, III, p. 234, 25, Diehl.

the learned but also on the authors of pagan apocalypses. The eschatological doctrine which triumphed at the end of paganism is in agreement with this theory, generally admitted by the science of the period. This doctrine is certainly of Chaldeo-Persian origin, and was spread in the first century especially by the mysteries of Mithras.[39] Then, in the second century, the Pythagorean Numenius introduced it into philosophic speculation. Man's soul was held to descend from the height of heaven to this sublunary world, passing through the planetary spheres, and thus at its birth it acquired the dispositions and the qualities peculiar to each of these stars. After death it went back to its celestial home by the same path. Then as it traversed the zones of the sky, it divested itself of the passions and faculties which it had acquired during its descent to earth, as it were of garments. To the moon it surrendered its vital and alimentary energy, to Mercury its cupidity, to Venus its amorous desires, to the sun its intellectual capacities, to Mars its warlike ardour, to Jupiter its ambitious dreams, to Saturn its slothful tendencies. It was naked, disencumbered of all sensibility, when it reached the eighth heaven, there to enjoy, as a sublime essence, in the eternal light where lived the gods, bliss without end.

In the mysteries of Mithras a ladder composed of seven different metals served as a symbol of this passage of souls through the spheres, astrology placing each of the planets in relation with one of these metals, lead with Saturn, gold with the sun, silver with the moon and so on.[40]

But in opposition to this pantheism which, while identifying God with the universe, placed the chief home of divine energy in the celestial spheres and particularly in the highest of them, the sectaries of Plato transported

[39] Cf. my Mysteries of Mithras, Chicago, 1903, p. 145; below, Lecture VI, p. 169; VII, p. 187.

[40] Origen, Contra Celsum, VI, 21; cf. Monum. mystères de Mithra, I, p. 118.

the supreme Power beyond the limits of the world and made of him a Being no longer immanent, but transcendent and distinct from all matter. This conception became more and more predominant in pagan theology as Stoicism lost influence in favour of Neo-Platonism. This God, "ultramundane and incorporeal, father and architect" of creation,[41] had his seat, it was thought, in the infinite light which extended beyond the starry spheres. Religion called him sometimes the Most High (Ὕψιστος), sometimes Jupiter, but gave him at the same time the epithets "Uppermost," "Insuperable" (*summus, exsuperantissimus*).[42] It was this celestial Father whom the elect souls aspired to join, but only those who had attained to perfection succeeded in doing so, as we shall see in our last lecture. The others stayed, in accordance with their degree of purity, in a lower zone of the successive stages formed by the atmosphere, by the planetary circles, and by the heaven of the fixed stars, which were the "visible gods," opposed to the spiritual world.[43]

*　*　*　*　*

This was the last conception of paganism and on the whole it was to impose itself on men for many centuries. Judaism had already made concessions to the astronomical theories of the "Chaldeans," and had borrowed from them the idea of seven stories of heavens, an idea which we find developed in particular in the apocryphal Book of Enoch. It also belonged to Christianity almost from the beginning, and the gnostics gave it a large place in their speculations. But especially Origen, who borrowed it directly from the Greek philosophers, lent the authority of his name to the doctrines of astral eschatology. According to him, souls, after they have sojourned in Paradise, which he imagined as a remote place of earth where they learn terrestrial truths, rise to the zone of the air

[41] Apuleius, *De dogm. Plat.*, I, 11.
[42] *Archiv für Religionsw.*, IX, 1906, p. 323 ss.
[43] See, *e.g.*, Plotin., III, 4, 6; *cf.* Lecture VIII, p. 213.

and there understand the nature of the beings who people this element. But if they are free from all material weight, they cross the atmosphere rapidly and reach "the dwellings of the heavens," that is, the celestial spheres. There they grasp the nature of the stars and the causes of their movements. Finally, when they have made such progress that they have become pure intelligences, they are admitted to contemplate the reasonable essences face to face and see invisible things, enjoying their perfection. Although Origen was condemned by the Church, his ideas were not abolished. Since the Christian lore adopted the ancient conception of the world's structure, as formulated by Ptolemy, it had necessarily to admit that souls traversed the planetary circles in order to reach that "supermundane light" in which they found perfect beatitude. Dante's Paradise, with its choirs of angels and its classes of the blessed, distributed among the superimposed spheres of the heavens, is a magnificent testimony to the strength of the tradition which antiquity bequeathed to the Middle Ages. Before this tradition could be destroyed, Galileo and Copernicus had to ruin Ptolemy's system and open up to the imagination the infinite spaces of a limitless universe.

IV

THE WINNING OF IMMORTALITY

A FUNDAMENTAL difference distinguishes the conception of immortality as it appears in the religion of the Roman Empire from our modern ideas. Immortality, as we conceive of it, follows on the very nature which we ascribe to the human soul. It is affirmed by some, denied by others, in accordance with the character which each one attributes to the principle of conscious thought, but whenever credence is given to it, it is generally supposed to be absolute, eternal, universal. For the ancients, on the other hand, immortality was no more than conditional: it might not be perpetual and it might not belong to all men. According to the Platonists the soul, an incorruptible essence, a principle of life and movement, survived necessarily;[1] according to the Epicureans, being composed of atoms, it was dissolved at the moment of death.[2] But between these extreme opinions of the philosophers, the religion of the people remained faithful to the old belief that the shade must be nourished with offerings and sacrifices, that if it lacked sustenance it was condemned to waste away miserably. This conception, like not a few others which were fading away in the West, was revived when the Orientals imposed on the Roman world their more primitive and sometimes very crude beliefs. The normal destiny of the soul was therefore to survive the body for a certain time, then in its turn to disappear. A second death (δεύτερος θάνατος) completed the work of the first which gave the corpse over to corruption. The spiritual

1 See above, Introd., pp. 6, 41.
2 *Ibid.*, p. 7.

essence which had abandoned the body was annihilated after it. Such was the inevitable necessity imposed on mankind. Immortality was a privilege of divinity. The man who was exempted from the common lot of his kind was therefore the equal of the gods; he had risen above his perishable condition to acquire the everlasting youth of the Olympians, the unlimited duration of the stars which travel the heavens, the eternity of the Supreme Being.

If he became a god after his death it was sometimes because he had been one ever since his birth. For men were not all born equal: if each of them possessed the *psyche* which nourished and animated the body, yet all men did not equally receive the divine effluence ($\pi\nu\epsilon\hat{v}\mu\alpha$) which gave reason. This reason, which distinguished man from the beasts, was akin to the fires of the stars; it established between man and heaven a community of nature ($\sigma\nu\gamma\gamma\acute{\epsilon}\nu\epsilon\iota\alpha$) which alone made it possible for him to acquire a knowledge of divinity,[3] the "gnosis" of God and of the world which He animated. This special grace also exempted him who obtained it from the passions and weaknesses to which the inclinations of the flesh exposed him. It made him pious, temperate and chaste: he was holy (*sanctus*).[4] It communicated to him a lucidity and power lacking to the common run of mortals. He penetrated the secrets of nature and commanded the elements; he received revelations and was capable of prophetic divination. Inversely, every exceptional quality was regarded as superhuman; every extraordinary act seemed a miracle. The most enlightened spoke merely of celestial inspiration. "*Nemo magnus vir sine quodam adflatu divino,*" said Cicero.[5] The many saw in these privileged beings earthly incarnations of all the Olympians. From the moment of their appearance on the earth these men were really gods; their soul kept its higher nature in all

[3] See above, Lecture III, p. 96.
[4] Link, *De vocis "Sanctus" usu pagano*, Königsberg, 1910.
[5] Cic., *De natura deor.*, II, 66, § 167.

its purity; it would indubitably return after death to its place of origin. Such are the leading ideas which explain the belief in the immortality of the heroes.

Among those who escaped the common law of death because they were divine, first of all, were the kings. In all times kings have been looked upon as of superior essence to the rest of mankind, and the ancient East approximated them or made them equal to the heavenly powers. The Hellenistic realms, in Egypt, Syria, Asia Minor, raised the cult of the monarch to the rank of a state institution; and the Caesars inherited this homage, which was rendered to them by their subjects even in their lifetime, first in the East and then throughout the Empire. The powerful chief who delivered his state from the scourge of invasion and ensured it peace and welfare, accomplished a work which seemed to be beyond the ability of man, and he was adored as a present god ($\epsilon\pi\iota\phi\alpha\nu\dot{\eta}s$ $\theta\epsilon\delta s$, *praesens numen*), a saviour ($\sigma\omega\tau\dot{\eta}\rho$). Sometimes the god incarnate in him was specified; and he was looked upon as a manifestation of Zeus, Apollo, or another. Very ancient but still active beliefs gave him the power to command nature as well as men. If the fields were fertile, if the flocks and herds had increased, these were benefits received from the godlike sovereign. No miracle was beyond his accomplishment. He was the providence of his people, having indeed the power of foreseeing and foretelling the future. According to Manilius,[6] it was to kings, whose lofty thoughts reached the heights of the sky, that nature first revealed her mysteries. The pagan theologians affirmed, indeed, that the souls of kings came from a higher place than those of other men, and that these august personages borrowed more from heaven than the common crowd of mortals.[7] And thus, death had no sooner carried them off from the earth than their souls once again rose to the stars, who welcomed them as their

---

[6] Manilius, I, 41; *cf.* Boll, *Aus der Offenbarung Iohannis,* 1914, p. 136 ss.
[7] Pseudo-Ecphant. ap Stob., *Anth.,* IV, 7, 64 (IV, p. 272 ss., Wachsmuth); Hermes Trism. ap. Stob., *Ecl.,* I, 49, 45 (I, p. 407, W).

equals (*sideribus recepti*). It was thought that an eagle or the chariot of the sun bore them away.[8] It may seem strange that the senate should deliberate as to whether or not a deceased emperor deserved apotheosis, and should refuse or accord him official canonisation. But this act is in conformity with all the ideas we have described, since the monarch's benefits and victories were the proof of his divine origin, and since, if he had committed crimes and caused misfortunes, he was thus shown to be in no respect a god.

In the remote ages of ancient Egypt, the Pharaohs were the first whom Osiris consented to identify with himself, or whom their father Ra bore away in the solar boat, but little by little the rites practised in order to ensure eternity to the sovereign were extended to the magnates surrounding him. Thus immortality was a kind of posthumous nobility bestowed on the great servants of the state, or usurped by them, long before the rest of the people obtained it. In Greece, also, kings were the first to be the objects of a cult as protecting heroes, but after them other classes of eminent men received the same title and the same adoration, in particular the founder of a city, its lawmaker who had given it a constitution and the warrior who had victoriously defended it. In the same way as fabulous demigods, Castor and Pollux or Hercules, had in heaven become brilliant stars as a reward for their earthly deeds, they also were public benefactors who by their works and their virtues had shown themselves worthy of the same "catasterism." These ideas passed to Rome with the Stoic philosophy. After having given a list of those who had triumphed in the wars of the Republic, Cicero lays down as a fact that not one of them could have attained so far without the help of God;[9] and elsewhere he states more explicitly:[10] "To all who have saved, succoured or aggrandized their country, a fixed

---

[8] See below, Lecture VI, p. 156 ss.

[9] Cic., *Nat. deorum*, II, 66, § 165.

[10] *Somn. Scipionis*, 3; *cf. Pro Sestio*, 68, § 143.

place in which they shall enjoy everlasting bliss is
assigned in heaven, for it is from heaven that they who
guide and guard cities have descended, thither to reascend." The ex-consul Cicero claimed apotheosis for the
great men of the state: this was the republican transformation of the doctrine of the divinity of kings.

Pagan theology was to give much wider extension to
this doctrine. In a curious passage Hermes Trismegistus[11]
explains that there are royal, that is to say divine, souls
of different kinds, for there is a royalty of the spirit, a
royalty of art, a royalty of science, and even a royalty of
bodily strength. All exceptional men were godly, and it
was not to be admitted that the sacred energy which
animated them was extinguished with them.

Pious priests, like kings, were judged, or rather judged
themselves, to be worthy of immortality. Who could more
justly deserve a share in the felicity of the gods than
those who on the earth had lived in their company and
known their designs? He who had thus been in communication with the godhead and learnt his secrets was raised
above the condition of humanity. This sacred knowledge,
this gift of prophecy, this "gnosis," which was inseparable from piety, transformed him who had obtained it,
set him free even in life from the condemnation of fate;
and after death he went to the immortals whose confidant
he had been here below.

The philosophers and theologians who treated of the
nature of the Divine Being shared the blessed lot of the
priests and soothsayers who interpreted His will. Their
doctrine came to them by inspiration from on high, or at
least so they readily believed. Their intelligence, which
was lit by a divine ray, penetrated the world's mysteries
and subjected it to their will. *Philosophus* became a
synonym for thaumaturge. Even in this life the superior
mind of the philosophers allowed them to escape the
necessities by which other men were oppressed, and this

---

11 Hermes Trismeg. ap. Stob., *Ecl.*, I, 49, 69 (I, p. 466, Wachsmuth).

reason returned after death to the source of all intelligence.

But all knowledge came from God. It was He who gave light to the wise man, absorbed in austere research, and caused him to discover truth. It was He too who inspired the poet, who worked in him when enthusiasm carried him away; He likewise who gave to the artist the faculty of apprehending and expressing beauty, to the musician the power to recall by his chords the sublime harmony of the celestial spheres. All who gave themselves up to works of the intellect had a part in the godhead. They were purified by the high pursuit of spiritual joy and freed thereby from the passions of the body and the oppression of matter. For this reason the Muses are frequently represented on tombs; beautiful sarcophagi are decorated with the figures of the nine sisters. Thanks to these goddesses, mortals were delivered from earthly misery and led back towards the sacred light of the heavens.

Thus the spirits of all men distinguished above their fellows were one day to find themselves gathered together in the dwelling-place of the heroes. This conception made the future life a reward for eminent service rendered to the state or humanity. Its origin certainly went very far back: it is found among primitive peoples, in reference to the famous warriors of the tribes, and it never ceased to be accepted in ancient Greece. But towards the end of the Roman Republic it was more generally admitted than ever before. It was in harmony with the constitution of an aristocratic society in which it seemed that even posthumous honours should be reserved for the elect. Some modern thinkers and poets have shared the ancient feeling which inspired it. Carducci, who disliked the critics of Milan, thought that they might well perish wholly, but that the great spirits like Dante, whom he interpreted,— and doubtless also this interpreter himself,—were saved.[12]

[12] Maurice Muret, *Les contemporains étrangers,* Paris, I, p. 30.

Matthew Arnold also in an admirable sonnet strongly defends the faith in a limited immortality. Let me recall to you the last verses:

> "And will not then the immortal armies scorn
> The world's poor routed leavings? or will they
> Who fail'd under the heat of this life's day
> Support the fervours of the heavenly morn?
> No! The energy of life may be
> Kept on after the grave, but not begun,
> And he who flagg'd not in earthly strife,
> From strength to strength advancing—only he,
> His soul well-knit and all his battles won,
> Mounts, and that hardly, to eternal life."

*   *   *   *   *

But this proud doctrine vowed to final destruction the mass of humble men, the multitude of the miserable, that is to say, those who, because they endured most in this world, must most aspire to seek in another the happiness which was here denied them and the retribution which should repair the injustice of their earthly lot. This doctrine of the immortality of the few made low station in life a misfortune which was prolonged beyond the grave. To the immense company of the wretched, who suffered without consolation, the religions of the East brought a "better hope," the assurance that by certain secret rites the mystic, whatever his rank, whether senator or slave, might obtain salvation. The virtue of the liturgical ceremonies made him equal to the immortals (ἀπαθανατίζειν). This was the secret of the rapid spread of these exotic cults in the Latin world.

Every day the stars disappear beneath the horizon to reappear in the east on the morrow; every month a new moon succeeds the moon whose light has waned; every year the sun is reborn to new strength after his fires have died away; every winter vegetation withers to bloom again in the spring. The gods of nature—Attis, Osiris, Adonis—also rose again after they had been slain; the gods of the stars resumed their glowing ardour after darkness had overwhelmed them. Their essential quality was to be for ever "living" or "unconquered" (*invicti*). Their career was a perpetual triumph over death. The struggle implied was, under the influence of dualism, recognised to be an unceasing battle between two powers disputing possession of the world. Thus the mystic who had become god, who had part in the divine energy, also acquired the power to conquer death. Oriental religions looked upon earthly existence as a fight from which the just man issued victorious. Immortality was a triumph won over the powers of evil, of which the most implacable was death. The souls of the elect were crowned like athletes and soldiers; their wreath was the "crown of life," often represented on funeral monuments.[13] The Greeks sometimes, and the Etruscans frequently, had personified death as a horrible monster who frightened those whom he approached. But the idea of making death into the adversary of mankind, from whose empire pious and strong souls might escape, spread only with the reception of the Oriental beliefs.

This mythological conception of salvation was combined in the mysteries with another, which was more scientific, that of fatalism, which was the chief dogma imposed by astrology on the Roman world. Death is for man the most inevitable and the hardest necessity. *Fatum* often denotes the unalterable term of life; and this end, which diviners could foresee but could not delay, ought, according to the law of our kind, to overtake the soul as well as the body. But the Oriental cults never ceased to claim that the celestial powers who escaped the rule of Destiny, which extends only to the sublunary world, were also able to withdraw thence their faithful followers. As the emperor was not subject to Fate because he was god, so he who had been initiated and had acquired the same quality was, as a funeral inscription expressed it,

13 See my *Études syriennes*, p. 63 ss.

"exempt from the lot of death."[14] Those who had taken
part in the occult ceremonies of the sect and were instructed in its esoteric doctrines were alone able to pro-
long their existence beyond the term fixed by the stars
at their birth. By the virtue of these rites pious souls were
withdrawn from this fate-ridden earth and were led,
enfranchised from their servitude, to a divine world.

Thus those who had acceded to a religious initiation
obtained eternal life, like the great men whose celestial
origin had predestined them thereto. By what rites was
wrought this "deification" ($\dot{\alpha}\pi o\theta\dot{\epsilon}\omega\sigma\iota\varsigma$), or rather this
"immortalisation" ($\dot{\alpha}\pi\alpha\theta\alpha\nu\alpha\tau\iota\sigma\mu\dot{o}\varsigma$)?

The soul, enclosed in the body, was by its very contact
with matter exposed to pollution, "as pure and clear water
poured into the bottom of a muddy well is troubled."[15]
The mysteries never conceived the soul as absolutely immaterial: it was a subtle and light essence, but one
coarsened and weighed down by sin, which thus altered
its divine nature and caused its decomposition and loss.[16]
In order therefore that immortality might be ensured to
the soul, it must be cleansed of its stains. The pagan
religions employed a whole set of ablutions and purifications for restoring his first integrity to the mystic. He
could wash in consecrated water in accordance with certain prescribed forms. This was in reality a magic rite:
the cleanliness of the body wrought by sympathy a veri-
table disinfection of the inner spirit, the water clearing
off its taints or expelling the evil demons which caused
pollution. Or else the initiate sprinkled himself with or
drank the blood either of a slaughtered victim or of the
priests themselves. These rites arose from the belief that
the fluid which flows in our veins is a vivifying principle,
able to communicate new existence.[17] The man who had

[14] CIL, VI, 1779=Bücheler, *Carm. epigr.*, 111, 23: "(Me) sorte mortis
eximens in templa ducis. . . ."
[15] Pseudo-Lysis ap. Jamblich., *Vit. Pyth.*, 17, § 77.
[16] See Introd., p. 29; Lecture VII, p. 184 s.
[17] *Cf.* Lecture I, p. 51.

received baptism by blood in the *taurobolium* was reborn for eternity (*in aeternum renatus*),[18] and when, foul and repulsive, he left the sacred ditch, he was adored as a god by those present. Elsewhere purifications by air and fire were found united to that by water, so that the different elements all had part in the purgation.[19] All these cathartic ceremonies had the effect of regenerating him who submitted to them, delivering him from the domination of the body, making him a pure spirit, and rendering him fit to live an immaculate and incorruptible life.

A similar belief in a transference to the soul of bodily effects partially explains why unctions were still employed in the liturgy of the mysteries. By rubbing himself with perfumed oil the wrestler in the palaestra and the bather after the perspiration of the sweating-room strengthened their limbs and rendered them supple. Ancient medical science deals at great length with the propitious action of numerous ointments, and by their means magic worked not only sudden cures but also prodigious metamorphoses. The aromatic unguents, which had marvellous antiseptic qualities, served to ensure the conservation of an embalmed corpse. Similarly, in the cult of the mysteries, unctions gave the soul an increase of spiritual force and made it capable of prolonging its existence for ever. As rubbing with unctuous substances was a practice of the thermae, so it was of the temples after the liturgical bath. In the anointing of kings and the ordination of priests they communicated to man a divine character and higher faculties, and this idea has been preserved down to modern times. But, above all, as ointments preserved mortal remains from putrefaction, so the consecrated oil and honey became a means by which the soul was rendered incorruptible and immortality was bestowed upon it.

The most efficacious means of communicating with the godhead which the mysteries offered was, however, that

[18] CIL, VI, 510=Dessau, 4152.
[19] Servius, *Aen.*, VI, 741.

of participation in the ritual banquets. These banquets are found in various forms in all these religious communities. We have seen that among the votaries of Dionysos his feasts, in which the consecrated wine was drunk, gave a foretaste of the joys reserved for the initiate in the Elysian Fields.[20] Drunkenness, which frees from care, which awakens unsuspected forces in man, was looked upon as divine possession, as the indwelling of a god in the heart of the Bacchantes. Wine thus became *par excellence* the drink of immortality, which flowed for the sacred guests in the meals of the secret conventicles. The heady liquid not only gave vigour of body and wisdom of mind, but also strength to fight the evil spirits and to triumph over death.

Sometimes honey, which was according to the ancients the food of the blessed, was offered to the neophyte and made him the equal of the Olympians. Elsewhere bread consecrated by appropriate formulae was held to produce the same effects.

But still another conception is discernible in the feasts of the mysteries and mingles with the first: it is thought that the god himself is eaten when some sacred animal is consumed. This idea goes back to the most primitive savagery, as is seen in the rite of "omophagy" in which certain votaries of Bacchus fiercely tore the raw flesh of a bull with their teeth and devoured it. Undoubtedly there was originally a belief that the strength of the sacrificed animal was thus acquired, like the superstition of the native African hunters who eat a slain lion's heart in order to gain his courage. Similarly, if a victim be regarded as divine, to consume it is to participate in its divinity. "Those," says Porphyry,[21] "who wish to receive into themselves the soul of prophetic animals absorb their principal vital organs, such as the hearts of crows, moles or hawks, and thus they become able to speak oracles, like a god." Similarly, the Syrians ate the

[20] See Introd., p. 35; *cf.* Lecture VIII, p. 204.
[21] Porph., *De abstin.*, II, 48.

fish of Atargatis, a forbidden food which was, however, provided for the initiate after a sacrifice; and those who partook of these mystic repasts were not, like the rest of men, vowed to death, but were saved by the goddess.[22]

All means of attaining to godliness were not so crude as these. An important part of the mysteries was the instruction which gave the sacred lore, the "gnosis." This "gnosis" included the whole of religious learning, that is to say, it was the knowledge of rites as well as of theological and moral truths. It taught above all the origin and the end of man, but it covered all the works of God, and, inasmuch as it explained creation, it formed a system of the world and a theory of nature. In fact the world, being wholly penetrated by a divine energy, was itself a part of God. The close alliance which exists between philosophy and the mysteries, and which is revealed to us especially in the Pythagorean and Hermetic literature,[23] is shown in the value thus given to science. This science, which in the East had always been sacerdotal, was not looked upon as a conquest of reason but as the revelation of a god. Illumined by this god, the initiate entered into communication with him, and consequently himself became divine and was withdrawn from the power of Fate. "They who possess the knowledge (γνῶσις) have deification as their happy end," said Hermes Trismegistus.[24]

The highest degree of this "gnosis" is the sight of the godhead himself, or to use the Greek word, "epoptism." By artifice or illusion apparitions were evoked and "epiphanies" produced.[25] A whole system of fastings and macerations placed the mystic in a fit state to attain to ecstasy. In the temple of Isis the faithful devotee merged

---

[22] *Cf. Comptes rendus Acad. Inscriptions*, 1917, p. 281 ss.

[23] See above, Introd., p. 37.

[24] Hermes Trismeg., *Poimandres*, I, 26: Τοῦτό ἐστι τὸ ἀγαθὸν τέλος τοῖς γνῶσιν ἐσχηκόσι θεωθῆναι.

[25] See below, Lecture VIII, 207.

himself "with inexpressible delight"[26] in the silent adoration of the sacred images, and when the rites had been accomplished and he felt himself transported beyond the confines of the world, he contemplated the gods of heaven and hell face to face. He who had had the vision of this ineffable beauty was himself transfigured for ever. His soul, filled with the divine splendour, must when its earthly captivity had ended live eternally in contemplation of the radiant beings who had admitted it to their company.[27]

*   *   *   *   *

The mysteries have thus a number of processes, some material and some spiritual, for producing the union with god which is the source of immortality. This union is first conceived as effected with the particular god honoured by a sect. As this god has died and has risen again, so the mystic dies to be reborn, and the liturgy even marks by its ceremonies the death of the former man and his return to a glorious life.

The fervent disciple to whom the god has united himself suffers a metamorphosis and takes on divine qualities. In magic this process is sometimes very grossly indicated: "Come into me, Hermes," says a papyrus,[28] "as children do into women's wombs, ... I know thee, Hermes, and thou knowest me; I am thou and thou art I." The old Egyptian doctrine of the identification with Osiris, which goes back to the age of the Pharaohs, was never given up in the Alexandrian mysteries, and the whole doctrine of immortality rested on it. As on the earth the initiate who piously observed sacred precepts received in his bosom the godhead, so after death the faithful became a Serapis if a man, an Isis if a woman. This beatification seems to have been conceived sometimes as an absorption into the

---

[26] Apuleius, *Metam.*, XI, 24: "Inexplicabili voluptate divini simulacri perfruebar."

[27] See *Oriental religions*, p. 100, and below, Lecture VIII, p. 210 ss.

[28] Papyr. of London, CXXII, 1 ss.; *cf.* Reitzenstein, *Poimandres*, p. 20.

heart of the divinity, sometimes as a multiplication of the divinity, who left to the deceased his own personality.

It was above all from Egypt that apotheosis in the form of a particular divinity spread first in the Hellenistic and then in the Roman world. As the Pharaohs became Osiris on the earth and after their death, so among the Ptolemies such names as Isis-Arsinoë and others similar are found, and the emperors were adored even in their lifetime as epiphanies of Apollo, Zeus or Helios.[29] Their subjects could obtain a lot as happy as that of the sovereigns. The mystics of Dionysos were early made divine, in imitation of those of Serapis, and became as many emanations of Bacchus; and finally under the empire a cult was rendered to the dead under such titles as Mars, Hercules, Venus, Diana and other Olympians.

Conceptions less in conflict with reason were taught by the astral cults of the Semitic East. The celestial powers here were higher, more distant, less anthropomorphic, and it was not imagined that a man could assume their form. Here the action of the god on the mystic recalled that of the stars in nature: it was regarded as an effluence, fallen from the ether, which penetrated the initiate, as an energy which filled him, as a luminous ray which lit his mind. Virtue from on high entered into the neophyte and transformed him into a being like the divinities of heaven.[30] He was glorified ($\delta o \xi a \sigma \theta \epsilon i s$) as a conqueror who had triumphed over demons and smitten down death; he was illuminated ($\phi \omega \tau \iota \sigma \theta \epsilon i s$) and penetrated by a supernatural light which disclosed to him all truth; he was sanctified ($\dot{a} \gamma \iota a \sigma \theta \epsilon i s$) and acquired unfailing virtue; he was exalted ($\dot{v} \psi o \hat{v} \tau a \iota$), that is to say his soul rose in rapture to the stars. Glory, splendour, light, purity, knowledge: all these ideas were confounded until they became almost synonymous and together denoted

[29] Riewald, *De imperatorum Romanorum cum certis dis aequatione*, Halle, 1912.

[30] *Cf.* Gillis Wetter, *Die "Verherrlichung,"* in *Beiträge zur Relig.-Wissenschaft*, II, 1914.

the transfiguration which was undergone by the soul
called to rise to ethereal regions, even on this earth and
while it was still joined to the body.

But this divine action, which tended to become purely
spiritual, was originally much more material. A very
coarse substratum to the theological ideas is still apparent in the texts which mention them. Magic, which was
addressed to the credulity of simple men, did not conceal
it at all. Here the ascension of the spirit appeared as a
journey to heaven. By appropriate formulae and processes the sorcerers pretended to secure immortality for
their adepts, making them fly, body and soul, through the
higher spheres to reach the dwelling of the gods.[31]

*   *   *   *   *

In short, the initiate of the mysteries believed that they
found in them a warrant of immortality. By the virtue of
the rites their souls were united to their god; thus they
became themselves divine, and were ensured an everlasting life. Inevitably, every Oriental religion affirmed that
it held the only sacred tradition leading surely to eternal
felicity. Outside the sect there was no certain salvation.
But philosophy always opposed these claims. Philosophy,
too, thought itself able to lead through wisdom to happiness in this world and in the next, and there was rivalry .
between it and the positive cults, as soon as it took on a
religious character and set up religious claims. The Neo-
Pythagoreans who formed esoteric communities opposed
their purifications and initiations to those of the mysteries. But the eschatological doctrine, of which Posidonius was, if not the author, at least the powerful
promoter, and which was to be taken up again and
transformed by the Neo-Platonists, exempted the wise
man from any obligation to religious observances as
ensuring his immortality. He was no longer in need of
sacraments and sacrifices, but could by his own unaided

31 See below, Lecture VI, p. 158.

force become a pure intelligence, win the complete mastery of himself by reason, and thereafter be certain of raising himself to the godhead.

At the most, certain thinkers granted a "propaedeutic" or preparatory value to ritual observances, and saw in them a means of predisposing the soul to ecstasy, but the mystic philosophers, of whom Plotinus represents the purest type, discarded for themselves all religious practices. Their proud doctrine places man alone face to face with God.[32] Or else, like Porphyry, they admit that sacred ceremonies can purify the spiritual or pneumatic soul but not its highest part, the intellectual soul; that they can raise it to the region of the stars but not bring it back to the Supreme Being. The late pagan philosophy asserts constantly and forcibly that the wise man's reason is able by itself, or rather through a celestial grace, without the intervention of any liturgy, to ensure its own return to its divine source. "As," says Porphyry, "he who is the priest of a particular god knows how to consecrate his statues, celebrate orgies, perform initiations and lustrations, so the true philosopher, who is the priest of the universal God, knows how to make His sacred images and to carry out His purifications and all the processes which will unite him to this God."[33]

Philosophers were therefore the priests of the world. Their functions were parallel to those of the actual priests but higher. They tended more and more to form a sacerdotal order which was separated from the rest of human society by its customs and its way of life. Like the mysteries they taught that piety, temperance and continence were the indispensable conditions of obtaining true knowledge. This "gnosis" was no longer a traditional theology revealed in the shadow of the sanctuary, but a scientific truth perceived by a grace-illumined reason. The philosopher took no part in the ceremonies of a

[32] See below, Lecture VIII, p. 212.
[33] Porph., *De Abstin.*, II, 49.

complicated ritual, but his prayer was the silent supplica-
tion of his intelligence seeking to understand creation. He
did not become absorbed in the contemplation of idols
but in the sight of the divine world and in particular of
the starry heavens. The end which this lonely cult strove
to attain was analogous to that sought by others in the
conventicles of the initiate—a divine revelation which
would give to the perfect wise man superhuman power,
which would make him a prophet, sometimes a wonder-
worker; and after death, already a god on earth, he went
to live in the company of the gods on high.

The lifting of the reason to heaven, source of all intelligence, was thus the pledge of astral immortality, as the
liturgical banquet was of the celestial feast. As physical
drunkenness, being divine possession, was a prelude to
the joy of the eternal repast, so spiritual ecstasy was the
sign of future deification.[34]

The ancients found impassioned words to depict this
communion of man with the starry heavens, and to express the divine love which transported the soul into
radiant space.[35] In the splendour of night the spirit was
intoxicated with the glow shed on it by the fires above.
Like the possessed and the Corybantes in the delirium
of their orgies, it abandoned itself to ecstasy, which set
it free from its fleshly wrappings and lifted it up to the
region of the everlasting stars. Borne on the wings of
enthusiasm it sprang to the midst of this sacred chorus and followed its harmonious movements. Reason,
illumined by the divine fires which surrounded it, understood the laws of nature and the secrets of destiny. It
then partook of the life of the light-flashing beings which
from the earth it saw glittering in the radiance of the
ether; before the fated term of death it had part in their
wisdom and received their revelations in a stream of

[34] See below, Lecture VIII, pp. 201, 207, 211.
[35] See my *Mysticisme astral dans l'antiquité* in *Bulletins de l'Acad. de
Belgique*, 1909, p. 264 ss.

light which dazzled even the eye of reason. This sublime rapture was an ephemeral foretaste of the endless felicity reserved for the sage when, after his death, rising to the celestial spheres, he penetrated all their mysteries.[36]

[36] See Lecture VIII, p. 210 ss.

V

UNTIMELY DEATH

IN the last lecture we endeavoured to show that in the ancient world immortality was at first conceived as being precarious and conditional, and that only the heroes, the exceptional men, who were in truth gods on earth, obtained apotheosis after their death. We afterwards saw that the mysteries extended the promise of eternal salvation to all the initiate, who by virtue of the rites were made equal to the gods, and finally that the philosophers contested the necessity of sacred ceremonies and affirmed that human reason by its own unaided power could win union with God.

We will now consider in more detail what lot was reserved for a special class of the dead, those whose life had been interrupted by an untimely end, and how in their case philosophy modified the old traditional beliefs.

If we turn over collections of ancient inscriptions we find, as when we go through our own cemeteries, a number of epitaphs in which the grief caused by the early death of a friend or relative is expressed. But in antiquity this sorrow was called forth not alone by regret for a loved being, too soon lost to sight, and by painful disappointment because of the irreparable ruin of the hopes to which his youth had given rise. Along with these human feelings, which are of all time and all societies, there were mingled in antiquity ideas which caused the loss of those who died before their time to seem more fearful and bitter.

Virgil's celebrated lines, in which he describes the descent of Aeneas to Hades, will be remembered:[1]

[1] Virg., *Aen.*, VI, 426 ss.

"Continuo auditae voces, vagitus et ingens,
Infantumque animae flentes in limine primo,
Quos dulcis vitae exsortes et ab ubere raptos
Abstulit atra dies et funere mersit acerbo."

"Ever were heard, on the outermost threshold, voices, a great wailing, the weeping souls of infants bereft of sweet life and torn from the breast, whom the ill-omened day swept off and whelmed in bitter death."

In an eschatological myth of Plutarch,[2] the traveller beyond the grave also sees a deep abyss, in which moan the plaintive voices of a multitude of children who had died at the moment of their birth and were unable to rise to heaven. It has been shown that the Latin poet and the Greek philosopher are here interpreters of an old Pythagorean belief, to which Plato alludes:[3] children who died young, like persons who met with violent deaths, the ἄωροι καὶ βιαιοθάνατοι, found no rest in the other life, but their souls wandered on the earth for the number of years for which their life would normally have lasted. The souls of the shipwrecked who perished at sea roamed the surface of the waters and sailors believed that they were incarnated in the seagulls.[4]

How did this belief in the miserable lot of innocent children arise? Its origin should probably be sought in that fear of death which haunts all primitive peoples, and it developed owing to the frequency in antiquity of infanticide by abandoning or "exposing" newly born infants. Remorse provoked terror. This conclusion is especially suggested because the fate of those who died prematurely was approximated to the lot of those who died violent deaths. Beings who had been prevented from completing the natural span of life were feared; their shades were conceived as being unquiet and in pain, because it was believed that they could return to disquiet and pain the

2 Plut., *De genio Socratis*, 22, p. 590 F.
3 Plato, *Republ.*, p. 615 C; *cf.* Norden, *Aeneis Buch VI*, 1903, pp. 11, 27.
4 Achill. Tat., V, 16.

living. The idea was entertained that a spirit brutally separated from the body came to hold it in horror and did not consent to inhabit the tomb until a reconciliation had been disobtained by expiatory ceremonies. Being grievously disincarnated, the soul became harmful. Souls, said the ancients, whom a cruel and untimely end has violently or unjustly torn from their bodies, themselves tend to be violent and unjust in order that they may avenge the wrong they have suffered.[5] It is no rare thing to find evidence in the inscriptions of a suspicion that a person cut off in the flower of his years has been the victim of some foul play; the curse of Heaven is called down on the head of his assumed murderer. The Sun, who discovers hidden crimes, is often invoked in Roman epitaphs against this unknown offender:[6] "Towards the Most High god, who watches over everything, and Helios and Nemesis, Arsinoë, dead before her time, lifts up her hands; if anyone prepared poison for her or rejoices in her end, pursue him," says an inscription of Alexandria. But the victim was himself believed to be capable of vengeance. It seemed incredible that one still full of strength and life should be entirely blotted out and that the energy which had animated him should also have disappeared suddenly, and the reprisals of this mysterious power were apprehended. This spirit pursued above all the murderer and, more generally, those who had given it cause for complaint. It showed itself to them in the form of terrifying monsters which tormented them. "As soon as I shall have expired, doomed to death by you," says the child in Horace whom the witches sacrificed, "I will haunt your nights like a Fury, I will tear your faces with my hooked nails, as the Manes gods can, and weighing on your unquiet hearts I will take sleep from your affrighted eyes.'"[7] Suetonius[8] relates that after the death

5 Tertull., *De anima*, 57.
6 Dessau, *Inscr. sel.*, 8497 ss.; *cf. Recueil des inscriptions du Pont*, 9, 258.
7 Horace, *Epod.*, 5, 92; *cf.* Livy, III, 58, 11.
8 Sueton., *Nero*, 34, 4.

of Agrippina, Nero was, on his own confession, often
troubled by the vision of her spectre and attempted to
calm her spirit by a sacrifice and an evocation which he
caused his magicians to make. The same historian
gravely recounts that the house in which Caligula was
murdered was every night haunted by dreadful apparitions until the time when it was destroyed by fire.[9] A
scholiast defines the *lemures* as "the wandering shades
of men who died before their normal time and are hence
redoubtable."[10] Even today popular belief in many countries attributes a maleficent power to the spirits of those
who have died a violent death.

These disquieting superstitions acquired new force
through the teachings of astrology, which by incorporat-
ing them in its system gave them a doctrinal foundation.
Astrology spread the belief, which was and is common to
all ancient and modern peoples of the East, that each
soul has a predetermined number of years to spend on
earth. The *mathematici* multiplied calculations and
methods in order to be able to predict the instant of death
predetermined by the horoscope. "This is the great work
of astrology, held by its adepts to be its most difficult and
by its enemies to be its most dangerous and blameworthy
operation."[11] But by an internal contradiction this
pseudo-science admitted that the natural end could be
hastened by the intervention of a murderous star ($\dot{\alpha}\nu\alpha\iota$-
$\rho\acute{\epsilon}\tau\eta\varsigma$): Saturn and Mars can in certain positions call
forth sudden death by accident, killing, execution. A frag-
ment attributed to Aristotle asserts that a Syrian mage
predicted to Socrates that he would meet such a fate.[12]
Sometimes the maleficent planets tear a nursing child

---

[9] Sueton., *Calig.*, 59.

[10] Porph., *Epist.*, II, 2, 209: "Nocturnas Lemures: umbras vagantes
hominum ante diem mortuorum et ideo metuendas."

[11] Bouché-Leclercq, *Astrologie grecque*, p. 404.

[12] Diog. Laert., II, 5, §45; *cf.* Lamprid., *Heliog.*, 33, 2: "Praedictum
eidem erat a sacerdotibus Syris biothanatum se futurum."

from its mother's breast before a single revolution of the
sun has been accomplished. All astrological treatises
devote chapters to these "unfed" children (ἄτροφοι) and
also to the *biothanati* whose life has been interrupted by
misfortunes of any kind. Petosiris was even concerned
to discover—Ptolemy declared such preoccupation to be
ridiculous[13]—what the stars reserved until the end of
their life for those who had gone through only a portion
of it. The texts which have been preserved—and often
expurgated—by the Byzantines give no more than a bare
indication of astral influences on the lot of men. In antiquity other more religious and more mystical works
doubtless existed in which the inauspicious action of the
murderous star, still affecting after death the souls torn
from their mortal wrappings, was shown.

Pythagorism, which was closely connected with astrology, took possession of these-ideas and adapted them to
its speculations. According to this philosophy one and
the same harmony presided over all physical phenomena
and was, like music, subject to laws of number. These laws
therefore were at work during pregnancy, and a complicated arithmetic was employed to show by a multiplication of days that a child might be born after seven or
nine months with power to live, but not after eight, for
such was the strange doctrine of the sect. Thus gestation
became a melody in which abortion was a false note.
Nature was said to be like an artist who sometimes
breaks an instrument of which he overstretches the
chords, and sometimes leaves them too slack and can produce no tune. Now, these harmonic laws necessarily determined not only the formation but also the end of man:
"There is a fixed relation of determined numbers which
unites souls to bodies," says a philosopher, "and while it
subsists, the body continues to be animate, but so soon as
it fails, the hidden energy which maintained this union is
dissolved, and this is what we call destiny and the fatal

[13] Ptolem., *Tetrabibl.*, III, 10 (p. 127, ed. 1553).

time of life."[14] When the term fixed by nature is reached, the soul departs without effort from the body in which it can no longer exercise its office. But when the soul is violently ejected from the body and the link connecting them is broken by an external force, it is troubled and is afflicted by an ill which will cause it pain in the Beyond.

These ideas had sunk deep into the popular mind. The distinction between an end in conformity with nature and one unexpectedly provoked by extraneous intervention is often expressed in literature as well as in inscriptions. Thus the epitaph of a young woman of twenty-eight, who was believed to have been the victim of witchcraft, states that "her spirit was torn from her by violence rather than returned to nature,"[15] which had lent it to her; the Manes or the celestial gods will be the avengers of this crime. Still more frequently an opposition is found between an early death and *Fatum*. The hour of death is determined at the moment of birth:

"Nascentes morimur; finisque ab origine pendet."[16]

"At the moment we are born, we die; and our end is fixed from our beginning." He who reaches this term fixed for his life ends "on his day" (*suo die*); otherwise he dies "before his day" (*ante diem*).[17] The vulgar belief was that the intervention of a human or divine will could oppose the fated course of things and abridge the normal duration of existence. Often the expression occurs of a belief that a demon or, what is more remarkable, an evil god has carried off innocent children or young men whose life has thus been shortened.[18] But pagan theology undertook the task of re-establishing the order of nature thus

---

[14] Macrob., *Somn. Scip.*, I, 13, 1, probably after Numenius (*Revue des études grecques*, XXXII, 1921, p. 119 s.).

[15] CIL, VIII, 2756=Bücheler, *Carm. epigr.*, 1604.

[16] Manilius, IV, 16.

[17] *Cf.* Schulze, *Sitzungsb. Akad. Berlin*, 1912, p. 691 ss.

[18] Demon: Kaibel, *Epigr. Gr.*, 566, 4; 569, 3, etc.—Evil god: Dessau, 8498; *cf.* 9093: "Cui (*sic*) dii nefandi parvulo contra votum genitorum vita privaverunt."

disturbed by fortuitous accidents and by individual and unregulated interferences. The breaking of the laws of the universe was only apparent: a soul might by mischance or by a malevolent act be suddenly severed from its body, but, remaining obedient to Fate, it had thereafter to linger on earth until its appointed time was accomplished.

Its lot was supposed to be analogous to that of the unfortunate who had been deprived of burial (ἄταφοι, *insepulti*) of whom we spoke in our first lecture.[19] It circled about the corpse, which it could not abandon, or fluttered here and there near the place of burial or on the spot where the body which it had occupied had been assailed. Excluded from the abode of the shades these wandering souls flitted near the earth or on the surface of the waters, miserable and plaintive. The fear of never being able to penetrate into the kingdom of blessed shades seems to have inspired the following prayer, which occurs in a metrical epitaph of Capri:[20]

"You who dwell in the country of Styx, beneficent demons, receive me too into Hades, me the unfortunate who was not borne away in accordance with the judgment of the Fates, but by a hasty and violent death provoked by unjust anger."

These brutally disincarnated souls became like the swift and harmful spirits with which the air was filled: like them they belonged to the train of Hecate, the goddess of enchantment, and like them were subject to the power of magicians. At Lesbos, Gello, a young virgin carried off before her time, became a phantom which killed children and caused premature deaths.[21] The leaden tablets, which were slipped into tombs in order to injure an enemy, and the magic papyri of Egypt bear a large number of incantations in which these mischievous

[19] See Lecture I, p. 66 ss.

[20] Kaibel, *Epigr. Graeca*, 624.

[21] Rohde, *Psyche*, II⁴, p. 411; *cf.* Perdrizet, *Negotium perambulans*, 1922, p. 19 ss.

demons are invoked. In the same way a series of conjurations, dating from the third century and found in the island of Cyprus, appeal to the spirits of the dead thrown in the common ditch, "who have met their death by violence, or before their time, or who have been deprived of burial."[22] In general the sacrifice of newly born children, and the use of their vital organs and bones, was, and not without reason, a most frequent charge against sorcerers. Formulas preserved on papyrus recommend as powerful means to work a charm "a baby's heart, the blood of a dead maiden, and the carrion of a dog."[23] Witches were believed to steal children in order to use the entrails in their occult operations, a ritualistic murder analogous to that attributed by popular belief, in some countries, to the Jews. Cicero, Horace in an epode, Petronius in his romance,[24] and other authors bear witness to the extent to which this opinion was entertained. The epitaph of a young slave of Livia, wife of Drusus, relates his misfortune. Before he was four years old he was cut off by the cruel hand, the "black hand" of a witch, who practised her noxious art everywhere. "Guard well your children, ye parents," adds the epitaph.[25]

Likewise the murder of adults and the use made of objects which had belonged to executed or murdered persons is frequently mentioned. The wonder-workers believed that by practising with the bodies of this class of the dead, or with objects they had used, they became masters of their wandering souls and made them serve their designs. The nails of a crucified criminal, the blood-

---

[22] Audollent, *Defixionum tabellae*, 1904, p. 40, nr, 22 ss.; see above, Lecture I, p. 68.

[23] Wessely, *Griech. Zauberpap. aus Paris* in *Denkschr. Akad. Wien*, XXXVI, 1888, p. 85, l. 2577 ss., p. 86, l. 2645 ss.

[24] Cic., *In Vatin.*, 6, 14; Horace, *Ep.*, 5; Petronius, 63, 8.

[25] Bücheler, *Carm. epigr.*, 987:

"Eripuit me saga manus crudelis ubique,
Cum manet in terris et nocet arte sua.
Vos vestros natos concustodite, parentes."

Cf. Petronius, *l. c.*, and Lecture II, p. 61, n. 48.

soaked linen of a gladiator, were efficacious amulets.[26] Faith is still kept nowadays in the rope which has hanged a man.[27] The books which circulated under the name of Hostanes the Persian, Nectabis the Egyptian and other illustrious wizards dealt with evocations of ἄωροι and βιαιοθάνατοι.[28]

Thus a logical series of beliefs was pushed to its extreme consequence. At the moment of birth Fate fixed for each man the length of his career; if this were interrupted, the soul had to complete it in suffering, near the earth, and became a demon which lent its aid to diviners and sorcerers. This doctrine, supported by astrology and Oriental magic, imposed itself on many minds. Plato, who had found it among the Pythagoreans, alludes to it, and Posidonius seems to have dealt with it more at length in his treatise "On Divination" (περὶ μαντικῆς),[29] although we cannot tell in how far he supported it. But it encountered the objections of other Greek philosophers. The reproach made to this theory was that it left out of account morality and merited retribution, and brought together, as subject to the same misfortune, criminals condemned to capital punishment and children whose age had kept them from all sin. Feeling and reason at the same time protested against the cruel doctrine which vowed indifferently the innocent and the guilty to long torture. When accident or illness caused the death of a beloved son, could his parents make up their mind to believe that he would suffer undeserved chastisement? A distinction had to be made between categories of persons, and to this task the pagan theologians applied themselves. Let us follow them in their undertaking.

*   *   *   *   *

The ἄωροι are those who die "out of season," that is to say, in the wide sense of the word, those whose existence

26 Alex. Trall., I, 15, pp. 565, 567, Puschman.
27 *Cf.* Pliny, XXVIII, 12, § 49.
28 Tertull., *De anima*, 57.
29 Norden, *Aeneis Buch VI*, p. 41.

ends abnormally, but more particularly those who die young, who die prematurely. They include the ἀνώνυμοι, those who have received no name, who have not, that is, reached the ninth or tenth day of life, the ἄτροφοι, *non nutriti,* or babes who are still being fed at the breast or, according to the astrologers, are not yet a year old, and the ἄγαμοι, the *innupti,* who have died before the age of marriage and have therefore left no posterity to render them funeral rites.

None of these children and adolescents deserved, in the opinion of the sages, any chastisement. The Pythagoreans placed the age of reason, at which man is capable of choosing between good and evil and may be made responsible for his faults, as late as sixteen, that is, the age of puberty. Until that age the "naked" soul, without virtue as without vice, was exempt from all merit and demerit which would later attach to it. We know the unhappy lot to which, according to these philosophers, they were doomed. But other theologians considered that these souls, which had not been weighted by a long contact with matter, should fly more easily to celestial heights. Unsullied by earthly pollution, their purity allowed them to rise without difficulty to a better life in a happier abiding-place.[30]

It is hard to determine to what degree these moral ideas had penetrated the popular mind. The reaction against a superstitious belief often led to pure negation. Those who held that death put an end to all sensibility, were content to affirm that the child they wept had gone down into everlasting night, and that nothing was left of him but dust and ashes. Certain epitaphs hope that, if his Manes still have some feeling, his bones may rest quietly in the tomb. But mother's love was not to be satisfied with this negative assurance or to resign itself to anxious doubting. The people kept an unreasoning fear of the evils which awaited the ἄωροι and of those which might be

---

[30] Sen., *Dial.,* VI, 23, 1; Plut., *Cons. ad uxorem,* 11; *cf.* Dessau, 8481 ss.

expected from them. Some also believed that an ancestral
fault—such as was, according to the Orphic doctrine, the
murder of Zagreus, by the Titans—made all humanity
guilty from birth, and that this hereditary sin had to be
effaced by purifications.[31] Religion offered a remedy for
the ill to which, to speak with Lucretius, it had itself lent
persuasion. The custom of initiating children to the mysteries which was, at least at Eleusis, originally connected
with the family or gentile cult, became a means of pre-
serving them from the fatal lot which threatened them
and of ensuring their happiness in the other life. Thus
pueri and *puellae* are found admitted at the most tender
age among the adepts of the secret cults, both Greek and
Oriental, perhaps even consecrated from birth to the godhead. They are imagined as partaking in the Beyond of
the joys which these cults promised to those whose salvation they ensured. A child who has taken part in a ceremony of Bacchus lives endowed with eternal youth in the
Elysian Fields in the midst of Satyrs.[32] Others continue
the games proper to their years in another life, or if they
have reached the age of first love they still sport with
young Eros. Above all, however, the influence of the astral
cults, added to that of philosophy, brought about an
admission that innocent creatures ascended to the starry
heavens. An epitaph of Thasos[33] speaks of a virgin,
flower-bearer (ἀνθοφόρος) probably of Demeter and Kora,
who was carried off at the age of thirteen by the inexorable Fates, but who, "living among the stars, by the
will of the immortals, has taken her place in the sacred
abode of the blessed." At Amorgos, a child of eight was,
we are assured, led by Hermes to Olympus, shone in the
ether, and would henceforth protect the young wrestlers
who emulated him in the palaestra. Even the precise spot
in which he twinkled was fixed, the horn of the constella-

[31] See below, Lecture VII, p. 178.
[32] Bücheler, *Carm. epigr.*, 1233.
[33] Kaibel, *Epigr. Graeca*, 324.

tion of the Goat—an appropriate place for this little fighter.[34] Curiously, an epitaph of Africa, which repeats Virgil's very expression (p. 129), states, in contradiction to the poet, that a baby, "cut off on the threshold of life," has not gone to the Manes but to the stars of heaven,[35] and a relief of Copenhagen shows the bust of a little girl within a large crescent surrounded by seven stars, thus indicating that she has risen towards the moon, the abode of blessed souls.[36]

Examples of these premature apotheoses might be multiplied. I shall merely show, by a characteristic case, how it was possible for old popular beliefs to be combined with the new astral doctrine. The ancients attributed to the rustic nymphs the strange powers which the Greek peasant today recognises in beings which he still designates as the Nereids.[37] Sometimes these fantastical goddesses possess themselves of the spirit of men and change them into seers or maniacs (νυμφόληπτοι); sometimes their fancy is caught by handsome youths whom they carry off and oblige to live with them. But above all they love pretty children and steal them from their parents, not to harm them but in order that they may take part in their own divine pastimes. Doubtless it was at first to mountain caverns, near limpid springs, in the depths of tufted woods, that they bore him whom they made their little playfellow. Such were the archaic beliefs of the country folk. But the mysteries of Bacchus taught that an innocent child, thus rapt from the earth, mingled in the train of the Naiads in the flowery meadows of the Elysian Fields;[38] and when Paradise was transferred to

[34] Haussoullier, *Revue de philologie*, XXIII, 1909, p. 6; see above, Lecture III, p. 105.

[35] Bücheler, *Carm. epigr.*, 569: "Vitaeque e limine raptus . . . Non tamen ad Manes sed caeli ad sidera pergis." *Cf. ibid.*, 569, 611.

[36] See Lecture III, p. 99.

[37] Rohde, *Psyche*, II[4], p. 374, n. 2; Lawson, *Modern Greek folklore*, 1910 p. 140 ss.; *cf.* Dessau, 8748.

[38] Bücheler, *Carm. epigr.*, 1233; *cf.* Statius, *Silv.*, II, 6, 100.

the sky it was in the "immortal dwelling-place of the ether" that the nymphs, we are told, placed a little girl whose charm had seduced them.[39]

Transported thus to heaven, these loved beings were transformed by the tenderness of their relatives into protectors of the family in which their memory survived, or of the friends who shared regret for them. Whether they were called "heroes" in Greek, or as elsewhere "gods,"[40] they were always conceived as guardian powers who acknowledged by benefits the worship rendered them. Thus in the middle of the second century the *familia* of a proconsul of Asia, C. Julius Quadratus, honoured a child of eight years as a hero, at the prayer of his father and mother;[41] and at Smyrna the parents of a dearly loved child of four, raised to this baby as their tutelary god, a tomb on which an epitaph described in detail all his illnesses.[42]

These sentimental illusions are eternal. Nothing is more frequently seen on tombstones in our own Catholic cemeteries than such invocations as "Dear angel in heaven, pray for us," or even a figure of a winged baby flying away among winged cherubs. This faith is perhaps touching, but its orthodoxy is doubtful. For the doctors of the Church, except Origen, have, I think, never adopted the doctrine of Philo the Jew that human souls can be transformed into angelic spirits. But in the oldest Christian epitaphs the conviction is already expressed that, since children are without sin, they will be transported by angels to the dwelling of the saints and there intercede for their parents. "Thou hast been received, my daughter, among the pious souls, because thy life was pure from all fault, for thy youth ever sought only innocent

[39] Kaibel, *Epigr. Graeca*, 570, 571; *cf.* CIL, VI, 29195=Dessau, 8482: "Ulpius Firmus, anima bona superis reddita, raptus a Nymphis."

[40] *Cf.* Anderson, *Journ. hell. stud.*, XIX, 1899, p. 127, nʳ, 142, and below, note 42.

[41] Cagnat, *Inscr. Gr. ad res Rom. pertin.*, IV, 1377.

[42] Kaibel, *Epigr. Graeca*, 314.

play,"[43] says a metrical epitaph, once under the portico of St. Peter's. And another and older epitaph is as follows, "Eusebius, a child without sin because of his age, admitted to the abode of the saints, rests there in peace."[44] Still others end with the words "Pray for us," "*Pete pro nobis.*"

* * * * *

Thus little by little in antiquity the conviction gained strength and became predominant that, as Menander said with another meaning, whom the gods love die young.[45] As to individuals whose days were cut short by a violent blow, they were not uniformly in the same case. The theorists here distinguished among different categories of the *biothanati.*[46] The classification seems to have originated with the astrologists who claimed to enumerate, in accordance with the position of Mars and Saturn, all the kinds of death reserved for victims of these murderous planets, and to foretell whether these unfortunates were to be drowned, burnt, poisoned, hanged, beheaded, crucified, impaled, crushed to death, thrown to the beasts, or given over to yet more atrocious tortures. But the moralists here also made a point of separating the innocent from the guilty. Only the guilty were to suffer after death and only their souls were to become demons. For, side by side with those who had deserved capital punishment for their crimes, or who administered death to themselves, were others cut off by a fatal accident, perhaps even killed while performing a sacred duty.

[43] Bücheler, *Carm. epigr.*, 1439; *cf.* 1400:

"Vos equidem nati caelestia regna videtis
Quos rapuit parvos praecipitata dies."

[44] Cabrol et Leclercq, *Reliquiae liturgicae vetustissimae*, I, 1912, nr, 2917; *cf.* 2974; 3153.

[45] Menander's verse, " "Ον οἱ θεοὶ φιλοῦσιν ἀποθνήσκει νέος," is indeed translated into Latin in a Roman epitaph (Dessau, 8481).

[46] In Greek, βιοθάνατος is a popular form for βιαιοθάνατος. In Latin *biaeothanatus* is found only in Tertull., *De Anima*, 57, *biothanatus* everywhere else.

Such was the case of soldiers slain in battle. Logic ordered the theologians to place them among the *biothanati,* and so they are, for instance, in Virgil's sixth book of the Aeneid.[47] But death on the field of honour could not be a source of infinite ills for them, and it was generally admitted that, on the contrary, their courage opened for them the gates of heaven.

> "Virtus recludens immeritis mori
> Caelum,"

as Horace says.[48] The Greek theory of the divinity of the heroes here comes to temper the severity of an unreasonable and dangerous doctrine. According to Josephus,[49] Titus, when haranguing his soldiers, promised immortality to such as fell bravely, and condemned the others to destruction. "Who does not know," he asked, "that valiant souls, delivered from the flesh by the sword in battle, will inhabit the purest of ethereal elements, and, fixed in the midst of the stars, will make themselves manifest to their descendants as good genii and benevolent heroes? On the other hand, souls which are extinguished when their body is sick, vanish, even if they are free from all stain and defilement, into subterranean darkness and are buried in deep oblivion." In the military monarchies of the Hellenistic East, as in the Roman Empire, eternal life was certainly promised to those who had perished arms in hand, faithful to their military duty. We know that the same belief was transmitted to Islam: a Mussulman who dies in battle "in the way of Allah" is a martyr (*shahîd*) to whom the joys of Paradise are assured. The Jews, who had been reluctant to admit such ideas before, from the time of the Maccabees onwards associated with warriors those who sacrificed themselves in order to be faithful to their persecuted religion, and to these especially they promised a glorious immortality.

---

[47] *Aen.,* VI, 477 ss.
[48] Horace, *Od.,* III, 2, 21; *cf.* Introd., p. 13; Lecture IV, p. 113.
[49] Joseph., *Bell. Iud.,* VI, 5, § 47.

Faith in this celestial reward was later to cause the Christians, who won the martyr's crown, to face all sufferings.

*   *   *   *   *

The treatment which the gods reserved for another class of *biothanati* was more uncertain. In the Greek cities, as in Rome, moral reproof and posthumous penalties were anciently attached to suicide. The old pontifical law refused ritualistic burial to persons who had hanged themselves; and instead of funeral sacrifices it prescribed for these dead merely the hanging up of small images (*oscilla*) consecrated to their Manes,[50]—probably a magical, "sympathetic" rite, which was intended to purify their wandering souls by air, as other souls were purified by water and fire. The horrible appearance of men who died by strangulation had given rise to the belief that the breath of life had vainly sought to issue from their tightly closed throats.[51] A rich inhabitant of Sarsina in Umbria granted land for a graveyard to his fellow citizens, but excluded from the benefit of his gift those who had hired themselves as gladiators, had died by the rope by their own hand, or had followed an infamous calling.[52] This association shows how loathsome this kind of death was. Funeral colleges founded under the Empire introduced into their rules a clause stipulating that if anybody had for any motive whatsoever put himself to death, he should lose his right to burial.[53] This provision seems to have been inspired less by the fear that fraud would be practised on this society of mutual insurance against supreme abandonment, than by the conviction that funeral honours cannot deflect the curse which weighs on the suicide and renders his company undesirable for other dead.

[50] Servius, *Aen.*, XII, 603.
[51] Pliny, *N. H.*, II, 63, § 156.
[52] Dessau, *Inscr. sel.*, 7846: "Extra auctorateis et quei sibei [la]queo manu attulissent et quei quaestum spurcum professi essent."
[53] *Ibid.*, 7212, II, 5.

But there was against popular opinion and religion, which attached an idea of infamy to self-murder, a philosophical reaction which, among the Stoics, led to an entirely contrary moral judgment. The powerful sect of the Porch caused the doctrine to prevail that suicide was in certain cases commendable. It saw in this end the supreme guarantee of the wise man's freedom, and praised those who by voluntary death had withdrawn from an intolerable life. Cato of Utica, who killed himself lest he should survive liberty, was held to be the wise man's ideal, and as worthy of apotheosis as Hercules. He himself, who is shown to us by the historians as reading and rereading Plato's *Phaedo* before he pierced himself with his sword,[54] certainly hoped for the immortality of heroic souls. Here, as on other points, the Neo-Pythagoreans, and the Neo-Platonists after them, brought the minds of men back to the old religious beliefs. Plotinus, yielding to the opinion which still prevailed in his time, still authorises suicide in certain cases, but we know that his exhortations dissuaded his pupil Porphyry from putting an end to his days, when he was seized with a disgust for life. This latter philosopher afterwards resolutely opposed the Stoic doctrine. Although the soul, said the Pythagoreans and Platonists, is enclosed in the body as in a prison, in order to suffer chastisement, it is forbidden by God to escape therefrom by its own act. If it do so escape, it incurs from the masters of its fate infinitely harder penalties. It must await the hour willed by these masters, and then it can rejoice in the deliverance which it obtains at the term of old age. If it itself break the link which joins it to the body, far from ridding itself of servitude, it remains chained to the corpse, for necessarily it is subject to passion at the moment of death and thus contracts impure desires. The only liberation worthy of the wise man is that of the soul which still dwells in the body but succeeds in freeing itself from all fleshly lean-

[54] Plut., *Cato*, 68.

ings and in thus rising, by the force of reason, from earth
to heaven.[55]

The prohibition of voluntary death anticipating the
hour fixed by Providence for each man, was strengthened
and enforced everywhere by the Christian Church.

With yet more cause did those who had been condemned
to capital punishment seem to deserve posthumous torment and the pains reserved for the impious. These maleficent spirits, transformed to demons, continued to work
harm to the human race. The odium which attached to
the word *biothanati* ended by concentrating itself on
these two classes—those who had committed suicide and
those who had been executed. The horror which both
inspired was marked by the withholding of honourable
burial. Even in pagan times, sacred or civil law in
many places denied funeral honours to children who
died young, and to suicides—in order, says a text,[56] that
those who had not feared death might fear something
after death—and, above all, to criminals, whose corpses
were not deposited in a tomb but were thrown without
any ceremony into a common ditch (πολυάνδριον). In
Rome persons executed in prison were dragged with a
hook through the streets to the Tiber, where they were
flung into the water. There was in the fact that they were
deprived of funeral rites a second reason, besides their
guilt, for their suffering in the Beyond.[57] Families and
friends of the condemned endeavoured therefore to spare
them this fearful penalty, and could obtain from the
magistrates the surrender of their bodies to them. But
the authorities often refused this supreme consolation to
Christians who wished to pay this last duty to their
martyred brothers. By scattering abroad the ashes of
martyrs the pagans hoped to prevent their graves from
becoming the sites of cults.

The denial of a religious funeral was also from the

[55] *Cf. Revue des études grecques*, XXXII, 1921, p. 113 ss.
[56] Sen., *Controv.*, VIII, 4, end.
[57] See above, Lecture I, p. 64 ss.

earliest time onwards ordered by Church discipline and sanctioned by the Councils in the case of suicides, and was similarly extended, in virtue of the law in force, to malefactors. In the Middle Ages the corpses of criminals were still to be seen carried to a shameful charnel-place in Byzantium. For instance, the chronologist Theophanes[58] relates indignantly that in 764 the iconoclastic Emperor Constantine Copronymus caused the arrest of a hermit of Bithynia, who supported the cult of the images. The emperor's guards tied a cord round the monk's foot and dragged him from the praetorium to the cemetery, where, after cutting him to pieces, they flung his remains into the ditch of the *biothanati*. Curiously this word, *biothanati*, was derisively applied to the Christians themselves, either because they adored a crucified Saviour, or in mockery of the martyrs, who believed that through death by execution they earned a glorious immortality. The poet Commodianus returns this insult by applying the term to the pagans, whose way of life condemned them to everlasting flames.[59] The opprobrious word remained in use until the Middle Ages, when it denoted all whose crimes deserved capital punishment, so that the final meaning of *biothanatus* was gallows-bird, gallows-food.[60]

If the meaning of the word *biothanati* was thus restricted in the Latin world, the old ideas which it called forth have had a singular vitality in folk-lore, especially among the Greeks. The Greeks believe even today that such as perish by a sudden and violent death became *vrykolakes*.[61] Their bodies can again be reanimated, can leave the grave, and can travel through space with extreme rapidity as vampires and become so maleficent that mere contact with them causes loss of life. Suicides and victims of unavenged murders are particularly fear-

---

[58] Theophanes, *Chronicon*, p. 437, 3 ss., De Boor.
[59] Commodianus, I, 14, 8.
[60] Du Cange, *Glossarium*, s. v.
[61] Lawson, *Modern Greek folklore*, 1910, p. 408 ss.

ful. It was the custom as late as the eighteenth century
to open the grave of a dead man suspected of being a
vrykolakas, and if his body had escaped corruption, thus
proving his supposed character, it was cut into pieces or
burnt in order to prevent it from doing further harm. So
lively did the belief remain that the *biothanatus* could not
detach himself from his body, and that his existence,
which had been too soon interrupted, was prolonged in
the tomb.

VI

THE JOURNEY TO THE BEYOND

AS soon as belief took shape in an underground kingdom where gathered the shades which were separated from the body and from the grave, the idea
also arose of a perilous journey which the soul must make
in order to win to this distant abode. Such an idea is
common to many peoples of the world. In California, the
Mojave Indians are said to believe that the departed have
to find their way through a complicated maze in search of
the happy hunting grounds, which only the good souls
can reach, while the wicked wander painfully and end-
lessly. We know what minutely detailed rules are contained in the Egyptian Book of the Dead, rules to which
the deceased had to conform in order that they might
travel safely to the Fields of the Blessed. The Orphic
tablets, discovered in tombs in Italy,[1] have preserved
fragments of another guide to the Beyond. For instance,
the tablet of Petelia, which goes back to the second or
perhaps the third century B. C., begins thus: "Thou shalt
find to the left of the house of Hades a well-spring, and
by the side thereof standing a white cypress. To this
well-spring approach not near. But thou shalt find another by the lake of Memory, cold water flowing forth,
and there are Guardians before it. Say 'I am a child of
Earth and of Starry Heaven. But my race is of Heaven
(alone). This ye know yourselves. And so I am parched
with thirst and I perish. Give me quickly the cold water
flowing from the lake of Memory.' And of themselves
they will give thee to drink from the holy well-spring;

[1] See above, Lecture II, p. 74.

and thereafter among the other heroes thou shalt have lordship. . . ."[2]

These instructions, which accompanied the member of the sect to his grave,—he bore them about his neck like an amulet,—were supposed to enable him to keep from straying in his posthumous wanderings and help him to accomplish exactly all the acts necessary for his salvation. They were a sort of liturgy of the other side of the grave which would ensure eternal happiness to the faithful. "Courage (εὐψύχει) ; be valiant (θάρρει) ; no man is immortal on earth," such is the exhortation frequently expressed in epitaphs. It probably reproduces a ritualistic formula intended to sustain the shade which had to blaze its path in the Beyond.

The Etruscans also had *libri Acheruntici*, books of Acheron which were attributed to the sage Tages and which treated of the fate of the dead. These made known, in particular, what were the rites by which souls could be transformed into gods (*di animales*). Their very title betrays a Greek teaching, and there are reasons for believing that the teaching of the Pythagoreans was not without influence on their composition.[3] It is hardly doubtful that they were concerned with the path which the Manes of human beings must follow in order to go down into the infernal regions. The Etruscan *stelae* and cinerary urns often show this journey to Hades: sometimes the dead are placed, like heroes, in a war chariot; sometimes in a cart protected by a canopy and exactly copied from the peasants' carts; and often nothing would indicate that these travellers are but shades, were not the significance of the scene defined by the presence of some deity of the nether world, like Charon. The great sarcophagus of Vulci in the Boston Museum bears a fine representation of this type, where the character of the

[2] Transl. Harrison, *Prolegomena to the study of Greek religion*, 1903, p. 660.

[3] Thulin, *Etruskische Disciplin*, III, 1909, p. 58 ss.

travellers is shown by a winged Fury standing behind their carriage.

Thus the idea that the dead have to tramp a long road descending into the depths of the earth before they reach their last abode, was accepted in Italy as in Greece from a very ancient period. How did men imagine this road? Their conception of it is connected with a whole group of Pythagorean doctrines which go back to a remote age.

The old poetry of Hesiod already speaks of two roads of life, a short and easy road which is that of vice, and the path of virtue, which is at first steep and rugged but becomes less hard as soon as the top of the slope is reached. Everyone knows the use which the sophist Prodicus makes of this ancient comparison in the famous myth of Hercules at the crossroads.[4] In it, two women appear to the youthful hero, and one seeks to draw him to the path of deceitful pleasures while the other succeeds in conducting him to the path of austere labours which leads to true happiness. This same conception, which is transmitted through the whole of antiquity, inspired the Pythagoreans with the symbol of the letter Y, formed of a vertical spike topped by two divergent branches. The spike is the road common to all men until they have reached the age of reason and responsibility. Subsequently they must choose between the right and the left branches. The former, say these moralists, is steep and rough and at first requires strenuous effort, but when those who climb it have gained its summit they obtain a well-deserved rest. The other road is at first level and pleasant, but it leads to harsh rocks and ends in a precipice over which the wretched man who has followed it is hurled. This symbol was popular in antiquity as well as in the Middle Ages, a fact of which a curious proof, additional to those in the texts, has lately been found. This is a relief, accompanied by an inscription, dating from the first century of our era, which has been discovered at

[4] Xenoph., *Memorab.*, II, 1, 21; *cf.* Hesiod, *Op. et dies*, 287 ss.

Philadelphia in Lydia.[5] It decorated, as the epitaph shows, the tomb of a Pythagorean, and it is divided into compartments by mouldings in the form of the letter Y. Below, to the right, a child is seen, in the care of a woman who is designated as Virtue ('Aρετή); above, a plough-man, driving his plough, stands for the hard and per-severing labour of the good man, who, still higher, lies on a couch before a table like the guest at a "funeral banquet" because he has obtained the reward of his toil. On the left side there is also, below, a woman with a child, but she stands for wantonness ('Aσωτεία); above her a figure is indolently lying on a bed; and still further above, the same figure is seen falling into a gulf, head down-wards, in chastisement of his vices.

These naïve scenes decorated, as we have said, a burial place. Many other tombs are not so elaborate, but express the same symbolism by opposing the hard labour of man, represented on the lower part of the stele, to the rest which this same man enjoys on the upper part of the stone, that is, in heaven.[6] The symbol of the Y was early applied to the future life by the Pythagoreans, who trans-ferred the roads representing the courses of the moral and the immoral life to Hades. Their stories of the descent to the nether world depicted the journey of the dead in the same way, and it is still thus described in the sixth book of the Aeneid. The dead first follow a common road; and those whose lot is still undetermined wait in this first abode, just as on earth children are not yet sepa-rate at the uncertain age at which they have not yet made their decision for virtue or for vice. At the crossroads of earthly existence the choice must be made; at the cross-road of the infernal regions (τρίοδος) the judges of souls are seated,[7] and send to the right those who have by their merits made themselves worthy to enter the Elysian Fields, while they drive to the left the wicked who are to

5 Brinkmann, *Rheinisches Museum*, LXVI, 1911, p. 622 ss.
6 See below, Lecture VIII, p. 205.
7 See Lecture II, p. 76.

be hurled into Tartarus. For in both worlds "right" is to the Pythagorean, as to the soothsayers, synonymous with "good," and "left" synonymous with "evil."

The original conception was necessarily transformed and explained symbolically when the abode of virtuous souls was transported to heaven. The stories of the ancients were no longer taken in their literal sense, but an allegorical meaning, allowing them to be brought into harmony with the new beliefs, was given to them. Henceforward one of the two roads leads to the higher regions, the road, namely, of the Blessed (ὁδὸς μακάρων) or of the gods. The other, the path of men, is that which after long windings brings back to earth the impure souls who accomplish the cycle of their migrations and must be reincarnated in new bodies.

A passage of Cicero's *Tusculans*,[8] which is directly inspired by the *Phaedo* of Plato, is instructive as to the transformation which ideas underwent. "There are," it says, "two roads and two courses for souls which issue from the body. The souls which are sullied with human vice and have abandoned themselves to passions . . . follow a crooked path which leads them away from the dwelling of the gods; but for the souls which have kept their innocence and purity and have, while in human bodies, imitated the life of the gods, there is an easy return to the beings from whose abode they descended to the earth." In the same way Virgil, as we have said elsewhere,[9] is apparently faithful to the traditional topography of Hades, but does not regard it as really situated in the underground. There were even attempts to fix precisely the itinerary which souls had to follow in the upper spheres. Seneca pleasantly ridicules these beliefs in his satire on the apotheosis of Claudius, affirming that emperors went to heaven by the Appian Way. The Milky Way, originally regarded as the path of the sun,

---

8 Cic., *Tusc.*, I, 30, 72.
9 See above, Lecture III, p. 82.

remained, according to an opinion which persisted until
the end of antiquity, the road by which gods and heroes
rose to the zenith.[10] It was said to cut the zodiac in the
tropical signs of Cancer and Capricorn, and it was there
that those gates opened by which souls went down from
heaven to earth ·and rose from earth to heaven.[11] The
former of these gates was called the Gate of Men, the
other the Gate of Gods.

We will return later (p. 162) to the theories which assign
different dwellings in the starry spheres to pure spirits
and tell of their passing through the celestial gates. We
would merely note that the allegory of the two roads, of
which one is the road of God and heaven and eternal life
and the other that of Satan, hell and death, is found in
the most ancient Christian literature, and is justifiably
likened by Lactantius[12] to the Pythagorean Y, which is at
the origin of all the later symbolism.

*   *   *   *   *

But when the idea of a journey to the underworld had
been transformed into that of a journey to heaven, how
was the power of the dead to reach the upper spheres
explained? What force or what vehicle raised them
thither? Originally they made use of all the means of
locomotion. They went on foot, in a ship, in a carriage, on
horseback, and even had recourse to aviation.

Among the ancient Egyptians the firmament was conceived as being so close to the mountains of the earth that
it was possible to get up to it with the aid of a ladder.
The early texts of the Pyramids describe the gods help-
ing the king to climb the last rungs of the ladder, when he
ascended to their high dwelling. Such ideas are found
elsewhere, among the Chinese as well as in Europe. We
are told that a priest-king of a people of Thrace joined
tall wooden ladders together in order that he might go to

[10] See above, Lecture III, p. 94.
[11] *Cf. Comptes rendus Acad. Inscr.*, 1920, p. 277.
[12] Lactantius, *Inst.*, VI, 3 s.

Hera to complain of his unruly subjects.[13] Although the
stars had been relegated to an infinite distance in space,
the ladder still survived in Roman paganism as an amulet
and as a symbol. Many people continued to place in tombs
a small bronze ladder, which recalled the naïve beliefs of
distant ages. This means of attaining to the upper world
has been given to the dead man in several graves of the
Rhine border. In the mysteries of Mithras a ladder of
seven steps, made of seven different metals, still symbol-
ised the passage of the soul across the planetary spheres.[14]
Philo, and after him Origen,[15] interpreted Jacob's ladder
as the air through which the disincarnate souls ascended
and descended; and the patriarch's dream in the symbolism of the Middle Ages was still considered as a pledge
of the ladder of salvation leading the elect to heaven. A
naïve miniature of the illustrated manuscripts of St. John
Climacus—one of them is preserved in the Freer collection—shows monks climbing the heavenly ladder of virtues
and welcomed at the top by Christ or by an angel, while
winged demons try to pull them down and make them fall
into the jaws of a dragon below, which represents hell.[16]
On the other hand, even in antiquity the emblem of the
ladder had been adopted by magic,[17] which retained it
throughout the centuries, and to this day little ladders are
sold in Naples as charms against the *jettatura* or evil eye.

In Egypt the souls also travelled to the dwelling of the
gods in the boat of Ra, the solar deity. This idea does not
seem to have passed into the mysteries of Isis in the West
but in the East it was retained by the Manicheans. The
moon and the sun were the ships which plied through the

[13] Polyaen., VII, 22.

[14] See Lecture III, p. 107; *Monum. mystères de Mithra*, I, p. 118 s.;
II, p. 525.

[15] Philo, *De somniis*, I, 22; Origen, *Contra Celsum*, VI, 21.

[16] Charles R. Morey, *East christian paintings in the Freer collection*, New
York, 1914, p. 17 ss.

[17] Ladder among other magical emblems on terra cotta discs found at
Taranto; *cf. Revue archéologique*, V, 1917, p. 102.

heavenly spaces carrying the luminous spirits.[18] For the
Greeks it was to the Islands of the Blest, situated somewhere in the distant ocean, that ships transported the
dead. This crossing of the sea, peopled by monsters of
the deep, was one of the favourite subjects of the decora-
tors of Roman sarcophagi. But under the Empire the
Fortunate Islands, we know,[19] were often explained as
being the moon and the sun, washed by the ether, and it
was therefore to the moon that the bark of salvation had
to bear souls across the stormy waters of matter. The
Styx had become a celestial or aerial river; Charon, with
the help of the winds, caused pious souls to pass not to the
subterranean world but to the heavenly dwelling of
heroes.[20] The bark which should bear the Blessed to the
abode of delight, where they would live together, is often
represented in funeral sculpture,[21] and continued to be in
Christian art, the symbol of a happy passage to the shores
of Paradise. Epitaphs sometimes cause the passer-by to
wish the dead "Εὐπλοῖ," "A happy voyage!"[22]

The Etruscan tombs often show the dead man on horseback on the road of the underworld, and in early Greek
tombs terra cotta shoes and horses have been discovered
which were intended to make easier the long and dangerous journey to the country whence there is no return. But
in order that a rider may win to heaven his horse must be
provided with strong wings. Primitively these wings were
probably intended to indicate only the swiftness of this
mythical steed.[23] But in Roman times they undoubtedly
meant that it could fly up to the sky. The great Paris

[18] See above, Lecture III, p. 93.

[19] *Ibid.*, p. 96.

[20] *Cf. Revue de philologie*, XLIV, 1920, p. 75.

[21] *Cf.* Joseph Keil, *Jahresh. Instituts Wien*, XVII, 1914, pp. 138, 142, n.
13; Bormann, *Bericht des Vereins Carnuntum*, 1908-1911, p. 330, where *Itala
felix* applies not to the ship but to the dead woman.

[22] For instance, Dessau, *Inscr. sel.*, 8031.

[23] *Cf.* my *Études syriennes*, 1917, p. 99, n. 1. So on the beautiful chariot
of Monteleone in the Metropolitan Museum of New York (sixth century
B. C.).

cameo, said to represent the apotheosis of Augustus, shows a prince of his house, Germanicus or perhaps Marcellus, thus borne away by a winged courser.[24] There is a similar representation on a coin which commemorates the apotheosis of an empress, probably Faustina. The same Pegasus, who probably has nothing in common with Bellerophon's steed, appears again on a fragment of a relief recently discovered in England at Corstopitum (Corbridge-on-Tyne).[25] He is carrying off a personage, probably an emperor, who wears the *paludamentum* or military cloak and has his head bound with a radiate crown, on either side of whom are the Dioscuri, the symbols of the two celestial hemispheres. The dead are mounted on Pegasus because he was brought into relation with the Sun, who is the creator and saviour of souls.

For the same reason, because he was the sacred animal of Apollo, the gryphon served this purpose. Thus in the medallion which decorates the stucco vault of a tomb on the Latin Way this winged monster carries on his strong back a veiled figure, covered with a long garment, who can be no other than the shade of the dead man wrapped in the shroud.[26]

Throughout antiquity, however, the departed travelled most frequently in a chariot, which had in the Roman period become the chariot of the Sun-god.[27] The idea that the divine charioteer drives a team across the heavenly field existed in very early times in Babylon and Syria, as well as in Persia and in Greece. "The horses of fire and the chariot of fire" which carried up the prophet Elijah in a whirlwind[28] are very probably the horses and the chariot of the Sun. In the same way when Mithras' mission on earth was fulfilled, he was conveyed in the chariot of Helios to the celestial spheres over the ocean, as we see

---

[24] *Cf.* my *Études syriennes,* p. 91 s.

[25] *Ibid.,* p. 92, fig. 41.

[26] *Ibid.,* p. 94, fig. 42; *cf.* below, p. 165.

[27] *Cf. ibid.,* p. 95 s.

[28] II *Reg.,* 2, 11.

on the reliefs found in his temples, and the happy lot
which the hero had won for himself he granted also to his
followers. The emperors in particular were commonly
reputed to become companions of the Sun-god after death,
as they had been under his protection in life, and to drive
with him up to the summit of the eternal vaults. According to a papyrus recently found in Egypt,[29] Phoebus,
when informing the people of the death of Trajan and
the accession of Hadrian, stated in set terms, ''I have just
risen with Trajan on a car drawn by white horses, and I
come to you, O people, to announce that a new prince,
Hadrian, has made all things subject to him, by his virtue
and by the fortune of his divine father.'' The writers and
the figured monuments show us other deified rulers winning to heaven in a similar way. At the very end of
paganism an oracle, addressing Julian the Apostate, predicted that he would be ''conducted to Olympus in a
flaming chariot shaken by stormy whirlwinds, and would
reach the paternal palace of ethereal light.''[30] It was not
only princes who were privileged to be drawn by the
swift team of the royal star. The chariot appears on
tombs of very humble persons to suggest their lot in after
life.[31]

Yet more rapid was another method of mounting up to
the stars. Among all the peoples of the eastern Mediterranean basin the idea was anciently spread that the
essence or the spirit which animates man escapes from
the body in the shape of a bird, especially a bird of prey,
for in order not to perish this soul must feed on blood,
the principle of life. The gravestones and funeral vases
of Greece give us a large number of representations of
the bird-soul.[32] In the Roman period vestiges of this conception persisted. In Syria an eagle with spread wings

[29] Kornemann, *Klio*, VII, p. 278; *cf. Études syriennes*, p. 98, n. 3.

[30] Eunap., *Hist.*, fr. 26 (F. H. G. IV, 25; *cf. Études syriennes*, p. 104).

[31] See above, Lecture III, p. 102.

[32] Weichert, *Der Seelenvogel in der alten Literatur und Kunst*, Leipzig,
1902; see above, Lecture III, p. 93.

occupies on tombs the place filled elsewhere by the portrait of the dead man.[33] Magic had retained this ancient belief with not a few others, for superstition picks up many ideas that have dropped out with the progress of religion. Sorcerers asserted that they could cause wings to grow from the backs of their dupes, so as to enable them to soar up to heaven. One of the marvels which miracle-mongers most frequently boasted of working was that of ascending into the air. The phenomena of levitation are said to be produced at all periods. When writers tell us that the pure soul "flies away" to the sky on swift wings, the expression, which since Plato[34] has been often repeated, and is still in use nowadays, is no mere metaphor but rather a traditional expression, first taken in its material sense and preserved in language, ultimately acquiring a figurative meaning. A late epigram composed on Plato's burial place[35] says: "Eagle, why art thou perched above this tomb and why dost thou look at the gods' starry dwelling?—I am the image of Plato's soul who has flown away to Olympus. The earth of Attica holds his earth-born body." Lucian in his Icaromenippus ridiculed the claims of the philosophers, showing Menippus attaching wings to his shoulders in order that he might take his flight to the stars and thus learn the secrets of the world.

The original idea of the bird-soul was transformed into that of the soul lifted aloft by a bird. It was in Syria that this change took place.[36] A widely held belief in the Roman period was that the soul was carried away by an eagle, which in Syria was the bird of the sun. The sun being conceived as a winged disk which flew through the

[33] *Études syriennes*, p. 38 ss.
[34] *Phaedr.*, p. 246 C.
[35] *Anth. Pal.*, VII, 62=Diog. Laert., III, 44; cf. *Études syriennes*, p. 88:

Αἰετέ τίπτε βέβηκας ὑπὲρ τάφον; ἢ τίνος, εἰπέ,
ἀστερόεντα θεῶν οἶκον ἀποσκοπέεις;—
Ψυχῆς εἰμὶ Πλάτωνος ἀποπταμένης εἰς Ὄλυμπον
εἰκών· σῶμα δὲ γῇ γηγενὲς Ἀτθὶς ἔχει.

[36] Cf. *Études syriennes*, p. 57 ss.

celestial spaces could easily be connected with an eagle. The king of birds was the servant or the incarnation of the star-king, to whom he bore his precious burden. This is why an eagle, preparing for flight and holding the crown of victory, is a usual motif of sepulchral decoration at Hierapolis and throughout northern Syria. The powerful bird of prey lifted not with his claws, as he did Ganymede, but on his back, mortals who rose to heaven. This soul-bearing eagle passed to Italy with the ceremonial of the apotheosis. At the funeral rites of emperors at Rome there was always fastened to the top of the pyre, on which the corpse was to be consumed, an eagle which was supposed to bear aloft the monarch's soul, and art frequently represents the busts of the Caesars resting on an eagle in the act of taking flight, by way of suggesting their apotheosis. The eagle, which is the bird of the Baals, solar gods, carries to his master those who have been his servants and representatives in the world below. This kind of aviation was not peculiar to monarchs. The eagle often has this meaning in funeral art. I will instance a stele, found in Rome and preserved in the museum of Copenhagen.[37] On this a young man, draped in a toga, is comfortably seated on an eagle, which is rising to the sky; to his right a winged child, bearing a torch, seems to point out the way to him. It is Phosphorus, the morning star, whom Roman art often represented in this form, before the chariot of the Sun. An altar recalls the cult of which the dead man will henceforth be the object on earth, and a wreath on the pediment stands for the victory which he has won over death.

All these supposed methods of reaching heaven are most primitive: they start from the supposition that a *load* has to be lifted up; they hardly imply a separation of body and soul; and they are antecedent to the distinctions which philosophers established between different parts of man's being. They are religious survivals of very

[37] *Études syriennes*, 1917, p. 87, fig. 39.

ancient conceptions which only vulgar minds still interpreted literally. These mechanical means of raising oneself to the starry vault carry us back to an extremely low stage of beliefs. Hence theologians no longer accepted them save as symbols. Other doctrines of a more advanced character were developed and these constituted the true teaching of the great Oriental mysteries, just as they had secured the adhesion of thinking men. They connected the ascent of the soul after death with physical and ethical theories and thus caused sidereal immortality to enter into the order of the universe.[38]

The first of these theories was that of *solar attraction*. We have already described the doctrine, certainly of eastern origin, that the sun by a series of emissions and absorptions projected souls onto the earth and drew them back to itself.[39] This unceasing action of the resplendent luminary of day was exercised through the force of its rays,[40] and very old Greek ideas here mingled with the "Chaldean" theory. The Pythagoreans already believed that the glittering particles of dust which danced ceaselessly in a sunbeam (ξύσματα) were souls descending from the ether borne on the wings of light. The air, they said, was "full of souls," we might say "of germs" or "microbes."[41] They added that this sunbeam, passing through the air and through water down to the depths of the sea, gave life to all things below.[42] This idea persisted under the Roman Empire in the theology of the mysteries. Souls descended upon the earth and reascended after death towards the sky, thanks to the slanting rays of the sun which served as the means of transport. The sun is the ἀναγωγεύς, "he who brings up from below." On Mithraic reliefs one of the seven rays which surround the head of Sol Invictus (θεὸς ἑπτάκτις) is seen

[38] See Introd., p. 28.
[39] See Lecture III, p. 100.
[40] *Études syriennes*, p. 106 s.; *cf*. Lecture III, p. 101.
[41] See Lecture I, p. 59.
[42] Diog. Laert., VIII, 1, 27.

disproportionately prolonged towards the dying Bull, in order to awake the new life that is to spring from the death of the cosmogonic animal. "The Sun," says the Emperor Julian, "by the invisible, immaterial, divine and pure essence which dwells in its rays, attracts and raises the blessed souls."[43]

In this theory it is to the power of the Sun, the great cosmic divinity, that the ascension of the soul is due. According to another doctrine the cause of this ascension is the physical nature of the soul.

This latter doctrine is set forth with great precision by Cicero in the Tusculan Disputations, and by Sextus Empiricus, doubtless after Posidonius.[44] The soul is a fiery breath, that is to say, its substance is the lightest of the four elements which compose our universe. It necessarily therefore has a tendency to rise, for it is warmer and more subtle than the gross and dense air which encircles the earth. It will the more easily cleave this heavy atmosphere since nothing moves more rapidly than a spirit. It must therefore in its continuous ascent pass through that zone of sky where gather the clouds and the rain and where blow the winds,[45] and which by reason of exhalations from the earth is moist and misty. When finally it reaches the spaces filled by an air which is rarefied and warmed by the sun, it finds elements similar to its own substance and, ceasing to ascend, is maintained in equilibrium.[46] Henceforth it dwells in these regions which are its natural home, continually vivified by the same principles as those that feed the everlasting fires of the stars.

We shall presently see how the Platonists modified this Stoic doctrine, and substituted that of the "vehicle" (ὄχημα) of souls.

These theories made it easier than the first one had

---

[43] Jul., *Or.*, V, p. 172 C.

[44] Cic., *Tusc.*, I, 42 ss.; Sextus Empir., *Adv. Math.*, IX, 71, 4; *cf.* above, Introd., p. 29.

[45] Winds and souls, see below, Lecture VII, p. 185.

[46] See below, Lecture VII, p. 186; *cf.* Lecture II, p. 81.

done to establish a firm connection between ethical beliefs concerning future destiny and physical theories
about the constitution of the universe and the nature of
man. The soul is never conceived by these theologians as
purely spiritual or immaterial, but when it abandons
itself to the passions it becomes gross; its substance
grows more corporeal; and then it is too heavy to rise to
the stars and gain the spheres of light.[47] Its mere density
will compel it to float in our mephitic atmosphere until
it has been purified and consequently lightened. Thus the
door is opened to all doctrines concerning punishment
beyond the grave. We shall show in another lecture[48] how
the soul was to be purified by passing through the elements which moved in sublunary space—air, water and
fire.

But, side by side with physical ideas, mythological beliefs always retained their sway. According to the common creed, the air was peopled with troops of perverse
and subtle demons. They were, it was thought, the guilty
souls whose faults condemned them to wander perpetually near the surface of the earth. They took pleasure in
inflicting a thousand tortures on their fellow souls, when
these, by their impiety, were left defenceless against
them. But succouring powers protected the good against
these perverse spirits. Thus the atmosphere became the
scene of an unceasing struggle between demons of every
kind, a struggle in which the salvation of the soul was at
stake.

The dangers to which the soul was exposed did not
always end when, after having crossed the most dangerous zone of the air, it reached the moon.[49] Those who believed that souls must pass through the planetary spheres
conceived these as pierced by a gate guarded by a
commander (ἄρχων) or, as they were also called, by toll

[47] See Introd., p. 29; cf. Lecture VII, p. 185.
[48] See below, Lecture VII, p. 185.
[49] See above, Lecture III, p. 93, and p. 96 s.

gatherers (τελώνια). The mystics claimed to supply their initiates with the passwords which caused the incorruptible keepers to yield. They taught prayers or incantations which rendered hostile powers propitious; by "seals" and unctions they made their followers immune against the blows of such enemies. These instructions, which were previously given to the dead in order to facilitate their descent to the nether world (p. 148), now served to make the ascent to heaven easy. In this matter the magicians emulated the priests, even claiming to show to their clients the way leading to heaven during life. The papyrus of Paris, wrongly called the "Mithraic Liturgy,"[50] affords the most characteristic example of this superstitious literature.

But, above all, the secret cults claimed to supply the soul with a guide to lead it during its risky journey through the whirlwinds of air, water and fire and the moving spheres of heaven. Plato in the *Phaedo* had already spoken of this demon leader (ἡγεμών) of the dead,[51] and the same word is applied to the "psychopompos," whether demon, angel or god, not only by Neo-Platonist philosophers but also in epitaphs. Thus the funeral inscription of a sailor, who died at Marseilles,[52] says: "Among the dead there are two companies; one moves upon the earth, the other in the ether among the choruses of stars. I belong to the latter, for I have obtained a god for my guide." This divine escort of souls frequently retains the name of Hermes in conformity with the old mythology, for Hermes is the Psychopompos who leads the shades to their subterranean abode and moreover summons them and brings them back, in another migration, to the earth. An epigram belonging to the first century of our era apostrophises the deceased with these words: "Hermes of the winged feet, taking thee by the hand, has conducted thee to Olympus and made thee to

---

[50] Dieterich, *Eine Mithrasliturgie* 2, 1910.
[51] Plato, *Phaedo,* p. 107 D, 108 B.
[52] Kaibel, *Epigr. Graeca,* 650=*Inscr. Sic. Ital.,* 2461.

shine among the stars.''[53] But often the rôle of escort
devolved on the Sun himself. We have seen (p. 157) that
at the end of paganism the star-king is figured as carrying mortals in his flying chariot; and the emperor Julian,
at the end of his satire on the Caesars, represents himself
as addressed by Hermes, who states that in causing him to
know Mithras he rendered propitious to him this leader-
god (ἡγεμόνα θεόν), who will enable him to leave the
earth with the hope of a better lot.

In these beliefs we see persisting to the end of paganism the old conception that heroes could be carried off to
heaven, body and soul.[54] It was never entirely given up
by popular faith, and appears notably in ideas as to the
apotheosis of the emperors, although learned theology
rose in arms against it and affirmed that nothing terrestrial could be admitted into the ethereal spheres. Antinous and Apollonius of Tyana are thus said to have
been borne away and to have continued without interrup-
tion the life they had begun on earth.[55]

*   *   *   *   *

We are thus brought to ask ourselves how, at the very
time when the conception of the journey of the dead was
being transformed, the idea entertained as to the physical
character of the dead also underwent a change. Let us,
in conclusion, seek briefly to trace the course of this
evolution.

Originally, as we said at the beginning of these lectures, two beliefs as to life beyond the grave existed
together. On the one hand, the illusion was kept that the
corpse which lay in the grave continued in some obscure
way to live, feel and nourish itself there. Side by side with
this simple faith the idea was maintained that the soul
is a breath, emitted by the dying man, which floats in
the atmosphere and which reproduces, when it makes

[53] Haussoullier, *Revue de philologie*, XXIII, 1909, p. 6; *cf.* Lecture III,
p. 105.

[54] See above, Lecture IV, p. 112.

[55] *Cf.* Rohde, *Psyche*, II⁴, p. 376 s.

itself visible in dreams and apparitions or in remembrance, the outward appearance of the person from whom it issued.[56]

These two conceptions of life beyond the grave are combined in the nature with which the inhabitants of the infernal regions are credited, and give these fantastic beings a character full of contradictions. Cicero justly remarks that acts are attributed to them which would be conceivable only if they had bodies. Thus they are supposed to speak, although they have neither tongue, palate, throats nor lungs.[57] The common belief was indeed that the shades fed, even in their deep abode, on the offerings made on their burial places; and the pains which might be inflicted on them presupposed that they had retained the sensibility and needs of men; while the pleasures accorded to them in the Elysian Fields were in part very material—to participate in a banquet was an essential part of them.[58]

Hence, when the dead showed themselves, they were sometimes given the appearance not of the living being but of the corpse: it was the body, as it was when buried, which issued from the entrails of the earth. Ennius, when he showed Homer appearing to him in a dream, said that the shades were "of prodigious paleness,"[59] and the idea is often expressed that ghosts are bloodless in colour. Not only are their faces wan: their mouths are mute; they are the *taciti,* the silent Manes. Much more, it is sometimes in the form of skeletons that they return to terrify men. The most usual way of figuring the soul in funeral sculpture is to show a person completely wrapped, save for his face, in a long garment, the shroud in which his body was buried.[60]

But on the other hand, side by side with this more or

---

56 See above, Lecture I, p. 45 ss., 59 ss.

57 *Cf.* Cic., *Tusc.,* I, 16, 37.

58 See below, Lecture VIII, p. 199 ss.

59 Lucretius, I, 124: "Simulacra modis pallentia miris."

60 See, for instance, above, p. 156.

less unconscious belief as to a survival of the body, the
soul continued to be regarded as a light breath. The
beings who peopled the infernal regions were imagined
as almost immaterial forms. They were called "shades"
(σκιαί, umbrae) or "images" (εἴδωλα, simulacra). The
former term implies, besides the idea of a subtle essence,
the notion that the inhabitants of the dusky spaces underground were black, and this is in fact the colour often
given to them. It is also the colour of the victims offered
them and of the mourning garments worn in their honour.
These sombre phantoms, which passed unnoticed in the
darkness of night, returned after the sunset to haunt the
houses of men, and this is why the *Inferi* or beings of
the nether world are above all appeased by nocturnal
sacrifices.

The words εἴδωλον, *simulacrum, imago,* especially express the complete resemblance of the dead to the living.
Are not the beings who return to talk with us in dreams
exactly like the persons we have known? This tenuous
image was compared to the reflection seen on limpid
waters or on the polished surface of metal.[61] Both alike
reproduced the features and colour and imitated the
movements of those whom they faithfully expressed. This
is why magicians often made use of mirrors in order to
evoke the spirits of the departed.[62] As to the nature of
these *simulacra,* the ancients agree in declaring them to
be material, for how otherwise could they convey sensual
impressions? But their substance is of an extreme subtlety. They are forms which are corporeal but empty,
flimsy, impalpable, often of such rarity that they remain
invisible. They are compared to the wind, for the wind
is the air in motion, to a vapour, to a smoke which escapes
so soon as its restraint is attempted.

This shade, formed of a light fluid, has a form which is
necessarily malleable and yielding. The fact is thus ex-

[61] *Cf.* Proclus, *In Rempubl.,* I, p. 290, 10 ss., Kroll.
[62] On this *katoptromanteia, cf. Revue archéologique,* V, 1917, p. 105 ss.;
Ganschinietz in *Realencycl.,* s. v.

plained that souls can take on various appearances and
sometimes let themselves be seen as terrible monsters,
especially if they are the souls of criminals who have
become maleficent spirits.[63] Heroes, on the contrary,
whose virtue has enabled them to be borne to heaven,
appear to be of more than natural stature when they
descend from the ether; they are surrounded by a radiant
nimbus, and their resplendent beauty strikes with admiration those who perceive them.

But here the ancients were faced with the question as
to whether that part of the human composition which won
to heaven was the same as that which descended to the
infernal regions.

As to this puzzling question there arose in the Alexandrian period a theory unknown to ancient Greece,—we
have already touched on this point[64]—the theory that man
is formed not of two elements but of three, namely, the soul
(ψυχή, *anima*), the shade (σκιά, εἴδωλον, *umbra, simulacrum*) and the body (σῶμα, *corpus*). This doctrine
claimed to be justified by a passage in Homer, in fact an
interpolation, as to the apotheosis of Hercules, but it was
manifestly borrowed from Egyptian religion by the
Pythagoreans of Alexandria. For Egyptian religion is
"polypsychic" and distinguishes different kinds of souls.
So the *ka* or "Double" has been explained as a living and
coloured projection of the individual whom it reproduced
feature by feature, which inhabited the tomb, but could
leave it and return to it as freely as a man to his
house. The *baï*, on the other hand, is thought to be a more
refined matter which enclosed a portion of the celestial
fire and which departed to another world. Certain Alexandrian Pythagoreans therefore admitted that when the
soul was not entirely purified, it remained joined to its
idolon in the infernal regions, which were for them situated in the atmosphere, but they held that when it had

---

[63] See above, Lecture V, p. 130.
[64] See above, Lecture II, p. 79.

entirely freed itself from matter it rose towards the
ether, and left only the *idolon* in the neighbourhood of the
earth.[65]

This theory was to be variously transformed, but it is
at the foundation of all the subsequent development of
the doctrines as to the return of the soul to heaven. The
triple division most usually adopted is not the one I have
just cited but the division into reason ($\nu o\hat{v}s$ or $\pi\nu\epsilon\hat{v}\mu\alpha$),
soul ($\psi v\chi\acute{\eta}$) and body. What becomes in this case of the
image ($\epsilon\check{\iota}\delta\omega\lambda o\nu$)? The theologians assimilated it to the ir-
rational soul or $\psi v\chi\acute{\eta}$, as opposed to the higher understanding. This image thus became the seat not only of vegeta-
tive and unconscious life—a theory which would be in
conformity with the Homeric sense of the word—but also
of sensitive and emotional life. This soul or shade at first
remained united to the *nous*, which it surrounded with its
vaporous envelope. Even after it had left the earthly
body, reason was still imprisoned in an aerial body: the
two dwelt in the infernal regions, that is, in sublunary
space, until they had been purified by the elements. They
then, as we have seen elsewhere,[66] left the atmospheric
Hades in order to be admitted into the Elysian Fields,
that is to say, into the moon. There the thin veils in which
reason was still wrapped were dissolved. Reason, a sublime essence, rose again towards the sun and the higher
spheres.

So the shades of the old mythology had become a garment of which reason rid itself, when it left this lower
world to attain to its celestial home. But the theologians
disputed at length on the origin of this psychic integument. When it was admitted that the passions and emo-
tions were due to the action of the planets, the $\epsilon\check{\iota}\delta\omega\lambda o\nu$,
being conceived, as we have said, to be the seat of sensi-
tive life, had necessarily to be formed in the seven
spheres, through which the soul passed as it descended

[65] *Cf. Revue de philologie*, XLIV, 1920, p. 237 ss.
[66] See Lecture III, p. 103.

to earth, and to be decomposed when it passed through them again in its ascension.[67] This is the doctrine supported by the Neo-Platonists. They merely apply a new name to this cloak of reason, that of vehicle (ὄχημα), which is at first synonymous with εἴδωλον as this word was last accepted. Plato in his myths had several times spoken of the chariot (ὄχημα) in which souls ascended, especially in the famous passage of the Phaedrus, where he depicted them as trying to follow the course of the gods towards the summit of heaven,[68] and above all in the Timaeus, where he says that God, having made men equal in number to the stars, caused them to mount on these stars as on a chariot.[69] This vehicle was, according to the philosopher's late interpreters, an ethereal envelope, analogous to the "astral body" of modern theosophists, which grew thicker and thicker by the accession of new elements, as the soul was gradually lowered to the earth;[70] and it was by the composition of these elements that the temperament of the newly born child was determined. This luminous body was attracted after death by stars of the same nature as those whence it derived its origin, and in particular by the sun, and it thus acquired a force of ascension which once again bore divine reason to the highest point of the heavens. We will not lay stress on the speculation of the last masters of the school, such as Jamblichus or Proclus, who imagined, on the subject of this subtle matter, yet more subtle distinctions and transformed the former conception of the "vehicle." It is enough that we have shown how the old belief in the shades who peopled Hades was modified, when it came to be thought that souls travelled in the air and among the constellations, until at last the Platonist theory of the psychic vehicle was reached.

[67] Cf. Lecture III, p. 107.
[68] Plato, Phaedr., 247 B; cf. Phaedo, p. 113 D.
[69] Timaeus, p. 41 D E.
[70] See above, Lecture III, p. 106 s., and Introd., p. 41; cf. p. 24.

VII

THE SUFFERINGS OF HELL AND METEMPSYCHOSIS

HOW did belief in the sufferings of hell develop? of what elements was it formed? through what vicissitudes has it passed?—these are questions which it is difficult to answer precisely, for the reason that the pains reserved for the impious in the Beyond were in the Greco-Latin world taught especially by mystic sects, who placed them in contrast to the bliss granted to the initiate. It is possible, however, to note the genesis and general evolution of the opinions on this point which reigned in the Roman Empire.

Already in the Odyssey three who are surpassingly guilty detach themselves from the grey crowd of the shades who lead an uncertain life in Hades—Tityus, Tantalus and Sisyphus.[1] All three committed grave assaults on the gods, who in revenge condemned them to eternal torture: the gigantic body of Tityus is unceasingly gnawed by vultures; Tantalus is plunged in a pond the water of which flees from his eager lips, while above him is a tree of which the fruit escapes from his hand as he wishes to seize it; Sisyphus unendingly rolls to the top of a hill a rock which always tumbles back down the slope. These souls, in order that their suffering may be more cruelly felt, have in Hades a vitality beyond that of the common run of the dead, who are pale, flimsy, half animate phantoms.[2]

To this Homeric triad of sufferers especially chastised

[1] *Odyssey*, XI, 576 s.
[2] *Cf*. Rohde, *Psyche*, I⁴, p. 61 ss.

by the divinity, further unhappy souls, whom an inexpiable crime had vowed to everlasting pains, were afterwards added: Ixion turning on the wheel to which he was
fixed, Theseus and Pirithous enchained, the Danaïdes
carrying water in a leaking vessel, and others. Thus was
formed a group of legendary personalities whose crimes
and punishments came to be the traditional themes of
every description and representation of Tartarus in
poetry and art until the downfall of paganism.

But these convicted souls were no longer conceived, as
they were by Homer, to be exceptional offenders on whom
the gods avenged a personal insult. They had come to be
the prototypes of men who, for like faults, would be similarly chastised, the terrible examples of the lot which
divine wrath reserved for all who provoked it. They were
explained as the incarnations of the different passions
and vices, the representatives of the various classes of
sinners on each of which a determined punishment was
inflicted.

The first authors of this new conception seem to have
been the Orphic and Pythagorean theologians. Homer
names only one class of criminals whom the Erinyes torture beneath the ground, the perjurers. But here again
the motive of the punishment is a direct provocation of
the gods; by the formula of execration which ended their
oath, the perjurers had surrendered themselves to divine
vengeance, if they broke their faith; and this is why a
place apart among the sufferers of the underworld was
always kept for them.

The Orphics, who were the first to separate in the underworld the region of Tartarus from the Elysian Fields,
were also innovators as regarded the character of these
contrasting dwelling-places. Notably, there was among
their books a Descent into Hades (Κατάβασις εἰς ῞Αιδου),
which described its joys and pains. If the blessed were
admitted to the flowery meadows where they enjoyed the
delight of a perpetual feast, the profane, those who had
not been purified by the rites of the sect, were plunged in

darkness and mire, which was either intended to recall the moral uncleanness of all who had not taken part in the cathartic ceremonies, or else implied that these shades were figured like the penitents who, seated in the mud of the road, proclaimed their sins to passers-by.[3]

Orphism conceived the suffering undergone beyond the tomb as an expiation. The soul which had not been able on earth to keep itself from the pollution of matter and to escape from the passions, thus found again the qualities which it had lost. After a fixed term, it returned to another life wherein it had another chance to render itself worthy of the lot of the Blessed—we shall speak presently of this transmigration. Moreover, the intercession of the living in favour of the dead, the sacrifices offered up on their behalf, could, according to the Orphics, deliver them from their pains.

But the Orphics taught also that side by side with those who thus purified themselves in infernal regions before returning to earth, there were others, more guilty, who were vowed to eternal punishment. The old Homeric belief was thus taken up and developed. The evil souls, whose ways nothing could mend, were immured for ever in the underground prison, where they became the companions of the great criminals whom mythology plunged in Tartarus. This capital distinction between the two classes of the inhabitants of hell, those condemned for a time and those condemned in perpetuity, was transmitted down to Virgil and appears distinctly in the Aeneid.

Infernal justice is a court of appeal from earthly justice. Like the City,[4] Hades has its tribunal, but the judges who sit there are infallible; it has its laws which are unremittingly applied to whoever has broken those of his country; it has its executioners, responsible for carrying out its sentences—the Furies, and later the demons. Similarly, the pains of Hades are always conceived as an

[3] Cf. Plut., De superst., 7, p. 168 D.
[4] Cf. above, Lecture II, p. 75.

imitation of those which were every day inflicted on criminals. The guilty were bound in unbreakable chains, as in
the prisons; the Erinyes struck them with their whips, as
they were flogged at the order of the magistrates; fierce
monsters bit them, as their bodies were thrown to the
beasts or devoured by them in an infamous charnel-place.
The old custom of retaliation continued to be followed in
the other world, where the dead were treated as in life
they had treated their victims.[5] Elsewhere we can recog-
nise an imitation of the torments inflicted on the accused,
who were subjected to torture to make them confess their
fault.

Penal law enacted a determined punishment for every
kind of offence; the law which ruled in Hades had similarly to inflict particular pains for each kind of fault.
This logical deduction led to a new development of penalties beyond the grave. As gradually the moralists and
criminalists detailed and classified the breaches of divine
and human law, so the authors of apocalypses multiplied
the categories of those who suffered in the nether world.
They imagined the most fearful tortures, in order to
frighten sinners and drive them to seek in some religious
purification a means of escape from so terrible a lot. In
a myth which Plutarch has introduced into his book on
the belated vengeance of the gods,[6] he shows us hypo-
crites, who have hidden their wretchedness under the
appearance of virtue, obliged to reverse their entrails so
that the inner side of them may be seen, haters who
devour each other, and misers plunged into and plucked
out from lakes of burning gold, icy lead and jagged iron.

The text which describes these sufferings of the other
world in greatest detail is the fragment of the apocryphal
apocalypse of Peter, which was found in Egypt some
thirty years ago and dates at least from the second century of our era. The vision of hell here opposed to that of
heaven is like a first sketch for the tragic picture of the

---

[5] *Cf.* Dieterich, *Nekyia*, p. 206 ss.
[6] Plut., *De sera num. vind.*, p. 567 B.

dwelling of the damned which Dante was to draw in his Inferno. The fragment enumerates a long series of criminals who are punished by black-robed angels and receive the treatment appropriate to the nature of their faults. Blasphemers are hanged by the tongue; the mouths of false witnesses are filled with fire; the rich who have been merciless to the poor roll, clothed in rags, on sharp and burning pebbles. Other tortures are like the sports of macabre fancy: thus adulterers are hanged by the feet, their heads plunged in burning mud; murderers are flung into a cave filled with serpents that bite them, the shades of their victims watching their anguish.

A learned philologist[7] has undertaken to prove that this repulsive picture of the dwelling of the damned had its origin in the Orphic books. If, however, he refers to ancient, genuine Orphism, he is certainly mistaken. The light fantasy of the ancient Greeks never laid heavy stress on the horrors of Tartarus; their luminous genius took no pleasure in describing these dark atrocities.[8] There is no evidence that they ever formulated, point by point, a penal code which applied in the kingdom of Pluto. The Romans, whose legal mind might have led them to do so, were kept from such aberrations by their lack of imagination. Their infernal mythology remained rudimentary: even Virgil, who is the interpreter of the Hellenic tradition, never alluded except in passing to the infinitely diverse forms of crimes and their punishments.[9] The Etruscans peopled the infernal regions with awful monsters: they gave Charon and the Erinyes a wild semblance which recalls the devils of the Middle Ages, but we never find them drawing up an inventory of the breaches of the moral law in order that a punishment might be applied to each of these.

Everything points to the conclusion that this infernal

[7] Dieterich, *Nekyia*, 1893 (2d ed. 1913).

[8] Even the devout Plutarch rejects them as superstitious imaginations; cf. *De superst.*, 167 A.

[9] *Aen.*, VI, 625-628.

theology developed in the East. The Egyptians described at length in the "Book of the Dead" the pains of those who despised the precepts of Osiris, and illustrated these sufferings with pictures. The only pagan writing in which we find a classification of sinners and of their torments, analogous to that contained in the revelation of the apocryphal gospel of Peter, is the Mazdean "Book of Arta Viraf," which, although of late date, has antecedents which certainly go back very far. The Persian religion, which more than any other brings the Spirit of Evil and his hordes of demons into relief, was certainly not unconnected with the development of infernal eschatology, even in the West, as is indicated by the fact that these demons succeeded the Furies as executors of the divine sentences. It was under the influence of these exotic religions that the descriptions were propagated of refined tortures, terrifying to the adepts of the conventicles in which they were revealed. The mysteries which spread under the Roman Empire accentuated the contrast between the delights of heaven and the sufferings of hell. These esoteric sects gave birth to the literature which was to be perpetuated through the Middle Ages, and inspire numbers of visionaries, poets and artists. Certain authors of treatises on demonology in antiquity must have revelled in inventing unheard-of atrocities, as later the hagiographers took pleasure in describing the inconceivable torments inflicted on martyrs.

Among all the forms of punishment that by fire predominates. The idea that the Erinyes burnt the damned with their torches is ancient, and the Pyriphlegethon is an igneous river surrounding Tartarus. Certain authors went beyond this. Lucian in his "True Histories" describes the island of the impious as an immense brazier whence rise sulphurous and pitchy flames. Thus was born into the world in the Greco-Roman period a doctrine which was to survive its fall and last to modern times. The ancients certainly connected this infernal fire with the treatment inflicted on those condemned to be burnt alive;

but this exceptional punishment could not inspire an eschatological conception which included all the dead. The opinion has been advanced that the choice of fire was due to the belief that this element purifies.[10] Fire would have been at first the means of destroying, in the Beyond as in this world, the uncleanliness of souls, before it became the instrument of their eternal torture. But a scientific theory seems here to have influenced religious faith. The physicians admitted the existence of an incandescent mass in the interior of the earth, which produced volcanic eruptions and hot springs. As Tartarus was situated in the uttermost depths of the underworld, it was conceived as a vast brazier in which the sulphur and bitumen vomited by the volcanoes were boiling for the punishment of sinners.[11]

But this adaptation of the pains of Tartarus to contemporary physics could not save them from philosophical criticism. While the pagan priests, to the terror of credulous minds, imagined more and more inhuman punishments for the guilty souls, the reaction of reason against these cruel inventions necessarily gathered strength. We have seen elsewhere how the polemics of philosophers forcibly attacked these life-poisoning beliefs and succeeded in a great measure in destroying them.[12] Even those who did not deny the future life rejected these fables of hell. There was an attempt to save the principle of posthumous retribution by replacing the doctrine of chastisement in Hades by that of the metempsychosis. We now will try, while considering this theory of transmigration in its various aspects, to show how such substitution was effected.

*   *   *   *   *

[10] Dieterich, *op. cit.*, p. 197 ss.

[11] Punishment by fire is mentioned for the first time in Philodemos, Περὶ θεῶν, XIX, 16 ss. Philodemos being a Syrian, it is not unlikely that this tenet is of Oriental origin. *Cf.* Diels, *Abhandl. Akad. Berlin*, 1916, p. 80, n. 3.

[12] See above, Introd., pp. 8, 17 s., and Lecture II, p. 83.

The mind of savages does not, like our science, distinguish between three kingdoms of nature. It supposes the same energy to animate all the beings who surround us, all of whom are taken to be like ourselves. The primitives often attribute human or even divine intelligence to beasts; and the belief is found throughout the two hemispheres that the spirits of the dead can incarnate themselves in animals and even lodge in plants. Men refrain from the slaughter or gathering of certain species, from eating their flesh or fruit, for fear of hurting a chief or relative who has gone to inhabit them. This animistic basis is common to a number of different peoples and is at the foundation of the system of metempsychosis.

But that which makes the grandeur of this theory, which won countless adepts throughout the centuries and the world, is that it transformed this naïve idea, which had no moral bearing, into a doctrine of retribution and liberation. To come back to the earth, to imprison itself in a body which soiled and tortured it, became a punishment inflicted on the guilty soul. The soul could not attain to supreme felicity until it had purified itself by long suffering and had gradually, through a cycle of rebirths, freed itself from carnal passions.

It is infinitely probable that this doctrine of reincarnation in the bodies of animals was in Greece a foreign importation. Herodotus thought that it came from Egypt,[13] but it does not seem to have existed in that country in ancient times in the form of a regular succession of transmigrations. On the other hand, Greek metempsychosis shows a resemblance, striking even in details, to one of the fundamental conceptions of the religious thought of India, that of *samsâra,* which was accepted as a dogma there long before the birth of Buddhism. The most probable opinion is that this idea made its way across the Persian Empire and thus reached the Orphics and Pythagoreans. It is, however, not unlikely that, like

13 Herodotus, II, 123.

Babylonian astrology, Hindu eschatology was propagated
as far as Egypt at a comparatively recent date, that is,
about the sixth century B. C., and that the information
given by the father of history may be at least partly
correct, Egypt having served as an intermediary between
India and Greece.

We have not, however, to discuss here this problem of
the origins of metempsychosis, nor to follow the development of the doctrine in ancient Greek philosophy. In the
period with which we are concerned, it had already long
been traditional in the Pythagorean and Platonic schools,
it was not only a philosophical theory but also a tenet
admitted by several religions. We can leave unanswered
the questions of whether, as the ancients affirm, the
Druids believed in it, being in this particular disciples of
Pythagoras, and of whether the Etruscans were persuaded to it by the teaching of the philosopher of Croton.
It is, however, certain that transmigration was in the
East an article of widely held belief. We find it accepted
by the mysteries of Mithras and by Manicheism, and it
survives to our own day in Syria among the sects of the
Druses,[14] the Yezidis and the Nosaïris.[15]

What was its form in the Roman period, and how was it
brought into harmony with traditional or acquired ideas
as to the future life?

The descent of the soul from heaven to earth is a fall;
the body is a grave in which this soul is buried, a prison
in which it is captive. These old Pythagorean doctrines
were unceasingly renewed and repeated down to the end
of antiquity. But the Orphic idea that this degradation
was the chastisement for an original sin, the consequence
of a crime committed by the Titans, who were the authors
of our race, and that this hereditary taint of guilt had to
be atoned for by their descendants, was either entirely

[14] The Druses have even preserved the ancient doctrine that the number of
souls is always the same in the world. *Cf.* Silvestre de Sacy, *Religion des
Druzes*, 1838, II, p. 459.

[15] Dussaud, *Les Nosaïris*, Paris, 1900, p. 120 ss.

forgotten or else, at the least, hardly regarded. The equally ancient conception that a bitter and cruel necessity constrained souls to incarnate themselves, was, on the contrary, emphasised in consequence of the spread of astrological fatalism. Their alternate descent and ascent was conceived as governed by a cosmic law, like the progress and regress of the planets.[16] The cycle of eternal generation (κύκλος γενέσεως), which is eternal, like the revolutions of the heavenly bodies, causes mind to circulate through matter which it animates.

This transmigration could be conceived in various ways. A first theory, in which the influence of Stoic pantheism can be recognised, lays stress on the identity of individual souls with the universal soul, of which they are particles. One single divine principle awakens life in all nature. It passes from being to being, quickening their various forms, and that which is said to be death is no more than a migration. The number of the souls that people the earth is determined from the beginning; they change their dwellings but not their essence. Hardly has the human soul left one body before it enters another. This continuous travelling causes it to go through all the degrees of the animal hierarchy. It will pass, successively, into a bird, a quadruped, a fish, a reptile, and then return to man. This is why it is impious to devour the flesh of our "lower brothers" and why the sage must practise vegetarianism. Some thinkers, however, drawing logical conclusions from the admitted premises, asserted that the life of the vegetable kingdom derived from the same migration as that of the animal kingdom and that the soul of man could enclose itself in plants. It was to this teaching that Seneca alluded when he gave the name of *Apocolocyntosis*, "Transformation to a Pumpkin," to his satire on the apotheosis of the emperor Claudius.

This eschatological doctrine had in reality nothing in common with morality. If an uninterrupted chain unites

16 See above, Lecture III, p. 101.

the existence of all species, if life propagates itself fatally
from man to the lower beings, this necessity seems to
exclude all hope of posthumous reward. In order to bring
the need of a retribution in after life into agreement with
the belief in the fatal circle of migrations, it was stated
that the good entered the souls of peaceful and tame
animals, the wicked those of wild beasts. This is why
Alexander of Abonotichos predicted to a devotee that he
would be in after life first a camel, then a horse, and end
by being a great prophet like himself.[17] Hermes Trismegistus even claimed to know that the just became eagles
among birds, lions among quadrupeds, dragons among
reptiles, dolphins among fish.[18] But the lot even of these
privileged souls might not seem very enviable. The moralists, therefore, relaxed the rigour of the system and
exempted noble spirits from bestial degradation. All souls
were no longer condemned to dwell in the bodies of
animals, but only those whose low inclinations had
assimilated them to brutes. They inhabited the species
which best conformed to their instincts. Thus debauchees
became hogs in another life; cowards and sluggards, fish;
the light-minded and frivolous, birds.[19] The pagan theologians ingeniously and laboriously interpreted the story of
Circe's changing the companions of Ulysses into beasts
as an allegory of metempsychosis. *Circe* became the *circle*
of the reincarnations which were undergone by those who
emptied the magic cup of pleasure, and whence the wise
Ulysses escaped, thanks to Hermes, that is, to reason
which instructed him.[20]

Transmigration thus became less an inevitable law of
nature than a punishment of the guilty. But this punishment did not overtake only those who were reborn in
animal shape. All physical defects and moral taints,

---

[17] *Cf.* Lucian, *Alex.*, 43.

[18] Hermes Trismeg. ap. Stob., *Ecl.*, I, 49, p. 398, 16 ss., Wachsmuth.

[19] Tim. Locr., p. 104 E.

[20] Ps.-Plut., *Vita Homeri*, 126; Porph. ap. Stob., *Ecl.*, I, 49, 60, p. 445,
Wachsmuth.

which afflict man from his entry into the world, were the consequence of his crimes in an earlier life. The old Pythagoreans combined the doctrine of the metempsychosis with that of the pains reserved for the wicked in a hell beneath the earth. But we have seen how the belief in the tortures of Hades was combated until it yielded and was discredited.[21] Metempsychosis dared to do without these incredible subterranean tortures and thereby acquired a new importance. It supplied the means of maintaining the dogma of posthumous retribution without imposing a blind faith in the foolish fables of the poets: souls were held to pass immediately from one body to another without leaving the earth, rising or sinking in the scale of beings in accordance with their merits or demerits. Thus Hades becomes our corporeal life in which we expiate the faults of a previous life. The Furies are the passions which strike us with their whips and burn us with their torches.[22] The ingeniousness of the theologians found an explanation for each of the tortures described by the old mythology. Tantalus threatened by the rock is the man obsessed by the fear of heavenly wrath; Tityus, whose entrails are devoured by vultures, is the lover whose heart is gnawed by care; Sisyphus rolling his rock becomes the ambitious man who exhausts himself with vain efforts; the Danaïdes carrying water in a leaking vessel, which empties as it is filled, are the insatiable souls who give themselves up to pleasure and never have enough of enjoyment. Even the old precepts of the Pythagorean school were twisted from their ordinary meaning and became symbols of this eschatology. A popular tabu, admitted by the sect, was formulated in the sentence, "If thou leave thy dwelling, turn not round lest the Erinyes pursue thee." The first meaning of this prohibition, which is known to the folk-lore of many places, is that to turn round as one leaves one's house is

21 See above, p. 176.
22 See above, Lecture II, p. 78.

to run the risk of being assailed by the spirits who haunt the threshold. But the doctors of Neo-Pythagorism did not thus understand the saying. For them, the dwelling was the body, the Erinyes the passions: when souls left the body they must not return thither or the passions would attach themselves to them and make them their victims.[23]

*   *   *   *   *

Here, however, we touch on another form of metempsychosis. The ancients make a distinction between the doctrine of reincarnation or "reincorporation" (translating exactly the Greek word μετενσωμάτωσις), and rebirth or palingenesis (παλιγγενεσία). This latter word is not here taken in the Stoic sense of the eternal return of things, a series of cosmic cycles in which the same phenomena are exactly reproduced.[24] It is used to designate a transmigration separated by intervals, a process which is not continuous. In the first kind of metempsychosis there is, properly speaking, no rebirth, for the soul does not leave the earth, but there unceasingly accomplishes its circular journey through the living world. On the contrary, according to the second theory, it does not immediately resume possession of a body. It remains disincarnate for a long period of years—for Virgil as for Plato the number is one thousand—and thus leads a double existence of which its passages to this world take up only the lesser part. It is not even fatally constrained to redescend to the earth: if it has kept itself free from all corporeal defilement, it will soar to heaven and dwell there for ever.

But if, during his sojourn on the earth, man has given himself up to the pleasures of the senses, his soul becomes attached to his body. At first it cannot separate itself from the corpse, around which it circles, plaintively regretting the joys it has lost. It desires again to enter

[23] Cf. *Revue de philologie*, XLIV, 1921, p. 232 ss.
[24] Above, Introd., p. 13.

the flesh which was the instrument of its voluptuous-
ness; it seeks a dwelling which will allow it to continue
the sensual habits which have become its second nature.
And so, when the time is accomplished, it is seized with
an irresistible love for the body in which it is to enclose
itself again; a fascination, like a magic charm, draws
it to this object of its desires, which is to cause its misery.
The fatality driving it to incarnation and suffering is not
here an inevitable law of the universe but an inner necessity, a destiny which it has made for itself. The cosmic
Ananke has become psychic.

Thus every vicious tendency contracted by the soul
during its abode in this world has for this soul consequences which their long duration makes more momentous. If virtue enables it to rise upward at each new birth
and to acquire, as the ages revolve, an ever increasing
perfection, perversion of character produces effects which
are calamitous not only in this life but also in several
other lives through the centuries. Moral laws are no less
infallible than physical laws. Right or wrong, every act
has to be paid for with harm or benefit in the long chain
of incarnations. By his acquired disposition, man determines his future throughout a sequence of generations;
the evil he suffers is to be imputed not to the creator but
to himself. A bust of Plato found at Tivoli and now preserved in San Francisco[25] has graven on it the following
sentence of the Master as to the lot of immortal souls:
"The fault is the chooser's; God is without fault"—
Αἰτία ἑλομένῳ, ὁ θεὸς ἀναίτιος.

The very fact of birth was a pain for the soul, since
it tore it from its celestial home and plunged it into
a soiled and troubled world; consequently it was not
necessary for the soul's chastisement that it should
descend into the body of animals. Indeed, certain thinkers
rejected this kind of metempsychosis: a reasonable spirit

[25] Museum of the University of California; Kaibel, *Inscr. Sicil. et Ital.*,
12, 1196. The sentence is taken from *Republ.*, X, 617 C.

could not, they held, dwell in a being deprived of reason. Transmigration occurred therefore exclusively from man to man and from beast to beast. Such was the opinion defended by Porphyry and Jamblichus, who, in order to dispose of the texts of Plato which were contrary to this theory, upheld that he spoke figuratively, and that his "asses," his "wolves" and his "lions" signified persons who resembled these beasts in ignorance or ferocity.[26]

It is seen that this metempsychosis was getting far away from that which had its origin in the primitive beliefs. The "cycle of generation" was no longer conceived as a flux of life circulating throughout the variety of the animate beings peopling the earth, but as the descent and the ascent of a psychic essence, passing alternately from heaven to earth and from earth to heaven.

It is to these doctrines that Virgil alludes when in the Aeneid he shows us, gathered in a remote place of the Elysian Fields, the shades whom after a thousand years a god calls to come in a great troop to the river Lethe, there to drink the forgetfulness of the past, whereby "they begin again to wish to return to the body."[27]

*   *   *   *   *

But the poet also gives us precious hints as to the lot reserved for the soul in the interval between its incarnations. For palingenesis, unlike the doctrine of perpetual reincorporation, left a place for chastisement in the infernal regions. These were however situated, as we have seen, for the Pythagoreans and Posidonius, whom Virgil interpreted, not on earth but in the air. It was there that the soul had to purify itself from the stains acquired while

---

[26] Porph., *De regressu anim.*, fr. 11, Bidez=Aug., *Civ. Dei*, X, 30; Jamblich. ap. Nemes., *De nat. hom.*, 2; *cf.* Zeller, *Philos. Gr.*, V⁴, p. 713.

[27]   "Has omnes, ubi mille rotam volvere per annos,
         Lethaeum ad fluvium deus evocat agmine magno,
         Scilicet immemores super ut convexa revisant,
         Rursus et incipiant in corpore velle reverti."

                                        Aen., VI, 749-753.

it was in touch with the flesh. This pollution, we know,[28] was conceived in a very material form. The texts speak of a thickening of the subtle substance of which the soul is formed, of concretions encrusting it, of indelible marks with which the vices stain it. When the soul left the corpse, of which it kept the form, it first, as we have seen, floated in the ambient air. When it was not weighed down by the matter with which it had become impregnated, the breath of the atmosphere raised it gently and, gradually warming it, bore it to the heavens, and this is why the Winds are often represented on tombstones.[29] But these Winds, fierce divinities, could also cause the soul to expiate its faults bitterly. If it had lost its purity and lightness, the whirlwinds drew it into their vortex, the storms rolled and buffeted it, thus violently tearing away the crust which had become attached to it. The souls were thus freed from defilements contracted during life just as linen hung in the air is bleached and loses all odour.

Their passage through the air did not complete their purification. In the East the idea was old that above the firmament was found the great reservoir of the waters which fell to the ground as rain. Beyond, a burning zone must extend, where the heavenly bodies were lit, and a river of fire, identified with the Pyriphlegethon of the Greeks, was imagined. These old mythological ideas were brought into relation with Stoic physics: above the region of the winds stretched that of the clouds, in which the rain, the snow and the hail were formed, and higher still there was the burning air, in which the lightning flashed and which touched the starry spheres. The souls must blaze a path through these obstacles. After being tossed and blown about by the winds, they were drenched by rain and plunged into the gulf of the upper waters. They reached at last the fires of heaven, of which the heat scorched them. Not till they had undergone this threefold trial,

---

28 See above, Lecture VI, p. 162, and Introd., p. 29.
29 *Études syriennes*, p. 70.

in the course of which they had passed through countless years of expiation, did they at length find peace in the serenity of the luminous ether.[30]

Virgil,[31] in the passage already quoted, alludes to this doctrine when, in speaking of the souls, he says:

> ". . . Aliae panduntur inanes
> Suspensae ad ventos, aliis sub gurgite vasto
> Infectum eluitur scelus, aut exuritur igni."

"Some are exposed, hung lightly to the winds; as to others, the crime infecting them is washed away in a deep gulf or burnt by fire."

In an eschatological myth, which Plutarch[32] borrows from Demetrius of Tarsus, he shows us guilty souls who seek to reach the moon and who do not arrive thither, but are hunted and buffeted as by swelling billows, and others who have reached the goal, but are rejected and plunged from on high into the abyss. Similarly, Hermes Trismegistus depicts souls flung from the height of heaven into the depths of the atmosphere and delivered to the storms and whirlwinds of warring air, water and fire. Their eternal punishment is to be tossed and carried in different directions by the cosmic waves which roll unceasingly between earth and heaven.[33]

The passage of souls through the elements is represented symbolically on a funeral monument almost contemporary with the verses of Virgil, which was discovered near Scarbantia in Pannonia.[34] Above the portraits of the deceased, there appear first in the spandrels of this *cippus* two busts of the winds facing each other. Higher up, on the architrave, are two Tritons, and on each side of a trident two dolphins, which evidently represent the idea of the watery element. Finally, at the top

---

[30] See Lecture VI, p. 161; *cf.* below, Lecture VIII, p. 196.

[31] Virg., *Aen.*, VI, 740 ss.

[32] Plut., *De facie lunae*, p. 943 B.

[33] Ps. Apul., *Asclep.*, 28.

[34] *Jahresh. Institut Wien*, XII, 1910, p. 213.

of the stone, in the pediment, we see two lions. The lion, for physical and astrological reasons, was considered as the symbol of fire, the igneous principle.

We have seen[35] that for the doctrine which placed the limit of the dwelling of the gods and the elect in the zone of the moon, another was substituted according to which the souls, in order to regain the purity of their original nature, had to traverse the spheres of the planets to reach the heaven of fixed stars. The trials of purgatory had to be prolonged up to the entry into the dwelling of the blessed. The idea was, therefore, conceived of attributing each of the planets to one of the elements. The moon was the ethereal earth, Mercury the water, Venus the air, the sun the fire: and inversely, Mars was the fire, Jupiter the air, Saturn the water, and the sphere of the stars the celestial earth, in which lay the Elysian Fields. Thus the soul, in order to be saved, had to be reborn three times in virtue of a triple passage through the four elements.[36]

This last doctrine, which is connected with astrological speculations, seems to have had only a limited vogue and to have been of ephemeral duration. On the other hand, the idea of a purgatory situated in the atmosphere between our earth and the moon, a place in which souls were purified not only by fire but also by air and water, was long to survive the fall of paganism and to be propagated through the Middle Ages in the West as in the East. For Dante, purgatory still occupied a fiery zone stretched between the terrestrial and the celestial circles.

* * * * *

Was the soul which, after a long expiation, had reached the Elysian Fields and the sphere of the stars, always to descend thence, seized with a blind love for the body, and to pass again through the trials of another earthly life? No, the ancient Orphics already flattered themselves

---

35 See above, Lecture III, p. 107.

36 Macrob., *Comm. Somn Scip.*, I, 11, 8; Proclus, *In Tim.*, II, 48, 15 ss., Diehl.

that by their cathartic rites they obtained for the soul an escape from the fatal cycle of generation and regaining of heaven for ever. The Pythagoreans inherited this doctrine, which they kept until the Roman period. In spite of the contrary opinion of certain thinkers, pagan philosophers and priests generally taught that after pilgrimages, more or less long, after a succession of deaths and rebirths, the purified spirits returned to dwell for ever in their celestial country. It was to this goal that the mysteries promised to lead their initiate; this was the end which the sages flattered themselves that they attained by their virtue.

It will be understood that such a hope, combined with the suppression of eternal damnation in Hades, led necessarily to the doctrine of the eventual salvation of all souls. We know this system especially through Origen, but he merely reproduced a theory to which the evolution of pagan ideas had led.

We have seen that metempsychosis helped the philosophers to shake, if not to ruin, the belief in infernal punishment. But this belief again had power towards the end of antiquity, when the dualist sects which were the outcome of Persian Mazdeism were propagated and when Plato became the supreme authority in philosophy. We touched on this point, in another lecture,[37] when we showed how the idea of a demons' prison in the bosom of the earth triumphed.

Thus, when the Roman world was in its decline, men came back to the old threefold distinction of the Orphics and the Pythagoreans. The very guilty, who cannot be corrected, are hurled into Tartarus, where they suffer for ever the punishment of their incurable wickedness. Souls less corrupt are subjected to purification, either by passing through the elements or by undergoing successive reincarnations, and thus they regain their original nature before they are readmitted to their first dwelling.

[37] Lecture II, p. 87 ss.

Finally, the most perfect souls, those of the wise who have freed themselves from the domination of the body and have not let themselves be contaminated by matter, and those of the pious faithful, to whom religious lustrations have given back their purity or whom initiations to the mysteries have made equal to the gods, at once rise again to the celestial spheres.

In the next lecture we shall speak of the rewards reserved for them in the dwelling of the blessed.

VIII

THE FELICITY OF THE BLESSED

WE have seen how the evolution of religious faith caused the dwelling-place of the dead to move from the tomb to the nether world and from the nether world to the heavens. When the abode of souls was changed, all the ideas attached to the future life had to be transposed. In this lecture we shall endeavour to make clear how the opinions which were held as to the felicity of the blessed were thus transformed. We shall take up again matter which we have already touched upon in another connection and try to show the successive changes undergone by three manners of conceiving happiness in after life: the repose of the dead, the repast of the dead, and the sight of God.

The most ancient and originally the simplest of these conceptions was that of the repose of the dead. We know[1] that the dead who had not been buried in accordance with the rites were believed to find no rest in the tomb. A corpse had to be committed to the earth with traditional ceremonies in order that the spirit which animated it might have quiet. If this spirit were not subsequently nourished by offerings and sacrifices, it left its burial place and roamed the earth's surface like an animal driven by hunger. The shades inhabiting the tombs could also be evoked by necromancers and such disturbance broke in upon their rest most unpleasantly.

These archaic ideas were so deeply implanted in the popular mind that other beliefs never expelled them, but supervened and existed side by side with them without causing their disappearance.

[1] See Lecture I, p. 64 ss.

On tombs of the imperial period formulas like the following are often read: *"Hic requiescit,"* "Here rests," *"Quieti aeternae,"* "For eternal rest"—inscriptions which could be interpreted figuratively; but other wishes can only be taken to have a material sense, such as: *"Ossa quiescant,"* "May his bones rest," and *"Molliter ossa cubent,"* "May the bones lie softly." Poetry has preserved a number of similar phrases. Tibullus expresses the following wish for a loved woman: "May thy slender form rest well beneath the soft earth."[2]

The rest which the exact accomplishment of the rites gave to the dead was not physical only but moral also. The dead were *securi*—the word is properly applied to them—that is, they were exempt from care. Doubtless the care from which they were delivered by the cult of the grave, was first that of suffering from hunger and thirst,[3] but the "eternal security" (*securitas aeterna*)[4] they enjoyed was also the absence of all the fears and anxieties which haunt humanity.

When philosophy claimed to free souls from the superstitions of the past, it did not destroy the old conception of rest in the tomb but cleansed it from all material alloy. If it be doubtful whether anything of man survives, it is at least certain that death marks the abolition of the pains of this world and the end of its troubles. *Mors laborum et miseriarum quies,* is Cicero's definition.[5] Death restores us to that state of tranquillity in which we were before our birth.[6] The "eternal home" which shelters the remains of man is the silent temple in which he no longer has anything to fear from nature or from his fellows.

The Epicureans who made *ataraxia* their ideal of life, the Stoics who found theirs in impassivity (ἀπάθεια),

---

[2] Tibullus, II, 6, 30: "Sic bene sub tenera parva quiescat humo."
[3] Tertull., *De testimonio animae*, 4.
[4] *Securitati aeternae;* cf. Dessau, *Inscr. sel.*, 8025 ss., 8149.
[5] Cic., *Catil.*, IV, 7; cf. *Tusc.*, I, 11, 25; 49, 118.
[6] Sen., *Dial.*, VI, 19, 5.

could see in the anaesthesia of death the supreme realisa-
tion of such absence of emotion and passion. The corpse
lies as softly on its last bed as a man plunged in a deep
and quiet sleep. The burial place is indeed often consecrated to *Somno aeterno.*[7] This idea is expressed in a
thousand forms in literature and in epitaphs. A poor
grammarian of Como, who doubtless had had little reason
to congratulate himself on life, caused two lines of verse
to be engraved on his tomb:[8] "I fled the miseries of sickness and the great ills of life; I am now delivered from all
its pains and enjoy a peaceful calm." On an African
grave there are the following words: "After bearing a
heavy burden and after manifold toils, he speaks no
more, content with the silent dwelling in which he rests."[9]
We read elsewhere, "Life was a pain, death prepared me
rest."[10] The sentiment expressed by these inscriptions
and many more like them is no mere reflection of the
teaching of philosophers who denied the future life: it is
profoundly human. The melodious but melancholy apos-
trophe of Leconte de Lisle is well known:

"Et toi, divine mort, ou tout rentre et s'efface,
    Accueille tes enfants dans ton sein étoilé;
Affranchis nous du temps, du nombre et de l'espace
    Et rends nous le repos que la vie a troublé."

"O Death divine, at whose recall,
    Returneth all
        To fade in thy embrace,
Gather thy children to thy bosom starred,

---

[7] Dessau, *Inscr. sel.*, 8024 and note; *cf.* Cic., *Tusc.*, I, 41, 97; and Introd.,
p. 10.

[8] Bücheler, *Carm. epigr.*, 1274:
    "Morborum vitia et vitae mala maxima fugi.
    Nunc careo poenis, pace fruor placida."

[9] Bücheler, *ibid.*, 573:
    "Qui post tantum onus, multos crebrosque labores
    Nunc silet et tacito contentus sede quiescit."

[10] Bücheler, *ibid.*, 507: "Poena fuit vita, requies mihi morte parata est."

Free us from time, from number and from space,
And give us back the rest that life has marred."[11]

In the midst of all the tribulation of our tormented
existence, to how many minds, even those which have the
strongest religious conviction, have not the immobility
and insensibility of those who are no more sometimes
seemed like a deliverance? In antiquity also, this aspiration towards the moment when man will obtain remission
of all his travail does not necessarily imply the belief
that there is no hope beyond the cold sleep of the grave.
This yearning mingles with faith in immortality and is
transformed with it.

When it was believed that the dead went down into the
depths of the earth where lay the infernal kingdom,
another meaning was given to their rest. The funeral
eulogy of a noble woman who towards the end of the
Republican period saved the life of her husband, who had
been proscribed, ends with the naïve words: "I pray that
the gods thy Manes may grant thee rest and thus protect
thee."[12] The shades of the kinsmen of the dead must
receive their souls in the subterranean world[13] and thus
ensure their welfare. The road which must be travelled
before the abode of the elect was reached was long and
beset with dangers. The Book of the Dead in Egypt, the
Orphic tablets in Greece, were guides to the Beyond which
taught the dead not to stray from the right path and to
avoid the various dangers threatening them.[14] Many of
them, the impious who had to expiate their misdeeds and
the unfortunate to whom funeral duties had not been
rendered, wandered wretchedly on the banks of the Styx,
vainly longing to enter the "peaceful abode" of the Elysian Fields.[15] There, lying in the cool shade, the blessed

11 Transl. by J. C. Anderson (in my *Astrology and Religion*, p. 171).

12 Dessau, *Inscr. sel.*, 8393, 79: "Te di Manes tui ut quietam patiantur
atque ita tueantur opto."

13 See above, Lecture I, p. 68; II, p. 86, n. 39; V, p. 134.

14 See above, Lecture VI, p. 143.

15 Virg., *Aen.*, VI, 705: "Domos placidas."

enjoyed a felicity exempt from all care. Serene quiet in a sweet idleness cheered by joyous relaxation and wise conversation—such was the ideal which some mysteries[16] opposed to the weary agitations of earthly life and to the long sufferings of the sinful and vagabond soul. For the adepts of these doctrines the *secura quies* applied to the repose of the nether world, and this conception of beatitude beyond the grave is found to persist until the end of paganism.[17]

But we have seen that another doctrine triumphed in the Roman period, the doctrine that souls rise to the skies to live there eternally among the stars. In this great metamorphosis of eschatological beliefs what became of the idea of the repose of the dead? The question deserves to be more closely investigated, for the transformation had lasting consequences of which the ultimate effects can be felt even today.

The Pythagoreans were, as we have seen,[18] the first to promulgate the doctrine of celestial immortality in Greece and Italy. One of the allegories familiar to the teaching of the sect connected human destiny with the old myth of Hercules at the crossroads. The Greek letter Y, of which the stem divides midway into two, was in the school the symbol of this comparison—we have already alluded to it elsewhere.[19] When man reaches the age of reason two paths are open to him. One is smooth and easy but ends in an abyss: this is the way of pleasure. The other is at first rough and jagged—it is the hard road of virtue—but he who climbs to the summit of its slope can there *rest* deliciously from his weariness. Funeral reliefs represent this contrast naïvely: at the bottom of the stele the dead man is often seen accomplishing the labours of his career; at the top of the stone he is shown stretched at his ease on a couch.

---

[16] See Introd., p. 34 ss.

[17] *Comptes rendus Acad. Inscr.*, 1912, p. 151 ss.; *cf.* Bücheler, *Carm. epigr.*, 513.

[18] Lecture III, p. 95.   [19] Lecture VI, p. 150.

The meaning of the allegory is immediately apparent: the *quieta sedes* in which deserving souls are received, has become the sky. How was this idea developed?

Homer[20] had already described Olympus as "the immovable seat of the gods which is neither shaken by the winds, nor wet by the rains, nor touched by the snow, but is bright with a cloudless light." The Epicureans applied these lines of the poet to the serene dwelling where nothing occurred to modify the perpetual peace enjoyed by the gods.[21] And the founder of Stoicism had already taught that the pious souls, separated from the guilty, inhabited "tranquil and delectable" regions.[22] Both called this dwelling of the gods or the elect by the same name—*sedes quietae.*

We must here remember the distinction, established by the philosophers and often repeated, between the sublunary circle and the celestial spheres.[23] Above, the world of the eternal gods; below, the world of generation and corruption. There the pure ether always kept the same serenity; here the struggle of the elements called forth unceasing agitation and transformation. On one side reigned peace and harmony, on the other war and discord. The zone of the moon was the boundary between the two contrasted parts of the world, and "the limit between life and death."[24] It was when they had crossed it, that the souls entered the *quietae sedes* of the Blessed.

The very ancient idea of a fearful journey which the dead had to make in order to reach Pluto's subterranean kingdom was transferred to the space lying between the earth and the moon, for this was the region of the universe to which the name of nether world (*Inferi*)[25] was

---

[20] *Odyssey*, VI, 42 ss.

[21] Lucretius, III, 18 ss.

[22] Zeno, fr. 147 (von Arnim, *Fragm. Stoicorum*, I, p. 40): "Zeno docuit sedes piorum ab impiis esse discretas et illos quidem quietas ac delectabiles habitare regiones."

[23] See Introd., p. 25; Lecture III, p. 96.

[24] Macrob., *Somn. Scip.*, I, 11, 6: "Vitae mortisque confinium."

[25] See above, Lecture II, p. 81 s.

henceforth applied. As we have seen in the previous lecture,[26] when the soul, escaping from the body, was laden with material dross, it was tossed about for many centuries before it could again win to the ether. Shaken by the winds, swept to and fro by the opposing elements of air, water and fire, it had to endure a long torture before it was cleansed of the sin which weighed it down. When at length it was freed of every fleshly taint, it escaped from inward trouble also, from the pains and the passions provoked by its union with the body. "Then," says Seneca, "it tends to return to the place whence it has been sent down; there eternal quiet awaits it when it passes from the confused and gross to the clear and pure."[27] In the same way certain Neo-Platonists taught that souls which had lived well, rose to the celestial heights and rested there amid the stars. Even in this life the ecstasy, which gave them anticipated enjoyment of the future bliss, is described by them as a transport in which reason attains to absolute stability or equipoise, escapes from all movement and rests in the Supreme Being.[28] Peace in the celestial light: such is the highest form which the repose of the dead assumed in paganism.[29]

The various ideas which we have just analysed—those of the repose in the grave, the repose in the infernal regions and the repose in heaven—followed parallel courses during the centuries and in part passed from antiquity to the Middle Ages. But the distinction between them is not always clear. Even in paganism they were intermingled and in the course of time they were gradually confused. In no class of beliefs is the force of tradi-

---

[26] See Lecture VII, p. 185 s.

[27] Sen., *Consol. Marc.*, 24, 5: "(Animus) nititur illo unde demissus est; ibi illum aeterna requies manet e confusis crassisque pura et liquida visentem."

[28] Plotin., IX, 8, 9, p. 768 A; IX, 8, 11, p. 770 C.

[29] *Cf.* Aug., *Serm.*, CCLX (P.L. XXXVIII, 1132, 38): "Dixerunt Platonici . . . animas, ire ad superna caelorum et requiescere ibi in stellis et luminibus istis conspicuis."

tion greater than in those which centre in death, and the Christian peoples clung tenaciously to articles of faith which Jews and pagans had shared before them.

We have seen[30] that the masses did not easily give up their belief that the dead continued, in or about the tomb, a vegetating and uncertain life. Extreme importance was still attached to burial because the more or less unconscious conviction persisted that the soul's rest depended on that of the body. The dread of ghosts was still the inspiration for some ceremonies performed over the remains of the dead. Nay, a new apprehension was added to this, namely, the fear lest the dead whose bodies were torn from the tomb should have no part in the resurrection of the flesh.[31] The formula, *"Hic requiescit,"* "Here rests—," was transferred from pagan to Christian epigraphy, and the rest men wished to the departed was first the rest of the corpse, which was peacefully to await the Day of Judgment in its last dwelling.

These were doubtless vulgar prejudices rather than dogmas recognised by orthodoxy, yet they did not remain without influence on the teaching of the doctors of the Church. For instance, Saint Ambrose[32] enlarges on the thought, probably borrowed from some philosopher, that death is good because in it the body, source of our uneasiness, our troubles and our vices, rests, calmed for ever, while the virtuous soul rises to heaven. After the travail of existence the dead rest as man rests on the Sabbath day, and this was, it was explained, the reason why the seventh day was the day of the commemoration of the departed.

The idea of rest in the infernal regions has left no deep traces on the Christian faith, for which the subterranean world became the abode of the wicked. It was, however, somewhere in the bowels of the earth that the dwelling of the righteous who lived before the Redemption was

[30] Lecture I, p. 45 ss.
[31] *Ibid.*, p. 69.
[32] St. Ambrose, *De bono mortis*, 9; *cf.* Kaibel, *Inscr. Sic. It.*, 2117.

commonly placed, sometimes also that of children who
died unbaptised. They found there according to the Pela-
gians a "place of repose and salvation" outside the
kingdom of heaven.[33]

But in Roman times the idea of peace in the celestial
light was dominant among the Jews and Christians as
among the pagans. Thus the Book of Enoch shows us the
prophet carried off in a whirlwind to the heights whence
he perceived "the beds where the just rest" amid the
saints.[34] We can here point out exactly the most important
of the literary intermediaries through whom this conception was transmitted from paganism to Judaism and
from Judaism to Christianity. Towards the end of the
first century A. D., amid the desolation which followed
on the destruction of the Temple, a pious Jew, somewhere
in the East, composed and ascribed to the venerable
authorship of Esdras an apocalypse which enjoyed singular popularity until the time of its rejection by the
Church as apocryphal. The visionary who set it down
combines a number of pagan reminiscences with biblical
ideas. He promises eternal felicity to the just, and asks
himself what will be the lot of souls between the time of
their death and the end of the world. Will they be at rest
or will they be tortured? And the angel who inspires him
answers that when the vital breath has left the body to go
again to adore the glory of the Most High, the soul which
has violated the divine law will not enter the celestial
dwellings but will "wander amidst torments, for ever
suffering and saddened on seven paths." But the soul
which has walked in the way of God "will rest in seven
orders of rewards."[35] The sixth of these is the order in
which its face begins to shine like the sun and in which it
becomes incorruptible, like the stars; the seventh is that
in which it wins to the sight of God.

[33] Aug., *De anima*, II, 12.

[34] *Book of Enoch*, 39.

[35] IV *Esdr.*, VII, 91: "Requiescent per septem ordines"; *cf.* VII, 95
(p. 131 ss., Violet).

These are conceptions and even expressions which belong to astral immortality, and the Jewish author, like the pagans before him, everywhere contrasts the state of agitation filled with anguish reserved for the guilty with the blessed tranquillity which is the reward of a pious life.[36] The description of the celestial dwelling which Saint Ambrose borrowed from the pseudo-Esdras is singularly like that given by the philosophers of the earlier period: a place in which there is no cloud, no thunder, no lightning, no violence of winds, neither darkness nor sunset, neither summer nor winter to vary the seasons, where no cold is met with, nor hail, nor rain. But the Christian doctor, like the Jewish visionary, adds a new feature: there will be no more sun nor moon nor stars; the light of God will shine alone.[37]

The idea of repose in the eternal light was, thanks to the apocalypse of the supposed Esdras, to become one of those most frequently expressed by epitaphs and ritual. It was from this apocryphal work that the Roman liturgy borrowed the form of a prayer introduced into the office of the dead at least as early as the seventh century and still sung in the funeral service—*Requiem aeternam dona eis Domine et lux perpetua luceat eis.* "Lord, give them eternal rest and may perpetual light shine upon them."

*   *   *   *   *

The idea of the repast of the dead evolved, like that of their repose, as the conception of life beyond the tomb was gradually transformed, and it finally assumed a far higher significance than that originally attributed to it.

According to a belief found everywhere, the dead, as we know,[38] needed nourishment if they were not to suffer from hunger. Hence the obligation to make libations and sacrifices on the tomb and to deposit food and drink there.

[36] IV *Esdr.*, VII, 36, 38 (p. 146, Violet).
[37] Ambrose, *De bono mortis*, 12, § 53 (P.L., XIV, 154); *cf.* IV *Esdr.*, VII, 39.
[38] See Lecture I, p. 50.

The neglect of these sacred duties entailed consequences fearful to him who failed to fulfil them, just as their exact observance ensured him the good will of the spirits of the dead.

The custom of holding banquets which united the members of a family beside a grave at a funeral or on certain consecrated days, was connected with this belief. This custom was no mere rendering of an honour to one who had gone, no unmixed manifestation of piety or affection. The motive for these ceremonies was much more concrete. As we have stated elsewhere,[39] men were persuaded that the spirit of him who lay beneath the ground was present at the meal, took its place beside its kin and rejoiced with them. Therefore its share was set aside for it, and by consecrated formulas it was invited to drink and eat. Moreover the guests themselves ate copiously and drank deeply, convinced that the noisy conviviality of the feast was a source of joy and refreshment to the shade in the gloom of its sepulchral existence. Sometimes the dinner took place in a room within the tomb, specially set aside for such meetings, sometimes in one of the gardens which men delighted to make around the "eternal house" of the dead[40] and to which inscriptions sometimes give the name of "paradise" ($\pi a \rho \acute{a} \delta \epsilon \iota \sigma o s$).[41]

These are customs and ideas which are found everywhere from the time when history had its origin, practices and ideas to which under the Roman Empire the people still clung, and which even partially survived the conversion of the masses to Christianity, although the Church condemned them as pagan. Until the end of antiquity and even in the Middle Ages, banquets, at which wine flowed abundantly, were still held on anniversaries by kinsfolk and friends near the remains of those they loved.[42]

When, however, the conception of survival in the tomb

---

[39] See Lecture I, p. 54.
[40] Ibid., p. 57.
[41] Calder, Journal of Roman Studies, 1912, p. 254.
[42] See above, Lecture I, p. 55 ss.

was superseded or overshadowed by that of survival in
the nether world, the repast of the dead was also transferred thither. Henceforth it was in the Elysian Fields
that pious souls could take their place at the table of the
Blessed. The Orphics were the first to introduce into
Greece this new idea, which was, however, no more than
the development of a pre-Hellenic belief, and it spread
through the mysteries of Dionysos[43] to every part of the
ancient world: the ritualistic repasts in which the initiate
took part, the drunkenness which exalted their whole
being, were for the adepts of this cult at once a foretaste
and a warrant of the happiness reserved for them in that
eternal feast of the subterranean world in which a sweet
intoxication would rejoice their soul. That forgetfulness
of all cares which the divine liquor gave was connected
with Lethe, the water of which, according to mythology,
souls drank that they might lose all memory of their
former life.

An immense number of reliefs, scattered throughout
the whole extent of the Roman Empire, bear witness to
the popularity of the belief in this form of immortality.
The dead man who has been made a hero and whose
family comes to make sacrifices to him is stretched on a
couch and lifts the *rhyton* which holds the heady drink
of Bacchus, while before him, on a little table, dishes are
placed. These banquets took place, as we have said, in the
Elysian Fields, and the idea of the repast thus met and
combined with the idea of rest. The Blessed were imagined as lying on a soft bed of flowered grass, taking part
in a perpetual feast, to the accompaniment of music and
songs. Lucian in his "True Histories"[44] describes, with
ironical exaggeration, the joys of these guests who are
stretched comfortably among the flowers of a fragrant
meadow in the shade of leafy trees, and who gather, instead of fruit, crystal goblets, which fill with wine as soon
as they are placed on the table.

[43] See Introd., p. 35; Lecture IV, p. 126.
[44] Lucian, *Verae hist.*, II, 14.

In spite of the mockery of sceptics these beliefs still had some faithful partisans even at the end of paganism. A picture discovered in the catacomb of Praetextatus shows us a priest of the Thraco-Phrygian god Sabazios celebrating a mystic banquet with six of his fellows, and another fresco represents the introduction of a veiled woman into the garden of delights, where she has been judged worthy of being received at the table of virtuous souls.[45]

Sometimes in the reliefs of the "funeral banquet" the dead are seen wearing on their head the bushel (*modius*) of Serapis, with whom, after a virtuous life, they have been identified. This indicates a confusion, to which much other testimony bears witness, between the Bacchic mysteries and the cult of the Alexandrian god.[46] Serapis is the great master of the feast ($\sigma\nu\mu\pi\sigma\sigma\iota\acute{a}\rho\chi\eta s$),[47] the host who must in the nether world entertain those faithful to him. Thus the eschatological beliefs of the Nile Valley mingled with those of Greece. In the country of burning sun, where a straying traveller runs the risk of dying of thirst on the arid stretches of sand, the hope expressed above all others for him who accomplishes the great pilgrimage to the abode of the infernal divinities, is that he may find wherewith to quench his consuming thirst. "May Osiris give thee fresh water" is a wish which the votaries of the Egyptian god often inscribed on their tombs. Thus the repast in the other world was to be above all a refreshment (*refrigerium*). The word passed into Christian language to denote both earthly "*agape*" or sacred meal and the bliss of the other world, and even today the Roman Church prays for the spiritual "refreshment" of the dead.[48]

We touch here on a question which is not yet completely

---

[45] Best reproduction, Wilpert, *Pitture delle Catacombe Romane*, II, 132-133.

[46] See above, Introd., pp. 35, 37.

[47] Aelius Arist., XLV (VIII), 27 (p. 360, Keil).

[48] See my *Oriental Religions*, Chap. IV, end.

elucidated, that of the relation established between the funeral banquet and the salvation of those who took part in it.

In Rome from the end of the Republic onwards this banquet, amid the general decline of faith in immortality, was increasingly detached from the tomb and became a guild or domestic ceremony. The tendency was to reduce it to the repast of a family or confraternity, to the perpetuation among men of the memory of him whose features were preserved by a statue or picture. But the funeral cult acquired new meaning with the spread of Oriental religions. It did not cease to be useful to the dead who were its object, to whose subsistence in the beyond and safe arrival in the Elysian Fields it was still thought to be necessary. The offerings of the living sustained them on their dangerous and hard journey thither; the food and drink restored them on the long road they had to travel before they reached the place of everlasting refreshment.

But the funeral repast was also salutary to those who offered it, and not only because it ensured to them the good will of a spirit or demon capable of protecting them. This banquet, at which wine flowed profusely, was like the "orgies" of the Bacchic and Oriental mysteries, and the resemblance is partly explained by an identity of kind.

The ritual of the gods whose death and resurrection were commemorated—Bacchus, Osiris, Attis, Adonis— was probably a development of the funeral ritual, and the banquet of initiation was thus related to the banquet at the grave. On the one hand, it was believed that by a mystic union with the god, men could share his blessed lot after the transient trial of a death like his.[49] On the other hand, it was with a dead man that a repast was taken, but with one who also, in some sort, had become a god, who had preceded the diners into the other world and awaited

49 See Lecture IV, p. 122; Introd., p. 34.

them there. "Live happy and pour out wine to our Manes," says a Latin epitaph of Syria, engraved beneath a scene of libation, "recollecting that one day you will be with us."[50]

According to an opinion which often found expression, the shades themselves rejected whoever did not deserve to enter the abode of the Blessed, but willingly received the pious soul which had always fulfilled its duty towards them.[51] For admission to this club of posthumous diners a members' vote was necessary. Thus the funeral banquet took on the character of a mystic banquet; that is, it came to be conceived as a prelibation of the banquet at which the elect feasted in the other world. The wish which the guests made to each other—"Drink and live!"—became an allusion, no more to this earthly life, but to that other existence in which they would participate in the felicity of him who had gone before them and who would help them to rejoin him therein. The following advice, repeated elsewhere in various forms, is found on the tomb of a priest of Sabazios: "Drink, eat, jest and come to me . . . that is what you will carry away with you" (hoc tecum feres).[52] This is not to be understood here as an Epicurean invitation to enjoy life because all else is vain,[53] but a veiled expression of faith in the efficacy for the salvation of the initiate attributed to the joyous banquets which gathered men about a tomb.

The connection between the beliefs of the mysteries and the hopes attached to the funeral cult became more intimate as immortality brought the spirits of the dead nearer the celestial divinities. The idea that some few privileged mortals win admission to the banquet of the gods is very ancient. An inscription of Sendjerli in Syria, which goes back to the eighth century before our era, orders sacrifices to be made in order that the soul of King

---

[50] CIL, III, 14165.
[51] See Lecture I, p. 68; II, p. 86; V, p. 134.
[52] Bücheler, Carm. epigr., 1317=CIL, VI, 142; cf. Plato, Phaedo, p. 107D.
[53] As it is elsewhere; cf. Introd., p. 11.

Panamu "may eat and drink with the god Hadad,"[54] and Greek mythology told that certain heroes, such as Heracles, who had been carried off to heaven, had there become the table companions of the gods. Horace states that Augustus, borne to the ethereal summits, will there rest between Hercules and Pollux, "drinking nectar with his rosy lips."[55] But we have seen elsewhere that apotheosis, or deification, which was at first the privilege of an aristocracy, became the common lot of all pious souls,[56] and that the Elysian Fields were transferred from the depths of the infernal realm to the upper spheres of the world. The repast of the Blessed was thus transported to heaven.[57] This removal to the region of the stars seems to have been first made in the astral religion of Syria, but it was commonly accepted in western paganism. This is why in funeral reliefs of the Roman period, in which the dead are shown banqueting, such representations are placed in the upper part of the stele, above the scenes of earthly life which fill the lower portion of the stone. The emperor Julian is giving us a mocking picture of this repast of the heroes, when in one of his satires he shows us the shades of the Caesars at table immediately beneath the moon, in the highest zone of the atmospheres—in accordance with the ideas of the Stoics.[58] Men readily fashioned the heroes who tasted the joys of Olympus on the pattern of the celestial divinities—resplendent with light, clothed in garments of dazzling whiteness, their heads crowned with rays or surrounded by a luminous nimbus, singing, as in a Greek symposium, melodious hymns.

The philosophers of course gave a symbolical interpretation of the intoxication of the souls which took part in the feast, explaining it as the ravishing of reason pene-

54 Lagrange, Religions sémitiques², 1905, p. 493.
55 Horace, Od., III, 3, 12.
56 Lecture IV, p. 113 s., 116 ss.
57 See, for instance, Kaibel, Epigr. Graeca, 312, 13.
58 Julian, Caesares, p. 307 C; cf. Introd., p. 29; Lecture III, p. 98.

trated by divine intelligence. We will return to their doctrines presently.

The Jews of the Alexandrian period shared the belief in the celestial banquet with the Syrian paganism and transmitted it to the Christians. The Paradise of the elect was often conceived as a shady garden where tables were set out at which immortal guests passed their time in endless joy. Thus, not to mention better-known texts, Aphraates, a Syriac author of the first half of the fourth century, depicts the felicity of the Blessed, clothed in light, who are admitted to the divine table and are there fed with food which never fails. "There the air is pleasant and serene, a brilliant light shines, trees grow of which the fruit ripens perpetually, of which the leaves never fall, and beneath these shades, which give out a sweet fragrance, the souls eat this fruit and are never satiated."[59]

The representation of this feast of Paradise recurs several times in the paintings of the catacombs, but in them the wine is poured out by Peace (*Eirene*) and Charity (*Agape*). An allegorical explanation gave a spiritual meaning to the food and drink consumed by the elect. But the old idea which was at the root of all the later development, the idea of a material repast in which the dead participated, did not disappear from popular faith when the conception that souls rose to the sky was adopted, and in many countries it has not been obliterated even today.[60]

*   *   *   *   *

Even in the pagan period, as we have said, enlightened minds accepted the old descriptions of joyous feasts in fresh meadows only in a figurative sense. A less coarse conception of immortality suffered them to be looked upon only as symbols or metaphors. This conception of celestial beatitude originated not in the cult of the dead

[59] *Patrologia Orientalis,* I, p. 1014.
[60] See above, Lecture I, p. 55 s.

but in the cult of the gods. It was at first as material as preceding conceptions, but it became purified as the idea of psychic survival was spiritualised.

We have seen in another lecture[61] that the "sight of the god" who was adored was the highest degree of initiation. Theurgy flattered itself that it could evoke divine apparitions at will. These visions have been described to us by those who claimed to have been favoured with them.[62] Their character and their effects have moreover been analysed in detail in the treatise of Jamblichus, *On the Mysteries*. The impression most immediately produced by these epiphanies was a boundless admiration for their splendour. The incomparable beauty with which the gods were radiant, the supernatural light in which they were wrapped, had such an effect on men that they could hardly bear the effulgence and nearly lost consciousness, but their souls were flooded with unspeakable joy and purified for ever.

To this ineffable delight of a heart possessed of divine love there was added the highest revelation for the intelligence.[63] Must not the infallible "gnosis" be that which was the result of instruction received directly from the mouth of a celestial power which had come down to earth?

The devotees who had obtained the signal favour of this resplendent vision, were thenceforth united to the deity who had manifested himself to them, and were certain to share his immortal life. The fugitive pleasure which they had felt on earth would become a bliss without end in the kingdom of the dead. There they would see face to face the god who protected them and learn from him all that had remained hidden from them in this life.

These ideas, half religious, half magical, are very ancient, especially in Egypt, but they were transformed by astrolatry. Here the celestial powers had not to be

---

[61] Lecture IV, p. 121.

[62] For instance, by the physician Thessalus (under Nero); *cf. Cat. codd. astrol.*, VIII, 3, p. 137; VIII, 4, p. 257.

[63] *Cf.* Lecture IV, pp. 121, 125 s.

summoned by prayer or invoked by incantations in order that they might come and converse with the faithful, but were perpetually visible and offered themselves, day and night, to the veneration of humanity.

Henceforth the knowledge of divine things was no longer to be communicated by the words which the initiate believed that he heard in the silence of the sanctuary. It was revealed by a mysterious inspiration to him who had deserved it by a fervent observation of the heavens.[64] Thus by an illumination of the intelligence the astral powers unveiled their will and the secrets of their movements to their attentive servants. Here below this knowledge was always imperfect and fragmentary, but it would be completed in another world, when reason once more would rise aloft to the starry spaces whence it had descended.

This eschatological doctrine, which made astronomy the source of virtue and of immortality, could only be developed by a clergy devoted to the study of that science. Its first authors were doubtless the "Chaldeans," who transmitted it to Greece with their theories as to the divisions of the sky and the heavenly bodies. The most ancient writing in which this Oriental influence asserts itself clearly is the *Epinomis*, probably a work of the astronomer Philip of Opus, a disciple of Plato. Let us listen to his own words:[65]

"When man perceives the harmony of the sky and the immovable order of its revolutions, he is first filled with joy and struck with admiration. Then the passion is born in him to learn about them all that it is possible for his mortal nature to know, for he is persuaded that he will thus lead the best and happiest existence and will go after his death to the places suited to virtue. Then being veritably and really initiate, pure reason taking part in the only wisdom, he will spend the rest of his time in con-

[64] See above, Lecture IV, p. 126.
[65] P. 896 C; *cf.* p. 992 B.

templation of what is most beautiful among all visible things.''

This passage shows clearly the manner in which astrolatry modified ancient ideas as to the sight of a god, the reverential wonder felt in his presence by the faithful, the truth communicated to them and the immortality which completed their initiation. The doctrine of an intellectual reward for the Blessed was to attract scholars who in this world gave themselves up to study. Spiritual activity, which emancipates from material care and gives man nobility and virtue, seemed to them to be the only occupation worthy of the elect. If the theory that the Blessed would after death find this activity in the midst of the divine stars, is probably of ''Chaldean'' origin, it was developed by the Greek philosophers and in particular by Posidonius. It was also admitted into the Roman mysteries, which, being penetrated by the spirit of Oriental theologies, claimed to supply their adepts with a complete explanation of the universe.

We have already alluded to this system in speaking of astral mysticism.[66] Nature herself has destined man to gaze upon the skies. Other animals are bent to the earth; he proudly lifts his head to the stars. His eye, a tiny mirror in which immensity is reflected, the soul's door, open to the infinite, follows the evolutions of the heavenly bodies from here below. By their splendour they make men marvel and by their majesty compel them to veneration. Their complicated movements, ruled by an immovable rhythm, are inconceivable unless they are endowed with infallible reason.

The observation of the sky is not only an inexhaustible source of aesthetic emotion. It also causes the soul, a detached parcel of the fires of the ether, to enter into communion with the gods which shine in the firmament. Possessed with the desire to know them, this soul receives their revelations. They instruct it as to their nature;

66 See above, Lecture IV, p. 126.

thanks to them, it understands the phenomena produced in the cosmic organism. Thus scientific curiosity is also conceived as a yearning for God. The love of truth leads to holiness more surely than initiations and priests.

Of the numerous passages in which these ideas are expressed I will recall one which is well known but is not always well understood.[67] Virgil in his *Georgics* tells us what he looks to receive from the sweet Muses whom he serves, being "struck with a great love for them." Not, as one would expect, poetic inspiration but physical science. The Muses are to point out to him the paths of the stars in the sky, to explain to him the reasons for eclipses, tides and earthquakes and the variations in the length of the day. "Happy is he," the poet concludes, "who can know the causes of things, who treads underfoot all fear and inexorable fate and vain rumours as to greedy Acheron."[68] There is, in spite of a reminiscence of Lucretius, nothing Epicurean in the idea here expressed. The man who has won knowledge of Nature, which is divine, escapes the common lot and does not fear death because a glorious immortality is reserved for him.

For these joys which the acquisition of wisdom gives here below, partially and intermittently, are in the other life bestowed with absolute fulness and prolonged for ever. Reason, set free from corporeal organs, attains to an infinite perceptive power and can satisfy the insatiable desire of knowledge which is innate within reason itself. The Blessed souls will thus be able at once to delight in the marvellous spectacle of the world and to obtain perfect understanding thereof. They will not weary of following the rhythmic evolutions of the chorus of stars of which they form part, of noting the causes and the rules

---

[67] The true interpretation has been given by Bevan, *Stoics and Sceptics*, 1913, p. 112 s.

[68] *Georg.*, II, 489 ss.:
"Felix qui potuit rerum cognoscere causas,
Atque metus omnis et inexorabile Fatum
Subiecit pedibus, strepitumque Acherontis avari."

which determine their movements. From the height of their celestial observatory they will also perceive the phenomena of our globe and the actions of men. Nothing which happens in nature or in human society will be hidden from them. This speculative life (βιὸς θεωρητικός) is the only one on earth or in heaven which is worthy of the sage.

To observe the course of the stars throughout eternity may appear to us a desperately monotonous occupation, a rather unenviable beatitude. For the stars, shorn of their divinity, are for us no more than gaseous or solid bodies circulating in space, and we analyse with the spectroscope their chemical composition. But the ancients felt otherwise: they describe with singular eloquence the "cosmic emotion" which seized them as they contemplated their southern skies—their soul was ravished, borne on the wings of enthusiasm into the midst of the dazzling gods which from the earth had been descried throbbing in the radiance of the ether. These mystic transports were compared by them to Dionysiac intoxication; an "abstemious drunkenness"[69] raised man to the stars and kindled in him an impassioned ardour for divine knowledge. And as the exaltation produced by the vapours of wine gave to the mystics of Bacchus a foretaste of the joyous inebriation promised to them in the Elysian banquet, so the ecstasy which uplifted him who contemplated the celestial gods caused him to feel the happiness of another life while he was yet here below.[70]

"I know," says an epigram of Ptolemy himself,[71] "I know that I am mortal, born for a day, but when I follow the serried crowd of the stars in their circular course my

[69] Νηφάλιος μέθη, Philo., probably after Posidonius.
[70] Cf. Lecture IV, p. 126.
[71] Anthol. Palatina, IX, 577:

Οἶδ' ὅτι θνατὸς ἐγὼ καὶ ἐφάμερος, ἀλλ' ὅταν ἄστρων
μαστεύω πυκινὰς ἀμφιδρόμους ἕλικας
οὐκέτ' ἐπιψαύω γαίης ποσίν, ἀλλὰ παρ' αὐτῷ
Ζανὶ θεοτρεφέος πίμπλαμαι ἀμβροσίης.

feet touch the earth no longer: I go to Zeus himself and sate myself with ambrosia, the food of the gods.''

In the same way the intoxication produced by music, the divine possession which purified man by detaching him from material cares, caused him to taste for an instant the felicity which would fill his whole being when he should harken to the sweet harmony produced by the rotation of the spheres, the celestial concert which the ears of mortals are incapable of hearing, as their eyes cannot bear the brilliance of the sun. Men's instruments could cause the perception of only a weak echo of these delightful chords, but they awoke in the soul a passionate desire for heaven, where the unspeakable joy produced by the cosmic symphony would be felt.

The beatitude of the elect, as conceived by astral immortality, was a magnified projection to heaven of the joys which a religion of the erudite held to be most worthy of virtuous spirits. When pagan theology transported the abode of the most favoured souls outside the boundaries of the universe to a world beyond the senses,[72] the happiness of these souls could no longer consist solely in the sight and the hearing of the motion of the spheres. This entirely material conception of felicity in the Beyond had to be spiritualised. The ecstasy of Plotinus does not stop short at the visible gods of the firmament; in it the soul is transported beyond even the world of ideas and reaches, in an upward rush of love, the divine unity in which it merges, ridding itself of all consciousness and all form. This is the supreme goal which none can attain after death save him who has conquered perfect purity. But the aristocratic intellectualism of this philosophy reserved this union with the first Principle for an *élite* of sages. Paganism in its decline believed in a hierarchy of souls ascending to the divinity, in a scale of merit corresponding to various degrees of rewards: the majority lived among the stars and, divine like them, helped

[72] See Introd., p. 4.

them to govern the earth—we already know their blessed lot; others who were more perfect entered the intelligible cosmos[73] and their happiness, as it was imagined, is but a more exalted counterpart of the joys attributed to the former class. They were plunged in immovable contemplation of pure Ideas; forgetting earthly things, they were wholly absorbed by this intense activity of thought which was to them an inexpressible joy. Moreover, being set free from the bonds of their flesh and of their individuality, they could embrace in a single glance all the separate intelligences which together formed the divine *Nous,* and thus had a simultaneous intuition of everything, the direct comprehension of the ultimate reason of things.

Beatific vision of the splendour of God, immediate perception of all truth, mystic love for an ineffable Beauty—these were sublime speculations which were to be unendingly reproduced and developed after the fall of paganism. Unavailing efforts to represent a state inconceivable to any human imagination, they expressed the ardent yearning of religious souls towards an ideal of perfection and felicity. But this high religious spirituality had gradually broken away from somewhat coarse beliefs which had little by little been purified. The rapture which transported Plotinus to those summits where reason, bewildered as in a swoon, forsakes even thought in order to lose itself within a principle which is above all definition, is directly connected with the ecstasy which in the temples of Egypt came upon the devotee who, like the philosopher, conversed "alone with the lone god,"[74] whom the priest had evoked, and believed that in this vision he found a guarantee of eternal happiness.

[73] See Lecture III, p. 108.

[74] Μόνος πρὸς μόνῳ. The expression had been used by religion before being taken over by philosophy. *Cf. Le culte égyptien et le mysticisme de Plotin,* in *Monuments Piot,* XXV, 1922, p. 78 ss.

INDEX

Ablutions, 118; *cf.* "Lustration"

Absorption in God, 36 s., 42, 122

Acheron, 5, 8, 15, 27, 78, 80 s., 84 s., 149, 210

Achilles, 74

Adonis, 116, 203

Aeacus, 10, 75

Aeneid, 48, 82 s., 151; Aeneas, 74, 128; *cf.* "Virgil"

Africa, 93, 120, 139, 192

Age of reason, 137

Agricola, 18

Agrippina, 131

Ahriman, 89; *cf.* "Spirit of Evil"

Air full of souls, 26, 59, 160—purifies, 119, 143, 186; *cf.* Winds—Aerial bodies, 103, 168; *cf.* "Εἴδωλον"

Alexander of Abonotichos, 9, 23, 180

Alexander of Aphrodisias, 6

Alexander the Great, 62

Alexandria, 17, 20, 79, 96—cults, 36, 39; *cf.* "Isis," "Serapis"

Allegorical interpretations, 12, 21, 24, 42, 78 ss., 82, 86, 152, 180, 195, 206

Amorgos, 105

Andromeda, 104

Angels, 140

Anima, 59, 167; *cf.* "Soul"

Ante diem (death), 133

Antinous, 105, 164

Antipodes, 80 s.

Antonius Diogenes, 22

Aphraates, 206

Apocalypse of Peter, 173

Apocolocyntosis, 179

Apollo, 112, 123, 156—Musagetes, 101

Apollonius of Tyana, 23, 164

Apotheosis of heroes, 32, 205—of emperors, 102, 112 s., 156, 164—of Claudius, 179—of great men, 114 s.—in mysteries, 118 ss.—of children, 138 ss.

Appius Claudius Pulcher, 22

Apuleius, 108, n. 41

Aristarchus, 79

Aristophanes, 95

Aristotle, 6, 17, 77, 98, 131; *cf.* "Peripatetic"

Armenia, 52

Arnold (Matthew), 116

Asia Minor, 112; *cf.* "Cybele"

Astral body, 169

Astrolatry, 123, 207; *cf.* "Stars"

Astrology, 17, 28, 92 s., 96, 100, 102, 117, 187

Ataraxia, 8, 191

Atargatis, 121

Athribis, 93

Atmosphere, 25, 81, 162, 168; *cf.* "Hades"

Attis, 35 ss., 39, 116, 203

Augustus, 156

Avernus, 74

Axiochos, 79

Babylonia, 94, 156; *cf.* "Chaldeans"

Bacchus, 52, 120, 138 s., 202, 211—Bacchantes, 62—*cf.* "Dionysos"

Banquet; funeral, 53 ss., 200 ss.—ritual, 120 ss., 203 s.—eternal,

GREEK WORDS

Ἄγαμοι, 137
Ἀγιάζω, 123
Ἀγνεία, 24
Ἄγνωστος θεός, 41
Ἀειδής, (= Hades), 79
Αἰτία ἑλομένω, 183
Ἀναγωγεύς, 101, 160
Ἀναιρέτης, 131
Ἀναίτιος ὁ θεός, 183
Ἄνεμος, 59
Ἀνθοφόρος, 138
Ἀντίθεος, 89
Ἀνώνυμοι, 137
Ἀπαθανατίζω, 116, 118
Ἀπάθεια, 191
Ἀποθέωσις, 118; cf. "Apotheosis"
Ἄποροι τῆς ταφῆς, 68
Ἀρετή, 151
Ἄρχοντες, 162
Ἀσωτεία, 151
Ἀταραξία, 8
Ἄταφοι, 64; cf. "Insepulti"
Ἄτροφοι, 132, 137
Ἄωροι, 129, 136 s.

Βιαιοθάνατοι, 129, 141 ss.
Βίος θεωρητικός, 211

Γνῶσις (τοῦ θεοῦ), 23, 121 ss., 125, 207 ss.

Δοξάζειν, 123

Εἴδωλον, 7, 24, 79, 166 s.
Ἐκπύρωσις, 13 s.
Ἐπιφανὴς θεός, 112
Ἐπτάκτις θεός, 160
Εὔπλοι, 155
Εὐψύχει, 149

Ἡγεμονικόν, 30, 103
Ἡγεμὼν θεός, 163 s.

Θάρρει, 149

Κατάβασις εἰς "Αιδου, 171; cf. "Hades"
Κύκλος γενέσεως, 179

Μετενσωμάτωσις, 182

Νοῦς, 168; cf. 103, 213
Νυμφόληπτοι, 139

Ξύσματα, 160

Ὁδὸς μακάρων, 152
Ὄχημα, 41, 161, 169

Παλιγγενεσία, 182
Παράδεισος, 200
Πνεῦμα, 111, 168
Πολυάνδριον, 145

Σκιά, 166 s.
Συγγένεια, 96, 111
Συμποσιάρχης, 202
Σῶμα, 167
Σωτήρ, 112

Τελώνια, 163
Τρίοδος, 151

Υ, 26, 150 s., 194
Ὕψιστος, 41; cf. "Hypsistos"
Ὑψοῦσθαι, 123

Φωτίζω, 123

Ψυχή, 25, 59, 167; cf. "Psyche"